The Vocabulary of English Place-Names

(*Á–Box*)

The Vocabulary

of

English Place-Names

(*Á–BOX*)

edited by

David Parsons & Tania Styles

with

Carole Hough

Centre for English Name Studies
Nottingham
1997

Published by:
Centre for English Name Studies, Humanities Research Centre, Old Engineering Building, University of Nottingham, NG7 2RD.

Distributed by:
The English Place-Name Society, Department of English Studies, University of Nottingham, NG7 2RD.

ISBN 0 9525343 5 5

Typeset by David Parsons & Printed in Great Britain by Woolnough Bookbinding Ltd, Irthlingborough

Preface

The origins of this work lie in a research project entitled 'The Language of English Place-Names' funded by the Leverhulme Trust between 1992 and 1996. We are most grateful for the Trust's generosity over this period. Since that grant was exhausted, Tania Styles has been funded by the Humanities Research Board of the British Academy, and David Parsons by the University of Nottingham. We should like to express our gratitude to these bodies for their continued support. We have also always enjoyed the wholehearted support of the Council of the English Place-Name Society, and we thank them for that, and for helping with the printing costs of this book.

The first research associate on the project was Dr Carole Hough, who moved on to the University of Glasgow in 1995. Her achievements in Nottingham were considerable. She planned and set up a place-name database, establishing a powerful, intricately structured tool, which contains detailed information on each of 5000 elements. She compiled and published *The English Place-Name Survey: A Finding List to Addenda and Corrigenda* (Nottingham, 1995), involving a painstaking attention to detail. Last, but not least, she wrote a large number of draft entries for the present work, and has commented helpfully on subsequent drafts submitted to her. Each of these various contributions has been of great importance to the final publication.

We should also like warmly to thank the numerous other scholars who have read drafts of the work and offered corrections, additions and suggestions: Barrie Cox, who deserves special mention as the Academic Director of the Leverhulme project, Kenneth Cameron, Richard Coates, Paul Cullen, Gillian Fellows-Jensen, Margaret Gelling, John Insley, Peter Kitson, David Mills, Raymond Page and Victor Watts. Oliver Padel is another who has helpfully commented on the full range of material, but we are especially grateful to him and to Patrick Sims-Williams for their advice on the Celtic forms.

Most of all, we should like to thank Professor Christine Fell, though a few words here could not begin to express the debt that we and the project owe to her.

We hope that the *Vocabulary* will run to a series of nine or ten fascicles which can fairly quickly be revised and republished as a second edition in EPNS hardback format. This edition would take account of the corrections and additions that will inevitably come to light over the next few years, and we invite readers to bring them to our attention. The evidence offered by place-names requires, for a full appreciation, the expertise of a wide range of disciplines and thorough local knowledge; in preparing this work we are constantly reminded of our own limitations. Seventy-three years on, we should like wholeheartedly to endorse the words Professor Mawer wrote in the preface of his pioneering *Chief Elements Used in English Place-Names*: 'Many of [our] statements are clearly in the nature of suggestions rather than assertions and the whole attitude of the [editors] towards them is tentative and exploratory rather than dogmatic or final'.

D.P.
T.S.

26th July, 1997

Introduction

This work is a dictionary of the words that make up place-names in England. It has two predecessors, Allen Mawer's *The Chief Elements Used in English Place-Names* (Cambridge, 1924) and A.H. Smith's *English Place-Name Elements* (Cambridge, 1956). Mawer's work formed part of the English Place-Name Society's first volume, its main purpose 'to provide a useful companion to the successive county volumes of the English Place-name Survey, by presenting in concise and summary form a good deal of the matter which, as it is in the nature of "common form," would otherwise have to be repeated in each successive volume.' Smith's *Elements* followed the publication of twenty-three Survey volumes, covering nineteen counties, and reflects the huge increase in material that the project had brought to light. With such a wealth of detail at his fingertips, Smith chose to broaden the scope of the work. As well as providing an updated and expanded account of the more common elements, he decided to include rarer words, noting that 'the lexicographical results of over a quarter of a century's research . . . have been accumulating at a remarkable rate, which is perhaps not fully appreciated except by experts in this field'. The result was a two-volume reference work that has proved immensely valuable, not only to place-name specialists, but to many others: linguists (English, Scandinavian, Celtic and Romance), historians, archaeologists and geographers.

The main justification for the present work comes from another significant increase in available material. Since 1956 the EPNS has continued to publish prolifically, so that at the time of writing forty more Survey volumes dealing, at least in part, with another thirteen counties have appeared. A considerable amount of relevant research has also been published in books, journals and major new historical dictionaries. A revision taking this new material and research into account is by now clearly desirable. Moreover, it will be helpful again to broaden the scope of the work. Smith concentrated on material recorded before the late fifteenth century in major place-names, and omitted 'elements found in later minor-names and field-names'. From a language-historical point of view the rather arbitrary distinction between major, minor and field-names has little meaning; in broad terms, therefore, the aim here is to include all words first recorded before *circa* 1750 in any type of place-name. A closer description of the limits of the material will be given below.

The origins of this work as a revision of *English Place-Name Elements* will be apparent in a number of ways: the range of examples from early-edited counties or those that have not yet been surveyed are often retained (though thoroughly checked), as are various aspects of layout (including the indispensable ~ 'cognate with, related to, ultimately derived from') and, very occasionally, sequences of wording. Nonetheless, the extent of the revision is considerable: almost every retained entry has been recast, and a great many headwords have been added, resulting in a work running at three times the length of the comparable part of *Elements*. The adoption of a new title reflects the fact that in many respects this is a new work.

SCOPE

The material is drawn from all the place-names of present-day England, except for Cornish-language names in Cornwall and wholly Welsh names in border counties. For Cornish, O.J. Padel's *Cornish Place-Name Elements* (1985) provides a treatment far more thorough and authoritative than anything that could be attempted here, whilst the Welsh names of the borders must be taken with the study of place-names in Wales. Otherwise, material might in theory come from any class of place-name in any part of England. In practice, of course, many factors impose limitations. Nine counties have still to be treated by the English Place-Name Survey, while the early surveys were much less thorough than modern ones. The treatment here of different parts of the country varies accordingly. Some unsurveyed counties, such as Lancashire and Hampshire, are well served by independent publications and so are comparatively well represented. Others, such as Suffolk and Somerset, have been neglected; only a small selection of parish names can be included. The difference in coverage between these counties and the West Riding of Yorkshire, with its eight-volume survey including the names of buildings, streets and fields, need hardly be stressed. Great caution should clearly be exercised in drawing inferences about the distribution and frequency of terms from the present material. In entries for common elements, however, examples have none-theless been chosen to illustrate geographical range as well as variety of use; early examples have generally been favoured over later ones.

Words are included if they appear in names recorded before 1750. At the earlier end of the range, matters are less straightforward. The lack of a comprehensive modern edition of Old English charter boundaries is keenly felt, and no attempt has been made here to detail words found there but not surviving in place-names recorded after the Norman Conquest. On the other hand, where elements are included because they appear in post-Conquest records, relevant charter evidence has generally been cited. Note that place-name forming suffixes are included, but that the grammatical endings and other morphological segments included by Smith are not.

Personal names fall outside the scope of this work, with one exception:

Middle English occupational terms and the surnames derived from them can very rarely be distinguished; the class as a whole is included.

HEADWORDS

The headwords are drawn from a number of languages, each with its own conventions. The principal ones are as follows.

Brittonic elements are given under headwords meant to represent a common stage of British Celtic, before its separation into regional varieties. Professor Kenneth Jackson proposed emendations to Primitive Welsh, Cumbric and Cornish forms (JEPNS:1·43–52), intended to represent the stage at which British names were borrowed by Anglo-Saxons. Whilst these forms are valuable, and are quoted within entries, they raise problems of chronology, dialect identity, and not least, typography. Earlier forms close to those in Romano-British records avoid these problems. Note that the loss of the neuter gender in late British made it indistinguishable from the masculine, hence the large number of headwords with final, ambiguous, -o-.

Old English headwords are given in Anglian dialectal form, unless an element is recorded only in the south. As is traditional in place-name scholarship, Old English forms are used as the pegs on which to hang evidence from all dates. Clearly, a name first recorded in the later Middle Ages very often contains the Middle English reflex of an Old English term, and it is not intended to imply that such names were Anglo-Saxon coinages. For unattested simplex words likely to have existed in Old English, starred (reconstructed) forms are proposed. For unattested compounds made up of native elements, however, a starred Old English form is only used where a very similar phrase is used in Old English (e.g. *æcer-hēafod, *blæc-þorn). Otherwise, such compound headwords reflect the stage of the language when they are first attested, in names or elsewhere.

Scandinavian headwords are generally given in standard Old Norse (Old Icelandic) forms. Note that this is conventional and does not imply specifically West Norse origin for the elements in England. Words which seem to be limited to East Norse are given Old Danish headforms, however. Where West Norse does need to be specified, the abbreviation OWN is used.

Words of Old French origin are given Old French headwords, even where they have probably been taken into Middle English. Forms that appear to reflect Anglo-Norman developments are marked OFr (AN).

Middle English headforms are used for words which cannot be assigned with confidence to a single earlier stage of language.

ARRANGEMENT OF MATERIAL

Within an entry, evidence for a term is arranged in paragraphs, as follows: (*a*) as a first element in a compound, (*b*) as a simplex place-name, (*c*) as a final element, (*d*) as an affix. In place-name citations, modern names are printed in Roman type, the names of lost or unidentified places are in italics. Field-names are marked f.n., street-names st.n. (with the name of the town), building-names bdg.n. (with the name of the town). Later additions to place-names, like 'Farm', 'House', 'North' and 'South' are generally omitted.

The dates cited are those of the name's earliest record. Whereas EPNS collections give the earliest *possible* date or date-range first, in this work the earliest *certain* date is favoured. Thus 1279–91 rather than 1250–95, or 1407 rather than 1405–9. Regnal dates have been silently expanded, e.g. Hy2 [Henry II] is treated as 1154–89. Dates of Anglo-Saxon documents are frequently corrected in the light of recent scholarship; for this reason Anglo-Saxon sources are generally identified. Note in particular the convention of referring charters to Sawyer's catalogue in small type, e.g. S:214.

Where a document is preserved only in a later copy, the date of that copy is expressed as a round century in square brackets, e.g. 1234 [15th]. With Anglo-Saxon charters an attempt has been made to weed out the more obvious forgeries.

The county abbreviation which follows a place-name is for most counties also a reference to the source for the evidence. These sources are detailed following the abbreviation in the bibliography; where no page-reference is given, the name will be found in the work's index (unless a source other than the principal one is indicated in square brackets). Note the bibliographical style We:2·41 (i.e. *The Place-Names of Westmorland*, part II, page 41). Where a county abbreviation is not followed by a source (i.e. Co, Du, He, Nb, Sf, So) the authority is Ekwall's *Concise Oxford Dictionary of English Place-Names* (DEPN), unless otherwise stated. Similarly, for unfinished county surveys (Do, L, Nf, Sa, St), DEPN is the source unless a reference points elsewhere.

In compound place-names a suggestion for the other element is given in bold type in brackets; a provisional hand-list of these cross-references is printed after the main text. It is followed by a General Index, which incorporates a finding-list of headwords that have been omitted or altered from previous publications.

Abbreviations and Bibliography

a.	*ante* (before).
adj.	adjective.
adv.	adverb.
AFW	A. Tobler & E. Lommatzsch (eds), *Altfranzösisches Wörterbuch* (Berlin, 1925).
AHDW	E. Karg-Gasterstädt, T. Frings *et al.* (eds), *Althochdeutsches Wörterbuch* (Berlin, 1968–).
AN	Anglo-Norman.
AND	W. Rothwell, L.W. Stone & T.B.W. Reid (eds), *Anglo-Norman Dictionary* (London, 1992).
Anderson 1934–9	O.S. Anderson, *The English Hundred-Names* (Lund, 1934–9).
Arngart 1980	O. Arngart, 'Barstable: further notes towards an explanation', *Namn och Bygd* 68 (1980), 10–18.
ASC A	J.M. Bately (ed.), *The Anglo-Saxon Chronicle: a Collaborative Edition. Volume 3: MS A* (Cambridge, 1986).
ASC D	G.P. Cubbin (ed.), *The Anglo-Saxon Chronicle: a Collaborative Edition. Volume 6: MS D* (Cambridge, 1996).
ASC E	manuscript E of the Anglo-Saxon Chronicle cited from: C. Plummer (ed.), *Two of the Saxon Chronicles Parallel . . . on the Basis of an Edition by John Earle* (Oxford, 1892–9).
ASCh:1	A. Campbell (ed.), *Charters of Rochester*, Anglo-Saxon Charters I (British Academy, 1973). Cited by number, not page.
ASCh:2	P.H. Sawyer (ed.), *Charters of Burton Abbey*, Anglo-Saxon Charters II (British Academy, 1979). Cited by number, not page.
ASCh:4	S.E. Kelly (ed.), *Charters of St Augustine's Abbey Canterbury and Minster-in-Thanet*, Anglo-Saxon Charters IV (British Academy, 1995). Cited by number, not page.
ASCh:5	S.E. Kelly (ed.), *Charters of Shaftesbury Abbey*, Anglo-Saxon Charters V (British Academy, 1996). Cited by number, not page.
Asser	W.H. Stevenson (ed.), *Asser's Life of King Alfred* (Oxford, 1904).
ASWills	D. Whitelock (ed.), *Anglo-Saxon Wills* (Cambridge, 1930). Cited by number, not page.
Atkinson 1886	J.C. Atkinson, 'Notes on common-field names. Part II: Ofnam', *The Antiquary* 13 (Jan–June 1886), 150–2.
Aybes & Yalden 1995	C. Aybes and D.W. Yalden, 'Place-name evidence for the former distribution and status of wolves and beavers in Britain', *Mammal Review* 25 (1995), 201–27.
BCS	W. de G. Birch, *Cartularium Saxonicum* (London, 1885–99). Cited by number, not page.
Bd	Bedfordshire. A. Mawer & F.M. Stenton, *The Place-Names of Bedfordshire & Huntingdonshire*, EPNS 3 (Cambridge, 1926).
Bede	B. Colgrave & R.A.B. Mynors (ed. and trans.). *The Ecclesiastical History of the English People* (Oxford, 1969).
Bk	Buckinghamshire. A. Mawer & F.M. Stenton, *The Place-Names of Buckinghamshire*, EPNS 2 (Cambridge, 1925).
bdg.n.	building name.
Bishop 1935–6	T.A.M. Bishop, 'Assarting and the growth of the open fields', *Economic History Review* 6 (1935–6), 13–29.

Björkman   E. Björkman, *Scandinavian Loan-Words in Middle English* (Halle, 1900–2).
Brit   British (i.e. the common Brittonic stage of Celtic language).
Brk   Berkshire. M. Gelling, *The Place-Names of Berkshire*, EPNS 49–51 (Cambridge, 1973–6).
Brooks 1952-3   K.R. Brooks, 'Old English *ēa* and related words', *English and Germanic Studies* 5 (1952–3), 15–66.
C   Cambridgeshire. P.H. Reaney, *The Place-Names of Cambridgeshire & the Isle of Ely*, EPNS 19 (Cambridge, 1943).
Carlsson   S. Carlsson, *Studies on Middle English Local Bynames in East Anglia* (Lund, 1989).
CDEPN   V.E. Watts, *The Cambridge Dictionary of English Place-Names*, forthcoming.
Ch   Cheshire. J. McN. Dodgson, *The Place-Names of Cheshire*, EPNS 44–8, 54– (Cambridge, 1970–).
Charles 1963   B.G. Charles, 'The Welsh, their language and place-names in Archenfield and Oswestry', in *Angles and Britons: O'Donnell Lectures* (Cardiff, 1963), 85–110.
Charles 1992   B.G. Charles, *The Place-Names of Pembrokeshire* (Aberystwyth, 1992).
Co   Cornwall.
Coates 1982–3   R. Coates, 'English medieval Latin *bellerīca*', *JEPNS* 15 (1982–3), 20–3.
Coates 1988   R. Coates, 'Middle English *badde* and related puzzles', *NOWELE* 11 (1988), 91–104.
Coates forthcoming R. Coates, '*Box* in English place-names', *English Studies*.
Cockayne   T.O. Cockayne, *Leechdoms, Wortcunning and Starcraft of Early England* (London, 1866).
Cole 1985   A. Cole, 'Topography, hydrology and place-names in the chalklands of southern England: *funta*, *ǣwiell* and *ǣwielm*', *Nomina* 9 (1985), 3–19.
Cole 1987–8   A. Cole, 'The distribution and usage of the place-name elements *botm*, *bytme* and *botn*', *JEPNS* 20 (1987–8), 39–46.
Cole 1993–4   A. Cole, 'Baulking: an Anglo-Saxon industry revealed', *JEPNS* 26 (1993–4), 27–31.
Cox 1989–90   B. Cox, 'Byflete', *JEPNS* 22 (1989–90), 42–6.
CPNE   O.J. Padel, *Cornish Place-Name Elements*, EPNS 56–7 (Nottingham, 1985).
Cu   Cumberland. A.M. Armstrong, A. Mawer, F.M. Stenton & B. Dickins, *The Place-Names of Cumberland*, EPNS 20–2 (Cambridge, 1950–2).
D   Devon. J.E.B. Gover, A. Mawer & F.M. Stenton, *The Place-Names of Devon*, EPNS 8–9 (Cambridge, 1931–2).
dat.   dative.
Db   Derbyshire. K. Cameron, *The Place-Names of Derbyshire*, EPNS 27–9 (Cambridge, 1959).
DB   Domesday Book.
DCNQ   *Devon & Cornwall Notes & Queries.*
DEPN   E. Ekwall, *The Concise Oxford Dictionary of English Place-Names*, 4th edn (Oxford, 1960).

DES	P.H. Reaney & R.M. Wilson, *A Dictionary of English Surnames* 3rd edn (Oxford, 1991).
DEW	R. Hiersche (ed.), *Deutsches etymologisches Wörterbuch* (Heidelberg, 1986–).
Dietz 1981	K. Dietz, 'Mittelenglisch *oi* in heimischen Ortsnamen und Personennamen. II. Das Namen-element *Boi(e)* und die Etymologie von *boy*', *Beiträge zur Namenforschung* NF 16 (1981), 361–405.
Dietz 1985	K. Dietz, 'Ae. *bēocere* "imker", Me. *bīke* "bienennest" und die Ortsnamen auf *Bick-*', *Anglia* 103 (1985), 1–25.
DML	R.E. Latham *et al.* (eds), *Dictionary of Medieval Latin from British Sources* (London, 1975–).
Do	Dorset. A.D. Mills, *The Place-Names of Dorset*, EPNS 52–3 & 59/60– (Cambridge, 1977–).
Dobson 1940	E.J. Dobson, 'The etymology and meaning of *boy*', *Medium Ævum* 9 (1940), 121–54.
DOE	A. diP. Healey *et al.* (cds), *A Dictionary of Old English* (Toronto, 1986–).
DOST	W.A. Craigie *et al.* (eds), *A Dictionary of the Older Scottish Tongue* (Chicago, London and Aberdeen, 1937–).
Du	Durham.
Duignan 1912	W.H. Duignan, *Notes on Staffordshire Place-Names* (Oxford, 1912).
DW	J. Grimm & W. Grimm, *Deutsches Wörterbuch* 2nd edn (Leipzig, 1983–).
e.	early
EDD	J. Wright (ed.), *The English Dialect Dictionary* (London, 1898–1905).
Ek 1975	K.G. Ek, *The Development of OE æ (i-mutated a) Before Nasals and OE ǣ in South-Eastern Middle English* (Lund, 1975).
Ekwall 1917	E. Ekwall, 'Ae. *botl, bold, bodl* in englischen Ortsnamen', *Beiblatt zur Anglia* 28 (1917), 82–91.
Ekwall 1918	E. Ekwall, 'A few notes on English etymology and word-history', *Beiblatt zur Anglia* 29 (1918), 195–201.
Ekwall 1920	E. Ekwall, 'Några nordiska ortnamn i England', *Namn och bygd* 8 (1920), 85–96.
Ekwall 1926	E. Ekwall, 'Nord. *ā* "å" i engelska namn', *Namn och bygd* 14 (1926), 145–61.
Ekwall 1931	E. Ekwall, *Studies on English Place- and Personal-Names* (Lund, 1931).
Ekwall 1933	E. Ekwall, 'Names of trades in English place-names'; cited from Ekwall, *Selected Papers* (Lund and Copenhagen, 1963), 68–79.
Ekwall 1936	E. Ekwall, *Studies on English Place-Names* (Stockholm, 1936).
Ekwall 1957	E. Ekwall, 'English place-name elements', *Namn och bygd* 45 (1957), 133–46.
Ekwall 1963	E. Ekwall, 'A problem of Old Mercian phonology in the light of west midland place-names', *Namn och bygd* 51 (1963), 16–48.
Ekwall 1964	E. Ekwall, *Old English wīc in Place-Names* (Lund, 1964).
Ekwall 1965	E. Ekwall, 'A note on OE *bēce* 'brook, valley' in place-names', *Namn och bygd* 53 (1965), 22–5.
el.	element.

EPNE	A.H. Smith, *English Place-Name Elements*, EPNS 15–16 (Cambridge, 1956).
EPNS	English Place-Name Society; material from its collections.
ERN	E. Ekwall, *English River-Names* (Oxford, 1928).
Ess	Essex. P.H. Reaney, *The Place-Names of Essex*, EPNS 12 (Cambridge, 1935).
f.	feminine.
Feilitzen	O. von Feilitzen, *The Pre-Conquest Personal Names of Domesday Book* (Uppsala, 1937).
Fellows-Jensen 1977–8	G. Fellows-Jensen, 'A Gaelic-Scandinavian loan-word in English place-names', *JEPNS* 10 (1977–8), 18–25.
Fellows-Jensen 1980	G. Fellows-Jensen, 'Common Gaelic *áirge*, Old Scandinavian *ærgi* or *erg*?', *Nomina* 4 (1980), 67–74.
Fellows-Jensen 1986	G. Fellows-Jensen, 'Danish lake- and river-names in England', in V. Dalberg & G. Fellows-Jensen (eds), *Mange bække små* (Copenhagen, 1986), 59–74.
Fellows-Jensen forthcoming	G. Fellows-Jensen, 'Names and their usage: a suburban sidelight', in *Xenia Lideniana. Meddelanden från institutionen för nordiska språk och nordisk litteratur vid Helsingfors universitet*.
Field	J. Field, *English Field-Names: a Dictionary* (London, 1972).
f.n.	field-name.
Forsberg 1970	R. Forsberg, 'On Old English *ād* in English place-names', *Namn och bygd* 58 (1970), 20–82.
Fransson	G. Fransson, *Middle English Surnames of Occupation 1100-1350* (Lund, 1935).
Gelling 1974	M. Gelling, 'Some notes on Warwickshire place-names', *Birmingham and Warwickshire Archaeological Society Transactions* 86 (1974), 59–79.
Gelling 1988	M. Gelling, *Signposts to the Past*, 2nd edn (Chichester, 1988).
gen.	genitive.
Ger	German.
Gk	Greek.
Gl	Gloucestershire. A.H. Smith, *The Place-Names of Gloucestershire*, EPNS 38–41 (Cambridge, 1964–5).
Gmc	Germanic.
Gordon 1926–7	E.V. Gordon, 'Scarborough and Flamborough', *Acta Philologica Scandinavica* 1 (1926–7), 320–3.
Goth	Gothic.
GPC	R.J. Thomas *et al.* (eds), *Geiriadur Prifysgol Cymru* (Cardiff, 1967–).
Ha	Hampshire. R. Coates, *The Place-Names of Hampshire* (London, 1989).
Hallqvist 1948	H. Hallqvist, *Studies in Old English Fractured 'ea'* (Lund, 1948).
He	Herefordshire.
Higham 1977–8	M. Higham, 'The "erg" place-names of northern England', *JEPNS* 10 (1977–8), 7–17.
Hogg	R.M. Hogg, *A Grammar of Old English: I Phonology* (Oxford, 1992).
Hooke 1980–1	D. Hooke, 'Burial features in west midland charters', *JEPNS* 13 (1980–1), 1–40.

Hough 1994   C. Hough, 'Some ghost entries in Smith's *English Place-Name Elements*', *Nomina* 17 (1994), 19–30.
Hough 1995   C. Hough, '*Bonhunt*: an Essex place-name', *Anglia* 113 (1995), 207–12.
Hough 1995–6   C. Hough, 'The place-name Annesley', *JEPNS* 28 (1995–6), 45–9.
Hough forthcoming   C. Hough, 'Place-name evidence for Old English bird-names'.
Hrt   Hertfordshire. J.E.B. Glover, A. Mawer & F.M. Stenton, *The Place-Names of Hertfordshire*, EPNS 15 (Cambridge, 1938).
Hu   Huntingdonshire. See Bd.
IE   Indo-European.
Insley 1994   J. Insley, *Scandinavian Personal Names in Norfolk: a Survey Based on Medieval Records and Place-Names* (Uppsala, 1994).
Insley 1996   J. Insley, 'Bonhunt revisited', *Anglia* 114 (1996), 544–9.
IPN   A. Mawer & F.M. Stenton, *Introduction to the Survey of English Place-Names: Part 1*, EPNS 1 (Cambridge, 1924).
Ir   Irish.
Jackson 1948   K. Jackson, 'On some Romano-British place-names', *Journal of Roman Studies* 38 (1948), 54–8.
Janzén 1957   A. Janzén, 'Scandinavian place-names in England: I', *Names* 5 (1957), 193–207.
JEPNS   *Journal of the English Place-Name Society.*
Jordan   R. Jordan, *Handbook of Middle English Grammar: Phonology*, trans. and rev. by E.J. Crook (The Hague, 1974).
K   Kent. J.K. Wallenberg, *The Place-Names of Kent* (Uppsala, 1934).
KCD   J.M. Kemble, *Codex Diplomaticus Aevi Saxonici* (London, 1839–48). Cited by number, not page.
Kenyon   D. Kenyon, 'Addenda and corrigenda to E. Ekwall *The Place-Names of Lancashire*', *JEPNS* 17 (1983–4), 20–106.
Kirkham 1949   N. Kirkham, *Derbyshire Lead Mining Glossary*, Cave Research Group Publication 2 (Leamington Spa, 1949).
Kitson 1990   P. Kitson, 'On Old English nouns of more than one gender', *English Studies* 71 (1990), 185–221.
Kitson 1993   P. Kitson, 'Quantifying qualifiers in Anglo-Saxon charter boundaries', *Folia Linguistica Historica* 14 (1993), 29–82.
Kitson 1995   P. Kitson, 'The nature of Old English dialect distributions, mainly as exhibited in charter boundaries', in J. Fisiak (ed.), *Medieval Dialectology*, Trends in Linguistics Studies and Monographs 79 (Berlin and New York), 43–135.
Kitson 1996   P. Kitson, 'British and European river-names', *Transactions of the Philological Society* 94 (1996), 73–118.
Kitson forthcoming *A Guide to Anglo-Saxon Charter Boundaries.*
Krahe 1964   H. Krahe, *Unsere ältesten Flußnamen* (Wiesbaden, 1964).
Kristensson 1946   G. Kristensson, *Contributions to Middle English Lexicography and Etymology* (Lund, 1946).
Kristensson 1967   G. Kristensson, *A Survey of Middle English Dialects 1290–1350: the Six Northern Counties and Lincolnshire* (Lund, 1967).
Kristensson 1995   G. Kristensson, *A Survey of Middle English Dialects 1290–1350: the East Midland Counties* (Lund, 1995).
KPN   J.K. Wallenberg, *Kentish Place-Names* (Uppsala, 1931).

l.	late.
L	Lincolnshire. K. Cameron, *The Place-Names of Lincolnshire*, EPNS 58, 64–6, 71– (Cambridge/Nottingham, 1985–).
La	Lancashire. E. Ekwall, *The Place-Names of Lancashire* (Manchester and London, 1922).
Lat	Latin.
Laur 1992	W. Laur, *Historisches Ortsnamenlexikon von Schleswig-Holstein* 2nd edn (Neumünster, 1992).
Ldn	E. Ekwall, *Street-Names of the City of London* (Oxford, 1954).
Lei	Leicestershire. B. Cox, *The Place-Names of Leicestershire & Rutland* (unpublished University of Nottingham PhD thesis, 1971).
LexPoet	Finnur Jónsson (ed.), *Lexicon poeticum . . . Ordbog over det norsk-islandske skjaldesprog . . . af Sveinbjörn Egilsson*, 2nd edn (Copenhagen, 1931).
LEIA	J. Vendryes *et al.* (eds), *Lexique étymologique d'irlandais ancien* (Dublin and Paris, 1959–).
LHEB	K. Jackson, *Language and History in Early Britain* (Edinburgh, 1953).
Lindkvist 1912	H. Lindkvist, *Middle-English Place-Names of Scandinavian Origin* (Uppsala, 1912).
m.	masculine.
m.	mid(dle).
Mawer 1913	A. Mawer, 'Some unconsidered elements in English place-names', *Essays and Studies* 4 (1913), 55–71.
Mayhew 1908	A.L. Mayhew (ed.) *Promptorium parvulorum: the First English–Latin Dictionary*, Early English Text Society, Extra Series 102 (London, 1908).
McGarvie 1974–9	M. McGarvie, 'Bellerica, the place-name', *Somerset & Dorset Notes & Queries* 30 (1974–9), 353–4.
MCo	Middle Cornish.
MDu	Middle Dutch.
ME	Middle English.
MED	H. Kurath *et al.* (eds), *Middle English Dictionary* (Ann Arbor, 1956–).
MELS	M.T. Löfvenberg *Studies on Middle English Local Surnames* (Lund, 1942).
METT	G. Kristensson, *Studies on Middle English Topographical Terms* (Lund, 1970).
Middendorff	H. Middendorff, *Altenglisches Flurnamenbuch* (Halle, 1902).
Mills 1991	A.D. Mills, *A Dictionary of English Place-Names* (Oxford, 1991).
Mills 1996	A.D. Mills, *The Place-Names of the Isle of Wight* (Stamford, 1996).
MLat	Medieval Latin.
MIr	Middle Irish.
MLG	Middle Low German.
Moberg 1951	L. Moberg, 'Fornisländskans *biǫð* i östnordisk belysning', *Arkiv för nordisk filologi* 66 (1951), 38–51.
ModE	Modern English.
MW	Middle Welsh.

Mx	Middlesex. J.E.B. Gover, A. Mawer & F.M. Stenton, *The Place-Names of Middlesex*, EPNS 18 (Cambridge, 1942).
n.	neuter.
Nb	Northumberland.
NbDu	A. Mawer, *The Place-Names of Northumberland and Durham* (Cambridge, 1920).
n.d.	no date
Nf	Norfolk. K.I. Sandred & B. Lindstrom, *The Place-Names of Norfolk*, EPNS 61, 72– (Nottingham, 1989–).
Nicolaisen 1957	W.F.H. Nicolaisen, 'Die alteuropäischen Gewässernamen der britischen Hauptinsel' *Beiträge zur Namenforschung* 8 (1957), 209–68.
Nicolaisen 1971	W.F.H. Nicolaisen, 'Great Britain and Old Europe', *Namn och Bygd* 59 (1971), 85–105
Norw	Norwegian.
Nt	Nottinghamshire. J.E.B. Gover, A. Mawer & F.M. Stenton, *The Place-Names of Nottinghamshire*, EPNS 17 (Cambridge, 1940).
Nth	Northamptonshire. J.E.B. Gover, A. Mawer & F.M. Stenton, *The Place-Names of Northamptonshire*, EPNS 10 (Cambridge, 1933).
O	Oxfordshire. M. Gelling & D.M. Stenton, *The Place-Names of Oxfordshire*, EPNS 23–4 (Cambridge, 1953–4).
ODan	Old Danish.
OE	Old English.
OED	J.A. Simpson & E.S.C. Weiner (eds), *The Oxford English Dictionary*, 2nd edn (Oxford, 1989).
OEG	A. Campbell, *Old English Grammar* (Oxford, 1959).
OFr	Old French.
OFris	Old Frisian.
OGNS	J. Fritzner, *Ordbog over det gamle norske sprog* (Oslo, 1883–96).
OGNS (R&T)	F. Hødnebø, *Ordbog over det gamle norske sprog af Dr Johan Fritzner: rettelser og tillegg* (Oslo, Bergen and Tromsø, 1972).
OHG	Old High German.
OIcel	Old Icelandic.
OIr	Old Irish.
OLG	Old Low German.
ON	Old Norse.
ONP	*Ordbog over det norrøne prosasprog* (Copenhagen, 1989–).
OP	Cornish p.n. material provided by Dr Oliver Padel.
OSax	Old Saxon.
OSwed	Old Swedish.
OWN	Old West Norse.
Padel 1980–2	O.J. Padel, 'Welsh *blwch* "bald, hairless"' *Bulletin of the Board of Celtic Studies* 29 (1980–2), 523–6.
Parker 1984–5	M.S. Parker, 'Some notes on Barnby and related place-names in England', *JEPNS* 17 (1984–5), 5–13.
Parsons & Styles 1995–6	D. Parsons and T. Styles, 'Birds in *amber*: the nature of English place-name elements', *JEPNS* 28 (1995–6), 5–31.
pers.n.	personal name.

Pheifer 1974	J.D. Pheifer (ed.), *The Old English Glosses in the Épinal-Erfurt Glossary* (Oxford, 1974). Cited by number, not page.
pl.	plural.
prep.	preposition.
p.n.	place-name.
PNLand	M. Gelling, *Place-Names in the Landscape* (London, 1984).
PNRB	A.L.F. Rivet & C. Smith, *The Place-Names of Roman Britain* (London, 1979).
PrCu	Primitive Cumbric.
PrW	Primitive Welsh.
Quentel 1955	P. Quentel, 'Lamplugh (Cumberland)' *Ogam* 7 (1955), 81–3.
R.	River.
Rackham 1986	O. Rackham, *The History of the Countryside* (London, 1986).
Redin	M. Redin, *Studies on Uncompounded Personal Names in Old English* (Uppsala, 1919).
Ritter 1927–8	O. Ritter, '*bī-* in Ortsnamen', *Englische Studien* 62 (1927–8), 108–9.
r.n.	river-name.
Ru	Rutland. B. Cox, *The Place-Names of Rutland*, EPNS 67/9 (Nottingham, 1994).
Rumble 1987	A. Rumble, 'Old English *Bōc-land* as an Anglo-Saxon estate name', *Leeds Studies in English* 18 (1987), 219–29.
Russell 1988	P. Russell, 'The suffix *-āko-* in Continental Celtic', *Études Celtiques* 25 (1988), 131–73.
S	P.H. Sawyer, *Anglo-Saxon Charters: an Annotated List and Bibliography* (London, 1968). Cited by number, not page.
Sa	Shropshire. M. Gelling with H.D.G. Foxall, *The Place-Names of Shropshire*, EPNS 62/3, 70– (Nottingham, 1990–).
Sahlgren 1945	J. Sahlgren, '*Barnap*, rundanskt *Barni* och forntyskt *Barnulf, Athalbarn* m.m.', *Saga och Sed* (1945), 29–36.
SB	K. Brunner, *Altenglische Grammatik*, 3rd edn (Tübingen, 1965).
Sf	Suffolk.
sg.	singular.
Smith 1980	C. Smith, 'The survival of Romano-British toponymy', *Nomina* 4 (1980), 27–40.
SND	W. Grant *et al.* (eds), *The Scottish National Dictionary* (Edinburgh, 1931–76).
So	Somerset.
Sr	Surrey. J.E.B. Glover, A. Mawer & F.M. Stenton with A. Bonner, *The Place-Names of Surrey*, EPNS 11 (Cambridge, 1934).
SSNEM	G. Fellows-Jensen, *Scandinavian Settlement Names in the East Midlands* (Copenhagen, 1978).
SSNNW	G. Fellows-Jensen, *Scandinavian Settlement Names in the North West* (Copenhagen, 1985).
SSNY	G. Fellows-Jensen, *Scandinavian Settlement Names in Yorkshire* (Copenhagen, 1972).
St	Staffordshire. J.P. Oakden, *The Place-Names of Staffordshire*, EPNS 55– (Cambridge, 1984–).
Stevenson 1913	W.H. Stevenson, 'Senlac and the Malfossé', *English Historical Review* 28 (1913), 292–303.

st.n.	street-name.
Stratman	F.H. Stratman, *A Middle-English Dictionary*, 2nd edn, rev. by H. Bradley (Oxford, 1891).
Styles & Parsons forthcoming	T. Styles and D. Parsons, 'Place-names which ante-date the OED'
surn.	surname
Svensson	Ö. Svensson, *Saxon Place-Names in East Cornwall* (Lund, 1987).
Swed	Swedish.
Sx	Sussex. A. Mawer & F.M. Stenton with J.B. Glover, *The Place-Names of Sussex*, EPNS 6–7 (Cambridge, 1929–30).
Thuresson	B. Thuresson, *Middle English Occupational Terms* (Lund, 1950).
Townend 1994–5	M. Townend, '*Assandūn* and *Assatún*: the value of skaldic evidence for English place-name studies', *JEPNS* 27 (1994–5), 21–9.
W	Wiltshire. J.E.B. Glover, A. Mawer & F.M. Stenton, *The Place-Names of Wiltshire*, EPNS 16 (Cambridge, 1939).
TLF	P. Imbs *et al.* (eds), *Trésor de la langue française* (Paris 1971– 94).
Udolph 1994	J. Udolph, *Namenkundliche Studien zum Germanenproblem* (Berlin and New York, 1994).
Wa	Warwickshire. J.E.B. Glover, A. Mawer & F.M. Stenton with F.T.S. Houghton, *The Place-Names of Warwickshire*, EPNS 13 (Cambridge, 1936).
Watts 1988–9	V.E. Watts, 'Scandinavian settlement-names in County Durham', *Nomina* 12 (1988–9), 17–63.
Way 1843–65	A. Way, *Promptorium parvulorum sive clericorum . . .* (London, 1843–65).
We	Westmorland. A.H. Smith, *The Place-Names of Westmorland*, EPNS 42–3 (Cambridge, 1967).
Winchester 1986	A.J.L. Winchester, 'The distribution and significance of "bordland" in medieval Britain', *Agricultural History Review* 34 (1986), 129–39.
WNT	M. de Vries *et al.* (eds), *Woordenboek der Nederlandsche Taal* (The Hague and Leiden, 1882–).
Wo	Worcestershire. A. Mawer & F.M. Stenton with F.T.S. Houghton, *The Place-Names of Worcestershire*, EPNS 4 (Cambridge, 1927).
Wormald 1984	P. Wormald, *Bede and the Conversion of England: the Charter Evidence* (Jarrow Lecture, 1984).
Wt	Isle of Wight. H. Kökeritz, *The Place-Names of the Isle of Wight* (Uppsala, 1940).
Y	Yorkshire.
YE	East Riding of Yorkshire. A.H. Smith, *The Place-Names of the East Riding of Yorkshire and York*, EPNS 14 (Cambridge, 1937).
YN	North Riding of Yorkshire. A.H. Smith, *The Place-Names of the North Riding of Yorkshire*, EPNS 5 (Cambridge, 1928).
YW	West Riding of Yorkshire. A.H. Smith, *The Place-Names of the West Riding of Yorkshire*, EPNS 30–7 (Cambridge, 1961–3).
Zachrisson 1934	R.E. Zachrisson, Review of EPNS 6–10, *Zeitschrift für Ortsnamenforschung* 10 (1934), 243–51.

A

á ON, *f.* 'river, stream'. The ON gen.sg. *ár* is found in Ayresome YN. Spellings of several names in Cu and We, as *Wasagh* below, have been explained either as suggesting the existence of a variant ON **ah* or as showing Gaelic influence on names in *á* (see Ekwall 1926, Brooks 1952–3, Fellows-Jensen 1986:65–6).

Both *á* and OE *ēa* seem to be sources of the French-influenced *eau*, a common name for rivers and drainage channels in eastern England, as Great Eau L, perhaps to be identified with *A* c.1210 (ERN:140). Cf. *communis sewere vocat' le Seventowne Aa* 1430 L (cited by OED).

It is possible, but not likely, that Northumbrian OE developed a native **ā* beside *ēa* from which *á* would be formally indistinguishable (see Björkman:101, YW:4·218, but cf. SB:§128,2, OEG:§145).

(*a*) In settlement names with ON and OE elements, perhaps sometimes replacing OE *ēa*: Aby 1086 L (**bȳ**), Acaster 1086 YW (**cæster**), Ayresome 1119 YN (ON *hús*; see **hūs**), Ambleside 1090–7 [14th] We (**melr, sǽtr**), Ayton 1086 YN:100 [& JEPNS:3·34], 1086 YN:165 (**tūn**).

(*c*) With ON elements in many northern r.ns: Beela (*Beetha* 1190–9) We (***beð**), Brathay 1157–63 La–We (**breiðr**), Dowdyrigg 1170–84 We (**dauðr**), Aira Beck c.1250 Cu (**eyrr**), Greta 1200–30 YW–La, 1278 Cu, 1279 YN [& ERN:185] (**grjót**), Croco 1656 Ch:1·19 (**krókr**), Liza 1292 Cu (**ljóss**), Rawthey 1224 [17th] We–YW, Rothay 1275 We (**rauðr**), *Wasagh* (perhaps Wasdale Beck) 1292 We:2·173 (**vatn**), *Thordisa* 1108–14 YN (pers.n.). For *Borghra* and Borrowdale, see **borg**[1].

~ **á-mót, ēa.**

ONP *á*[1]; MED *ā* n.[2]; EDD *ea*; OED *aa*[1].

abbaie OFr, *f.* 'abbey, monastery'. The word derives from Lat *abbatia* which encompassed the meanings 'office, estate and property, jurisdiction of an abbot' and 'abbey'. ME borrowed OFr *abbaie* and Lat *abbatia* (as ME *abbatie, abbodie*), and both retain the range of meanings in the ME period, though they were coming to be separated (see OED *abbacy, abbatie, abbey*).

One instance of ME *abbodie* has been noted, Abdy 13th YW:1·107, where it is stated that two local monasteries owned land in the neighbourhood.

Since early documents are generally in Latin they tend to use *abbatia*, *conventus* or *monasterium*. The OFr/ME term appears fairly early in *the Abbay of Chester* 1349 [16th] Ch:5·35 for what is now Chester Cathedral.

Minor names relating to abbeys are quite common, as *Abbay flat* (f.n.) 1424 YW:2·81, *Abiegate* (f.n.) 1577–80 L:3·10, *Abbey Hill* (f.n.) 1647 Db:423, *Abbey Lane* (st.n. Gloucester) 1455 Gl:2·126. In Abbey Barn (f.n.; *ye Abbey* 1705) We:1·135, where there is no apparent relation to a monastic house, the use may be ironic.

~ Lat *abbatia*. For the *-d-* of *abbodie* see **abbod**.

AND *abbaie*; DML *abbatia*; MED *abbeie, abbat(h)īe, abbodīe*; OED *abbey, abbacy, abbatie*; DES *Abb, Abba, Abbay, Abdey*.

abbesse OFr, *f.* 'abbess'. The French form eventually supplanted OE *abbodesse* in general English usage. The pair alternate in Apesdown Wt, though the 'later' one happens to appear first (*Abbessesdune* l.13th, *le Abbedessedon* 1335). They have also both been identified in Abbotstone W, which certainly contains *abbesse* in some 14th-century spellings, as *Abbesseton* 1322 etc., and relates to ownership by the Abbess of Wilton, who is known to have held the estate in 1339. It is uncertain, however, whether earlier spellings, *Abbedeston* 1249 etc., contain *abbodesse*, as W:388 suggests, or whether they refer instead to previous ownership by an abbot (see **abbod**). There is a similar ambiguity in Rabson W.

(*a*) Apesdown 1272–1307 Wt (**dūn**), Abbotstone 1322 W, Rabson (*Abbedeston* 1242) W (**tūn**).

(*c*) As an affix often rendered by Lat *abbatissa* (*abbas* is later recorded in each instance, and probably represents confusion of *abbesse* with the Latin masculine *abbas*): Abbess Roding 1237 Ess, Melbury Abbas 1291 Do:3·129, Compton Abbas 1293 Do:3·99.

~ Lat *abbatissa*. See also **abbod**.

AND *abbeiesse*; MED *abes(se*; OED *abbess*; DOE *Abbess*.
DML *abbatissa*; DOE *abbodesse*; MED *abbatisse, abbodesse*; OED *abbatess, abbotess*.

abbod OE, *m.* 'abbot'. Beside *abbod* there was also *abbot*, the two forms representing separate borrowings from Lat *abbas* in the oblique cases (genitive *abbatis* etc.). Final *-d* seems to reflect late Latin pronunciation, while the form with *-t* is a later loan, and comes perhaps via OFr. It is not possible to draw a sharp line between them. DOE suggests that *-t* first appears in the second half of the 10th century, though *-d* continues to predominate through the 11th. (For a *-t* that is probably earlier, see *ad abbates land* 861 [13th] S:330 K; it may well be significant that these bounds are framed in Latin.) MED indicates that *-d* survives commonly in ME, though -*t* is usual by the end of the period. In the following examples, *abbod* spellings appear in all the names first recorded before the end of the 12th century, with the exception of Abbott's Barton Ha. *Abbot* forms tend to appear after 1200. Note that *Abbot* and *Abbod* are recorded as ME surnames (DES).

(*a*) *abbotesbrige* (f.n.) c.1290 L:2·218 (**brycg**), Abbotsbury 939–46 [18th] S:1727 Do (**burh**), *Abbott Crofte* (f.n.) 1341 YW:4·114 (**croft**), Awbridge 1086 Ha (**hrycg**), Abbot's Reading 1661 La (*****ryding**), Abbotstone c.970 [12th] S:1821 Ha:19, Abson c.1150 Gl (**tūn**), *le Abbotwath* (f.n.) 1481 YW:5·148 (**vað**), Abbot's Wood 1540 Sx (**wudu**).

(*d*) Frequent as an affix *Abbots* (sometimes rendered by the Latin genitive *abbatis*) and *Abbas* (Latin nominative *abbas*), denoting a monastic possession: Abbot's Bromley 1304 St, Abbotsham 1193 (*Hama* 1086) D, Abbott's Barton 1100–35 Ha, Astley Abbots 1291–2 Sa:1·21, Cerne Abbas 1288 Do [Mills 1991], Milton Abbas 1268 Do:3·219, Thorpe Abbots 1254 Nf.

~ Lat *abbas*, *abbatis*. See also **abbaie**, **abbesse**.

DOE *abbod*; MED *abbot*; OED *abbot*; DES *Abatt*.

*abonā Brit, 'river'. Despite its generic sense the element is never qualified in early sources: the general term may sometimes have been mistakenly borrowed into OE as a proper name, and there is some evidence that *Avon* was an alternative name of several rivers which survived bearing other Celtic names (ERN:22). On the other hand, un-compounded forms are evidenced in Romano-British sources, and unless the Romans were similarly mistaken it appears that *Avon* was acceptable as a simplex r.n. The PrW form of the element would have been **aßon*. See ERN:20–3, LHEB:558, PNRB:239–40, JEPNS:1·43.

(*b*) R. Avon 699–709 [11th] S:64 Nth–Gl ('Upper Avon'), 793–6 S:139 W–Gl ('Bristol' or 'Lower Avon'), 847 S:298 D, 933 [14th] S:424 W–Ha ('East Avon'), 972 S:786 Gl:1·3 ('Little' or 'Middle Avon').

The Bristol Avon is found already in Romano-British sources as *Abona*; it seems that the name was also transferred to the Roman settlement at the mouth of this river (PNRB:240). In later times several places are also named from the various rivers: as Avonmouth Gl (**mūða**), Aveton D (**tūn**).

Further instances in r.ns that have not survived are found in the OE bounds of S:175 (K) and S:573 (Do).

GPC *afon*; CPNE *auon*; cf. LEIA *ab*.

āc OE, *f.* 'oak-tree' is sometimes replaced by ON **eik** as in Eagle L and in the ME spellings of many Danelaw p.ns. It is frequent in OE charters in the names of boundary marks such as *on þa twisledan ac* S:754 Ha, *to wohan æc* S:1556 Gl, and also occurs as a first element in *of ac beara* S:440 So, *to tham ac holte* S:553 Gl. The dat.sg. *æc* survives in Each K, Radnage Bk, and the dat.pl. *ācum* in the various instances of Acomb and in Oaken St. The modern forms *Ac-* and *Oc-* are due to an early ME and a late ME shortening respectively; *Oak-* is usual in late p.ns or is a modern replacement of the older forms by standard English *oak*. On forms like Noke and Rock, which involve *atten* and *atter*, see **atte**. MELS:140–1 and Carlsson:82–3 give many further examples from ME surnames.

(*a*) Commonly with **tūn**: Acton 1002–4 [11th] S:1536 St:1·26, 1086 Sa (×5), 1086 Gl:3·1, 1086 Ch:3·126, Agden 1270 [17th] Ch:2·42, Aighton 1086 La, Aughton 1086 La:121, 1086 YE, 1320–46 La:179. Gelling suggests a possible association of the compound **āc-tūn* with the processing or distribution of oak timber (Sa:1·1–4; instances are mapped Sa:1·9).

With generics denoting 'wood': Ogbeare 1284 Co (**bearu**), *Acholt* 1100–35 Gl, Ackholt 1226 K, Knockholt 1197 K, Nackholt (*fram þære ac holte* 996 [14th] S:877) K [KPN:339], Occold 1086 Sf (**holt**), Akehurst 1318 Sx (**hyrst**), Acle 1086 Nf, Eagle 1086 L, Oakley 956 [15th] S:630 (cf. ASCh:5·21) Do:2·266, c.1002 [12th] Db [ASWills:17], 1060 [13th] S:1030 Bd, 1086 Ess:345, 1327 Do:2·4, 1443 Do:1·115 (**lēah**).

With other topographical generics: Oakdale (*Ockeden* 1257) YW (**denu**), Ogdown 1327 Brk (**dūn**), Okeford 939–46 [18th] S:1719 Do:3·178, 1086 Do:3·59, Shillingstone (*A[c]ford* 1086) Do:2·238 (**ford**), Acrise 1086 K (**hrīs**), Aqualate 1227 St:1·146 (*ge*-**lād**), Oxted 1086 Sr (**stede**), Oakwell 1333 YW (**welle**), Oakworth 1086 YW (**worð**).

(*b*) Acomb 1086 YW:4·228, 1222 YN, 1268 Nb, East Acomb 1242 Nb, Aike 1086 YE, Each 1086 K [DEPN], Noak 1327 Wo, The Noake 1320 Gl, Noke 1086 O, Oake 11th KCD:897 So, Oaken 1086 St, Oaks 1086 Sa:1·225, Rock (*Ak* 1224) Wo.

(*c*) With descriptive elements: *Vairoke* (surn.) 1312 Gl [METT:89] (**fæger**), *Gildenock* 1280 Do:3·93 (**gylden**), Harrock c.1260 La (**hār²**), *Pykedok'* (surn.) 1327 Gl [METT:82] (**pīced**), Radnage 1162 Bk (**rēad**), *Selioak* 1324 Db:198 (**sēlig**).

With words associated with religion: Cressage (*Cristesache* 1086) Sa:1·102 (**Crist**), Holyoaks 1086 Ru, Holyoake's Fm (*le Haliok* 1255) Wo:364 (**hālig**).

With a pers.n.: Hodsock 1086 Nt.

A group of names may allude to meeting-places: Matlock 1086 Db (**mæðel**), Skyrack Wapentake 1086 YW, Shireoaks 1100–35 Nt (**scīr**[1]). The latter element, meaning 'shire', cannot be separated from **scīr**[2] 'bright', which has been preferred for Shireoaks 1415 Db:527, 1461–83 Db:78.

~ **ācet, æcen, eik.*

DOE *āc*; MED *ōk(e*; EDD *oak*; OED *oak*; DES *Ake, Oak, Roke.*

*ācet OE, 'oak-wood'. MELS:142 notes further examples from Sr in ME surnames.

(*b*) The Hockett 1606 Brk, Hockett Wd 1791–2 Brk, *la Okette* (f.n.) 1294 Sr:359, *atto Okotto* 1327 Ha (Sx:18).

~ *āc, -et.*

DOE –; MED –; EDD –; OED –.

ād OE, *m.* and *n.* 'pyre, burning-place'. The term is used of a 'funeral pyre' in OE and ME texts. Forsberg 1970 indicates, however, that p.ns containing the element cannot be assumed to date from the period when early Anglo-Saxons practised cremation: names are found in areas where cremation burials are rare or unknown, while the recorded ME phrase *atten Ode* suggests that in at least one name the word was still meaningful in the 14th century (see **atte**). The guess 'ash heap' has still less to recommend it, and Forsberg suggests that 'limekiln' and 'beacon' are more likely specific meanings in p.ns. 'Limekiln' is a sense recorded for ME *ode* in the 14th century (though not noted by MED; see Forsberg 1970:51). There is no direct evidence for a sense 'beacon', but the sites of several examples lie appropriately on top of conspicuous hills, some of which certainly had beacons in later times. Forsberg argues that *on þat ealde ad* S:630 Do and *of þone ealdan ad* S:574 ?St might be OE examples of this usage.

Whatever its precise applications, the root sense of the word seems likely to have been 'site where fires were deliberately lit, burning-place'.

For *to þam ealdan ad fini* S:412 Ha, see ***fīnig**.

Outside OE charter bounds Forsberg identifies and discusses five instances of the element in minor names: *le Ode* 1286 O, The Nodes (*del Ode* c.1240) Wt [& Mills 1996:77], *la Ode* 1324 Wt, *le Oade* 1608 Wt and *Selestede ade* 1214 Roxburghshire (p.n.).

There are in addition several examples which, like The Nodes above, might contain a relic of the ME article *atten*: The Node 1282–5 Hrt, *atte Node* 1327 W, Nodehill (*atte Node* 1327) Wt:155, *le Node* (f.n.) 1543 Gl:1·137, Noads Copse 1591 Brk:332, *Nodeclose* 1630 Wt:229. There are relatively so many of these, however (and Forsberg lists further modern instances from Wt and Ha), that another element in *nod-* may be involved. Variation in OE grammatical gender between masculine and neuter may be dialectal (Kitson 1990:213).

~ OHG *eit* 'fire, burning-place, pyre'.

DOE *ād*; MED *ād*; EDD –; OED *ad* sb.[1]; DES *Noad*.

adela OE, *m.* 'filth, foul liquid', surviving as dialect *addle* 'stagnant water, urine'. Udolph 1994:298 maps the English element and Continental cognates.

OE also has a strong form *adel*.

(*a*) Addelhole 1547–53 D:305 (**hol**[1]), Addle Street, formerly -Lane (st.n. London) 1304 Ldn:102 (**lane**), *Adelmede* (f.n.) 1539 Gl:1·67 (**mēd**), *Adlemore* (f.n.) 1295 Ch:4·49 (**mōr**).

(*b*) Adel 1086 YW.

~ borrowed into MCo as *atal* 'rubbish, mining waste', which also appears as a p.n. element (CPNE).

DOE *adela*; MED *adel(e* adj.; EDD *addle* sb.[1] & adj.; OED *addle* sb. & a.

afnám ON, *n.* 'plot taken from common or undeveloped land'. In OWN prose texts *afnám* tends to mean 'a share reserved before the general division of property', while in 14th-century Swedish *afnām* is found with the meaning 'land severed from an estate'. In English usage, however, the term seems specifically to denote land newly enclosed for private cultivation (cf. Atkinson 1886, Ekwall 1918:195–6).

ME often has *of-*, from OE, and it is interesting that a parallel OE ***innām** (apparently the same process seen from the opposite viewpoint, a taking *into* cultivated land rather than *from* undeveloped land) seems to have existed independently. Moreover, OE *ofniman* is attested. The distribution of ME *ofnam*, however, suggests that it is an Anglicisation of the ON term.

The term is common in northern minor and f.ns. It is often unclear whether it is used as a name or a common noun.

(*a*) *Avena'croftes* c.1270 Cu:436 (**croft**).

(*b*) *Ofnam* (f.n.) 1160 YN:329, Haynholme 12th YW, *avenames* (f.n.) c.1208 YW:2·60, Yanham (f.n.) 1208–49 We:1·75, *Lavenum* (f.n.) 1252 YW:1·161, *Ofnumes* (f.n.) c.1255 Cu:165, Aynhems 1290 YW, *Afnames* (f.n.) e.13th Ch:4·198, Little Aynam (st.n. Kendal) 1409 We, Avenham 1591 La.

~ ON *nema* 'to take', ON *af*, OE *of* 'from'. Cf. ***innām**, **inntak**.

ONP *af·nám*; MED *ofnăm*; EDD –; OED –.

-age ME, *suffix*, originally in words adopted from French, but later added to English nouns to denote appurtenance or to form collectives. Used to turn a noun into a p.n. with the sense 'place where there are . . .': with plant-names Gorstage 1503 Ch:3·202 'place where gorse bushes grow' (**gorst**), *Thornage* (f.n.) 1357 Ch:4·191 'place where thorn-trees grow' (**þorn**), cf. Marlage (f.n.) 1839 Ch:1·62 (**marle**) 'place where there is lime-rich soil'.

agistement OFr, *m.* 'seasonal right of pasturage, rented pasture-land'. The pasture might be grazing land or woodland pasture for swine. There was a shortened ME form *agiste* which may have been formed directly from the verb, OFr *agister* 'to lodge, pasture'. Loss of initial *a-* (cf. OED *gistment*, *justment²*, *gist* sb.¹) appears to be due to its misreading as the indefinite article.

(*b*) Gist head (f.n.; *the least* 1660) We:2·62, Justment (*Agismont* 1713) D, Joistment (f.n.) 1801 Gl:1·40.

> AND *agistement*; DML *agistamentum*; MED *ağiste, ağist(e)ment*; EDD *agist* sb., *agistment*; OED *agistment*.

-āko- Brit, *adj. suffix*, used to form p.ns and r.ns. The sense implied by the suffix varies. Cam Beck, from **kambo-* 'crooked', would be 'the bent one'. York, from **eburo-* which may mean 'yew-tree', would probably be 'the place of yew-trees'. Note that **kambo-* and **krumbo-* are each apparently applied to rivers and hills in identical formations. For further possible instances in English r.ns see ERN:lxxviii. For discussion of the element in Britain and on the Continent, and of its transition from adjectival to name-forming suffix, see Russell 1988. The PrW form of the suffix would have been **-ǭg* (JEPNS:1·43).

In r.ns: Cam Beck 1169 Cu:7 (**kambo-*), Crummock Beck (*Crombok'* p.1150) Cu:10 (**krumbo-*), Wheelock 1086 Ch:1·38 [& Ch:2·273] (**swelo-*).

In hill-names: Cammock 13th YW:6·151 (**kambo-*), Crummack 1190 YW:6·229 (**krumbo-*).

Applied to sites that became habitations: York (Romano-British *Eburacum*) YE (**eburo-*), ?Haydock 1169 La (**sasjo-*).

~ **barrāko-*.

> GPC *-og*; CPNE *-ek*.

*alaunā Brit, of unknown meaning. An element widely attested on the Continent and in Roman Britain, generally as a r.n., though occasional examples suggest that it may have been applied to other topographical features. It is also found in personal, tribal and divine names, a range of applications which implies that the term was adjectival and broad in sense; suggestions have included 'mighty, holy', 'good', 'shining', 'speckled' and 'nursing'. Variation between *alaun- and *aloun- is problematic, and may reflect two distinct forms; for discussion, and reasons to see *aloun- as the source of PrW *alūn and the Welsh r.n. *Alun*, see Lambert 1990. The form *alaun- is hesitatingly retained here in the headword because it is much the more common spelling in Romano-British sources. These sources generally suggest an *ā*-stem, but occasionally an *o*-stem. See ERN:5–8, LHEB:309, PNRB:243–7, JEPNS:1·43, Kitson 1996:81.

(*b*) R. Aln (Romano-British *Alaunos*, *Alne* c.730 [Bede]) Nb, Ayle Burn (*Alne* 1347) Cu–Nb, R. Ellen (the Roman fort at its mouth is *Alauna*) 1171–5 [14th] Cu.

The R. Alne Wa is probably to be added, since another instance of Romano-British *Alauna* is likely to refer to the town of Alcester on its course, though this explanation would mean dismissing as corrupt the first Anglo-Saxon form (*Æluuinnæ* 716–37 [11th] S:94). The village of Alne c.1040 [12th] YN may also belong here, though the river that it stands on is now called the Kyle, which is itself supposed to be a Celtic name (see ***koilo-**).

The names of the various rivers are sometimes transferred to other names, as Allerdale Cu, Alnmouth Nb.

~ perhaps from the IE root found in ***alaventa**. The element has been considered pre-Celtic in origin; see Nicolaisen 1957:227–8 and 1971:98.

CPNE *alun.

*alaventa ?pre-Celtic, of uncertain meaning. An ancient r.n. supposed by Ekwall to be Celtic (ERN:11), but assigned by others to 'Old European', a stratum of western Indo-European language spoken on the Continent and in Britain before the arrival of Celtic. *alaventa is supposed to derive from the IE root *el-/*ol- 'to flow'. See Krahe 1964:35, Nicolaisen 1971:95, Kitson 1996:80–1, 85–6.

(*b*) Alwent Beck 1235–6 Du, R. Alwin c.1200 Nb, R. Allen 1275 Nb. Also in Allan Water c.1160 Scotland. See ERN:10.

The same IE root may be involved in ***alaunā** and in another possible pre-Celtic r.n., ***alma**, which is proposed for the R. Yealm 1309 D (see Nicolaisen 1957:225, Krahe 1964:36; cf. ERN:479–80).

ald OE, *adj.* 'old'. This is the OE Anglian form; in Kentish and West Saxon the form is *eald*. Standard English *old* derives from the midlands. In the north the regular development was to *ald*, and in the south to *eld* (which is reflected in earlier spellings of Oldbury K and Old Heath Ess). In the south-west, and especially Devon, initial *ea-* tends to produce a rising diphthong, as in the many instances of Yelland (also Yalland, Yolland) D; probably this is a sound-change belonging to the OE period (Hallqvist 1948:78–81). A similar development in Kent, cf. Yaldham and Yaugher, is later (Hallqvist 1948:102).

Formally the adjective cannot be distinguished from the OE pers.n. *(E)alda.*

(*a*) Particularly common with ancient and disused earthworks and fortifications: Albury 1086 Hrt:169, Aldborough (*Burg* 1086, *Aldeburg* 1145) YW, 1086 Nf, Aldbrough 1086 YN, 1086 YE, Aldburgh 1155 YN, Aldbury 1086 Hrt:26, Aldeburgh 1086 Sf, Oldbury 972 s:786 Gl:3·28, 1086 Sa, 1185 Gl:3·8, 12th Wa, 1302 K (**burh**), Oldcastle 1260 Ch:4·44 (**castel**), Aldwark 1086 YN, c.1140 Db, Aldwarke 1226 YW (*ge-weorc*).

With habitative elements, sometimes referring to individual buildings, sometimes relating long-established settlements to new ones, and sometimes—as in Aldwych Mx (see Gelling 1988:248)—indicating a former site: *Aldecroft* 1260 Ch:2·20 (**croft**), *Oldehale* (surn.) 1275 Wo [MELS:142] (**hall**), Aldam 1246 YW, Aldenham 1086 Hrt, Aldham 1086 Ess, 1086 Sf, Yaldham 1177 K (**hām**), Alport 1154–89 Db:183, 1282 La (**port²**), *Oldestrete* (surn.) 1327 So [MELS:143] (**strēt**), Alton 1298 Db:578, Old Town 1451 We:1·51 (**tūn**), Aldwick 1235 Sx, Aldwych 1199 Mx (**wīc**).

With other non-topographical elements, indicating former or long use: Aldford 1153 Ch:4·77 (**ford**), Old Heath a.1272 Ess (**hȳð**), Oldmixon 1200 So (**mixen**), *Old Park* 1340 We:1·191 (**parc**), Altofts c.1090 YW:2·119 (**toft**), Yelloways 1549 D (**weg**).

With terms for land, probably often referring to ground that has been long-cultivated; sometimes also to worn-out or fallow fields (see D: 1·lviii, Brk:865). EDD notes *old-land* as 'arable land which has been laid down in grass more than two years', but it also gives another—and rather different—specific sense: 'ground that has lain untilled a long time, and is now ploughed up', and several quotations make it clear that it is *at the time of re-use* that the term becomes applicable. Examples in p.ns include: Oldacres 1267 Du [NbDu:152] (**æcer**), Aldfield 1086 YW, 1200 Brk, Offal c.1250 C:74, Oldfield a.1162 YW:6·8 (**feld**), *Oldefallyngge* (surn.) 1286 St [METT:79] (**felging** 'fallow land'), Yaugher 1334 K (**gāra**), Oldham 1222–6 La (**holmr**), *Aldelond'* (surn.) 1260 So [MELS:142], Oldland 1086 Gl, Yelland 1275 D:311, 1281 D:359 (**land**).

With r.ns, generally referring to a former course of the river: Old

Avon 1539 Gl, *Old Ea* 1404 YW:7·133, Old Eye c.1226 [14th] L:1·38, Old River Ouse 1311 YE:10.

(*d*) As an affix, to distinguish an original from a newer settlement: All Cannings 1205 W (distinct from Bishop's Cannings), Old Sodbury 1385 Gl (distinct from Chipping Sodbury).

Kitson 1993:34–5 notes that the adjective is by far the most common qualifying element in Anglo-Saxon boundary clauses. For a range of examples, see Brk:774–5, where most of the categories set out above are exemplified in documents of the 9th–11th centuries, as *ealdan byrig* (**burh**), *ealdan dic* (**dīc**), *ealdan cot stowe* (**cot-stōw**), *ealdan wæg* (**weg**), *ealdan fyrh* (**furh**), *ealdan dune* (**dūn**), *ealdan broc* (**brōc**), *ealdan lace* (**lacu**), etc. The combination *ald-land* is attested in OE (S:389 D) and may already have had a specific sense; see DOE *eald-land*. Note that the OE adjectival inflection -*an* is preserved in some p.ns, as Aldenham Hrt.

DOE *eald*; MED *ōld(e* adj.; EDD *old*; OED *old*; DES *Old*.

aldormann OE, *m.* 'prince, nobleman, chief officer of a shire' came to mean in ME 'governor of a guild' and then 'magistrate in a city or borough'. It is attested as a ME surname (DES). The headform used here is Anglian; the word appears in its southern (West Saxon, Kentish) form, with *ea*-, in *to ðes ealdormonnes gemere* S:724 Brk:747.

(*a*) Aldermanbury (st.n. London) c.1130, *Aldermanbury* 1226 Bd (**burh**), Aldermaston 1086 Brk, Alderminster (*Aldermanneston* 1169) Wo (**tūn**).

~ OE *(e)aldor* 'an elder', **mann**.

DOE *ealdor-mann*; MED *alder-man*; OED *alderman*; DML *aldermannus*; AND *alderman*; DES *Alderman*.

alee OFr, *f.* 'alley, bordered passage'. The early use of the word is discussed and exemplified at length in Ldn:169–76.

(*a*) Ally Croft (f.n.) 1630 W:467 (**croft**), *Alley meadow* (f.n.) 1684 Db:644 (**mēd**).

(*b*) *the Alleyes* (f.n.) 1623 Gl:2·122.

(*c*) *Longe ally* (st.n. Tewkesbury) 1540 Gl:2·63 (**lang¹**), Millaley 1588 We (**myln**), Twisting Alley (f.n.) 1687 Ch:1·192 (**twisting**), *An' Alley* (st.n. Chester) 1543 Ch:5·9 (pers.n.), *Fridaysaley* (st.n. London) 1421 (?pers.n.), Panyer Alley (st.n. London) 1442 (inn n.), *Wringesaley* (st.n. London) 1363 (?pers.n.).

~ **bowling-alley**.

AND *alee*; DML *aleia*; MED *alei(e*; EDD *alley* sb.¹; OED *alley*.

áll ON, *m.* 'eel'.

(*a*) High Marr (*Alemar* 1218) YE:271 (**marr**).

OE ēl[1] is also replaced by its cognate in *Auburn* YE (**burna**), which is *Eleburne* 1086 but *Alburne* etc. from 1135–40.

~ ēl[1].

ONP *áll*[1].

almerie ME, 'storehouse, ambry' was early identified with forms from OFr *almosnerie* 'almonry, place where alms were distributed' (cf. **aumoner**). The words might be distinguished by the presence in the latter of a medial *-n-*, though even in the ME period spellings without are attested, cf. MED *aumenerī, aumery*. In p.ns forms often alternate between spellings with *-n-* and without: *The Almory/Ambry* in Westminster is *the Aumorie* in 1494, *the Amnerie* in 1593, and in 1603 is explained thus: '*The Elemosinary or Almory* now corruptly the Ambry, for that the Almes of the Abbey were there distributed to the poore' (cited in Mx:166 and OED). The semantic proximity of terms meaning 'place where food was stored' and 'place from which food was distributed' is clear, and the two may actually have converged in practice.

(*a*) *Almery Grange* 1538 Gl (**grange**, providing for the storehouse of Cirencester Abbey), *Amery house* 1724 Gl (**hūs**; a storehouse belonging to St Mary's Abbey, Tewkesbury), *le Ambree landes* (f.n.) 1601 L:3·160 (**land**).

(*b*) Almsbury (*the Amery* 1539) Gl, *le Amery* (f.n.) 1440 Ch:3·253 (a storehouse belonging to the abbot of Chester's grange at Ince).

(*c*) *Leuewynesamery* 1277 Ess:360 (pers.n.; owned by Waltham Abbey).

~ OFr *almarie*, MLat *armarium, almarium*.

AND *aumaire*; DML *armarium*; MED *almerīe*; EDD *ambry*; OED *ambry*.
AND *aumosnerie*; DML *elemosinaria*; MED *aumenerī*; OED *almonry*.

almr ON, *m.* 'elm-tree'.
(*a*) *Alinbalike* [for *Almbanke*] (f.n.) c.1200 We:2·167 (**banke**), *Almebergh* (f.n.) 12th YW:5·183 (**berg**), *Almcroft* (f.n.) 13th YW:4·64 (**croft**), Almsford 1576 YW (**ford**), Almholme 1232–7 YW (**holmr**), *le Almekeldecroft* (f.n.) 1288 YW:5·67 (**kelda, croft**).

~ **elm**.

ONP *almr*; MED *alme*.

alor OE, *m.* 'alder-tree'. Gen.sg. *alres* appears in Alresford Ha. Gen.pl. *alra* or dat.sg. *alre* lies behind the many early forms in *Alre(-)*. Variation due to metathesis is found already in the OE charter forms *on arlscagan/of alrscagan* S:255 D (**sceaga**). The OE word could not generally be distinguished from various related ON forms (OGNS *alr, alri, ölr*). Cf.

also ON **elri**.

Note the common development to *oller*, *owler* in parts of the midlands and north (EDD).

(*a*) Combined with words indicating or implying a watery site (including r.ns): Aller Beck 1513 We (**bekkr**), Arlebrook 1268 Gl (**brōc**), Alderbourne 1224 [15th] Bk, R. Enborne 749 [12th] S:258 (see ERN:148) Ha–Brk (**burna**), Alderford 1163 Nf, Alresford ?824–33 [12th] S:284 (cf. S:242) Ha (**ford**), Aldercar 1335 Db:436 (**kjarr**), Allerwash 1202 Nb (DEPN), Alrewas 942 [13th] S:479 (cf. ASCh:2·5) St (***wæsse**), Alderwasley 1251 Db (***wæsse, lēah**).

With elements meaning 'wood': Ollerbarrow 1406 Ch:2·24 (**bearu**), Alderholt 1285 Do:2·195 (**holt**), Alderley 1086 Gl (**lēah**), Ollershaw l.12th [13th] Ch:2·118 (**sceaga**).

With habitative generics: Alderton 1086 Sf, 1309 Sa, Allerton 1086 La, 1086 YW:3·242, 1086 YW:4·89, 1086 YW:4·137, Ollerton 1086 Ch:2·79, 1086 Nt, 1240 La, Orleton 1086 He, Owlerton 1310 YW (**tūn**), *Alretunstall* 1199–1216 [17th] Ch:2·31 (**tūn, stall**), Aldridge 1086 St (**wīc**).

With other elements: *Alrecumbe* (f.n.) 1148–79 Gl:1·159 (**cumb**), Ollersett 1216–72 Db (**sǽtr** or *ge*-**set**), Aldershot 1171 Ha (**scēat**).

(*b*) Aller 10th ASC A s.a.878 So, 1086 D:346, 1086 D:504, 1086 D:564, Arle 862 [14th] S:209 Gl.

(*c*) Longner 1086 Sa:1·182, Longnor 1121 Sa:1·182, 1086 St:1·136 (**lang**[1], in the OE construction **(æt þam) langan alre*), Lightollers 1246 La (**lēoht**), Bicknoller 1291 So (pers.n.).

An extraordinary group of Devon names contains animals and birds as first elements: Bulealler 1238 D (***bula**), Duckaller 1277 D (**dūce**), Hawkealter (*Hauekeallere* 1275) D (**hafoc**), Houndaller 12th D (**hund**[1]). Foxearle 1086 Sx may be a similar instance, though the forms are difficult and the suggestion of a by-form, or collective noun, *elre (Anderson 1934–9:3·102) lacks supporting English evidence.

~ ***alret, ælren, elri**.

DOE *alor*; MED *alder* n.[1]; EDD *aller* sb.[1], *alder*; OED *alder* sb.[1]; DES *Alder, Aldren*.

alpe ME, 'bullfinch' is likely in *Alpeleye* (f.n.) 1276 Gl:3·55 (**lēah**), though just possibly it is the derived surname (cf. Matilda Alpe 1275, DES).

~ of unknown origin.

MED *alpe*; EDD *alp*; OED *alp*[2]; DES *Alp*.

***alret** OE, 'alder copse'. Löfvenberg (MELS:1–2) presents many more examples from surnames in Sx and Sr, and discusses the formation. He notes several instances of *Nelrette* and the like which point to a mutated side-form **ælret*, **elret*. In that, and in most of the examples below, *n* has been attracted from the article *atten* (see **atte**).
(*b*) *le Aldrette* (f.n.) 1381 Sr:359, Nalderswood 1332 Sr, Naldred 1327 Sx:264, Naldrett 1279 Sx:157, Naldretts Copse 1332 Sx:135.
~ **alor, -et**.
DOE –; MED *aldret*; EDD –; OED –; DES *Aldritt, Arlet*.

***alto-** Brit, 'slope, cliff, hill' is probable in Alt c.1200 La, and may originally have referred to a long ridge in Brk surviving in Altwood 1241 (see Brk:54). In Auckland c.1050 [12th] Du [CDEPN] it may be combined with a Brit r.n.

Jackson (cited in Ch:3·xvi) dismisses the element as the original name of Holtridge (*Althurst* 1380, *Altrich* 1630) Ch:3·109 (**hyrst, hrycg**) on the grounds that *allt* tends to mean 'steep slope' and the slope is not there steep enough. The term, however, encompasses a range of meanings in the Brittonic languages, including 'inland slope, sea-shore, rock' etc. (see CPNE:4), and in early usage it might have had a similar range.

Beeston Ch:3·302 was interpreted as 'bee-stone' (though the first element is probably **byge²** 'commerce') and translated into 15th-century Welsh as *y Fêl Allt* 'the honey rock'—there is a precipitous crag at this place. *Allt* also appears in such wholly Welsh names as Allt Bough 1474 He (probably *bwch* 'goat') and Altwent 1334 He (*gwynt* 'windy'), cf. Charles 1963:94.
CPNE *als*; GPC *allt*; cf. LEIA *alt*.

ambo Lat, *adj.* 'both', usually referring to two villages of the same name forming one parish. This situation is variously described, cf. *Ludton* 1086, *duabus Luttunis* 1108–14, *Luttons two* 1650, *Luttons-Ambo* 1828 YE.
(*d*) Huttons Ambo YN, Luttons Ambo YE, Wendens Ambo Ess: cf. also Bradleys Both YW.

amer OE, a bird, probably 'a bunting'. The headword used here is a rationalisation of recorded spellings in Anglo-Saxon glossaries: *omer*, *amore*, *emer*, *emœr* (and cf. *clodhamer*, which may be parallel to the later 'clod-bird', used of the bunting). The evidence for this word and its appearance in p.ns is discussed at great length in Parsons & Styles 1996. It is most probably found in the OE charter forms *on omer lond* S:1329 Wo (**land**) and *Omermád* S:1036 Ess (**mēd**). Thereafter there are a series of formal possibilities, from names which show a number of early spellings without -*b*-, as Amberden 1086 Ess (**denu**), through names which consistently have -*b*-, including Amberley 1086 Sx and 1166 Gl (**lēah**), to names with consistent genitive *Ambres*-, as Ambrosden 1086 O (**dūn**), Ombersley 12th Wo (**lēah**) and Amesbury 873–88 [11th] s:1507 W (**burh**). We argue that all of these could contain *amer*, but that where there is an original -*b*- other explanations (including a personal name, tribal name or river-name) cannot formally be excluded. The regular combination of *Amber*- and *Ambres*- with elements that denote, or could denote, open country may give a little support to the suggestion that many of the names involve buntings.

~ OHG *amaro*, *golt-amaro* 'bunting, yellowhammer'.

DOE *amer*; MED –; EDD *yellow-ammer*, *yellow-omber*, *golden amber*; OED *hammer* sb.[2], *yellow-hammer*.

á-mót ON, *n*. 'meeting of rivers, confluence'. Cf. Beckermonds YW (see **bekkr**). Reasonably certain instances, suiting the topography, are:
(*a*) Ameshaugh 1314 Cu (**halh**).
(*b*) *Aymot* 1210 YN, *Amot* (f.n.) 1682 YW:6·271.

In addition the ON form alternates with OE **ēa-mōt** in River Eamont and Eamont Bridge (*æt Ea motum* c.1060 ASC D s.a.926, *Amoth* 12th, *Amot* c.1255 etc) We.

Other instances of ME *amot(e)* may represent **æmette** 'ant' (see **æmett-hyll**).

~ **á**, **mōt**, **ēa-mōt**.

ONP *á·mót*.

ampre OE, *f*. a weed infesting corn-fields, probably '(bur)dock, sorrel'; also used of a water plant, cf. *fen-ampre* 'water dock'. It may occur in:
(*a*) Ampleforth 1086 YN (**ford**), Emper Cotton (f.n.) 1536 Ch:4·110 (p.n.).

~ OHG *amphra*, Ger *Ampfer* 'sorrel'.

DOE *ampre*[2]; MED –; EDD –; OED –.

ān OE, *num./adj.* 'one, single'. In p.ns presumably sometimes with the further sense 'alone, isolated'.

The element cannot be distinguished from an OE pers.n. *An(n)a/On(n)a* (Redin:60).
(*a*) One Ash 1086 Db (**æsc**), Ancoats 1243 (earlier *Einecote* 1212, apparently with ON **einn**) La, Onecote 1199 St (**cot**), Ancroft 1195 [14th] Nb (**croft**), Onehouse 1052–66 [14th] Sf [ASWills:34], One Ho. (*Anhus* c.1166) Ch:1·140 (**hūs**), Anley 1086 YW, Olney c.1220 Nth, Only 1200 YW:3·99, Onneley 1086 St (**lēah**), Anston 1086 YW, Onston 1182

Ch:3·200 (stān), Antrey Lee (f.n.) l.13th Ch:2·267 (trēow, lēah).

~ ānlēpig, ānsetl, ānstīg, einn.

DOE *ān*; MED *ŏn* num.; EDD *an* num.adj., *one*; OED *an* a.¹, *an-* prefix (sense 3), *one* numeral, a., pron.

anchorage ModE, 'hermitage', first noted 1593 by OED.
(*a*) *Ankridge Hill* 1611 Ch:5·82 (identified with the site of *the Ankers Chappel* 1550).
(*b*) Ankerage (f.n.) 1842 Gl:3·41.

~ ancor.

OED *anchorage²*.

anchorite ME, 'recluse, hermit' is found as *Aumcorite* (f.n.) 1359 Do:2·191, apparently used elliptically for 'anchorite cell, hermitage'. A later reference to the same place is *Anchoriste* 1427, representing *anchorist*, a variant form here recorded in ME for the first time (cf. OED *anachorist* from a.1604, *anchorist* from 1651). The modern form of the f.n. is Anchor Md.

~ Lat *anachoreta* (from Gk), OFr *anacorite*; influenced by OE **ancor**.

MED *anchŏrīte*; OED *anchorite*; DML *anachoreta*.

ancor OE, *m.* 'recluse, hermit'. Beside this must have existed a feminine OE **ancre* 'anchoress'—in later use the OE words cannot be separated and ME *ancre* is applied to both sexes.
    The OE masculine term is also attested as a weak noun *ancra*.
(*a*) Anchor Church c.1270 Db:635 [& Db:3·viii], *Ankirkirk* (bdg.n. Richmond) 1479 YN:287 (**cirice**), *Ancarig* (the old name of Thorney) c.1150 ASC E s.a.656 C:280 (**ēg**), *Ankerhawe* (f.n.) 1497 Brk:75 (**haga¹**), *le Ancorhouse* (f.n.) 1608 YW:2·81, *le Ancris House* (Kendal bdg.n.) 1549 We:1·118 (**hūs**), Ankerwyke 1194 (cf. *in heremitorio Basingarum loco* c.1150) Bk:245 [cf. Sr:xl] (**wīc**).
(*b*) Ankers Knowl (*del Ancres* 1325) Ch:1·126.

~ Lat *anachoreta*, perhaps via Irish (OEG:§565); see also **anchorite**.

DOE *ancor²*; MED *ancre*; OED *anchor* sb.²; AND *ancre²*.

*ande- Brit, *intensive prefix* 'great, big' is found in *Anderitum*, the British name of the Roman fort at Pevensey Sx (***ritu-** 'ford'). The Anglo-Saxons adopted the name and transferred it to the forest which covered the Weald from Kent to Hampshire; note also the OE forms *Andredesleage* (**lēah**), *Andredesweald* (**wald**). Pevensey itself is *Andredescester* 10th ASC A s.a.491 (**cæster**). See Jackson 1948:54–5, PNRB:250–2; cf. LEIA *an-*.

*anger OE, 'grassland' is proposed on the basis of cognates (Mawer
1913:56–7). 'Grassland' is the most common sense in German (and
Middle Dutch) and the word is thought to be related to ON **eng** 'meadow'.
It may also be cognate, however, with ON **angr* 'inlet, bay' and other
words derived from a root **ang-* 'to bend'. There is therefore some reason
to be cautious about its precise early meaning. Moreover OHG *angar*
glosses Lat *arva* 'ploughed field' and Lat *forum* 'market-place' (see
AHDW *angar*², DW *Anger*, DEW *Anger*). Clearly the meaning of the OE
cognate is not easily established.

For Angerton La Ekwall suggests ON **angr* as an alternative, but
concedes that it is less probable (La:221–2). Ingram 1242 Nb appears to
contain **hām** or **hamm** (*Angerham* 1242 etc.), but given the frequency of
the dat.pl. name in the north it is perhaps a dat.pl. reinterpreted. The
word can be difficult to distinguish from **hangra** and **angle**.

(*a*) *Angerhale* 1268 C:131 (**halh**), Angerton 1187 Nb, 1278 Cu:144, 1293
La (**tūn**).

(*b*) Ongar 1043–5 [13th] S:1531 Ess:71 (?dat.sg.), Angerholme 1324 We,
Angram c.1190 YE, 1195–1200 YN:272, 1252 YN:191, 1276 YW:5·217,
1280 YW:4·252, 1324 La (all dat.pl.).

~ OHG *angar*, Ger *Anger* 'grassland, etc.'

DOE –; MED –; EDD –; OED –.

angle ME, 'angle, corner, point of land'; also 'outlying spot' without
reference to shape (MED, OED). ME and later usage probably derives
from OFr *angle*, and perhaps Lat *angulus*, though OE *angel*, ON *ongull*
'(fish-) hook' may also be influences—the Germanic and Romance terms
are ultimately related. No convincing instance earlier than the 13th century
has been noted in p.ns, and there is no particular reason to suspect that
OE or ON enters directly into the examples (though the possibility exists,
cf. Angeln, Schleswig-Holstein, which may lie behind the tribal name
Angle; see Laur 1992:127). Anglesey 12th C may involve the tribal name
(DEPN); alternatively it has been explained as an earlier *Angerhales-ēg*
(C:131), see *Angerhale* s.v. **anger*. This possibility introduces the
problem that *l* and *r* often interchange in medieval records. Thus Christ's
Piece C was formerly *Clayangles* but the first spelling is *Clayhangre* 1216
(C:40)—though spellings in *(h)angle* are much the more common, **anger*
cannot presumably be excluded from this, or from other instances.
Confusion with **hangra** is similarly possible.

Probable early instances are fairly scarce. For Angle 13th
Pembrokeshire see Charles 1992:2·672, where *Goldsmethesangle* 1362 is
noted in the same county. Beside Ovangle 1476 La (?1st el.) are noted the

13th-century f.ns *Low-angle, Ox-angle* (La:176). Note also *Fleghangelles* (f.n.) 1603 C:324 (**fleg**), *le Southangle* (f.n.) 1399 YW:2·19 (**sūð**) and *the Angel* (f.n.) 1677 St:1·98.

Later examples include Angle Corner 1668 C:263, Angle Farm c.1825 C:201 and The Angle c.1840 C:287, the latter two situated in outlying parts of their parishes. Angeldown 1843 Brk (**dūn**) is compared to an *Angledowne* 1639 Ha (Brk:492).

~ **anglet.**

AND *angle*[1]; DML *angulus*; MED *angle* n.[2]; EDD *angle* sb.[1]; OED *angle* sb.[2]; DES *Angle*.

anglet OFr, *m.* 'little angle or corner', first recorded in an English text c.1450 (MED).

(*b*) *les Anglettes* (f.n.) 1219 Hu [Bd:292].

~ **angle.**

AFW *anglet*; AND *anguilette*; MED *anglet*; EDD –; OED *anglet*.

ānlēpig OE, *adj.* 'single, solitary'. The forms of this word in OE are complex. The head-form given here represents a 'regular' Anglian development of the adjective, which is believed to combine **ān** 'one', and a form of *hlēapan* 'to leap' (cf. **hlēp*, 'a leap, something that is jumped'; but note also the rather different meaning of ON *einhleypr* 'single; unmarried and homeless'). The gradual obscuring of the original sense, whatever that was in OE, the consequent sporadic shortening of the second element, suffix alternation and dialectal developments all contribute to the range of attested spellings, which include all permutations but one of *æn-* and *an-* plus *-lypig, -lype, -lipig, -lipe, -lepig* and *-lepe*, as well as the shortened *ælpig* (cf. OEG:§204.2 n.3, §357, §468; Hogg 1992:§5.76, §6.30).

The term is commonly applied to isolated features in OE charter bounds: *of ðare anlipigan æc* S:470 W (**āc**), *oþ þone anlipigan þorn / on þone anlipian stan* S:476 So (**þorn/stān**), *on alpugan thorn* S:1549 Gl:2·92 (**þorn**) etc.

Otherwise it has only been noted in p.ns in *Aynlepythorn* (f.n.) 1244 YW:5·73 (**þorn**), *anlepihaudale* (f.n.) 1.12th [13th] L:2·113 (**haugr, deill**) and Wanlip 1086 Lei. The use of the simplex in the latter is unexplained.

DOE *ān-līpig*; MED *ŏn-lĕpī* adj.; EDD –; OED *anlepi, onlepy*.

ānsetl OE, *n.* 'hermitage' may appear in OE *ansætleh* S:1453 YW (**lēah**). The same compound has been suggested for Ansley 1086 Wa and for Annesley Nt (Hough 1995–6), though the spellings are not conclusive. A further name, Anslow St, appears to be excluded by the Anglo-Saxon charter spellings *ansidelege* S:920 and *(e)ansyðelege* S:930. There is yet another similar form in *Ansedeleg'* (f.n.) 1178–82 Db:463. Note that *ānsetl* would be hard to distinguish in combination with **lēah** from OE *ānsetla* 'hermit'. A simplex instance might be *the Ansill* (f.n.; *A(u)nsell feild* 1570) St:1·69.

Alternatively *anscetleh*, and perhaps some of the other names, might be related to OE *ge-sete* 'seat, habitation, house' and northern dialect *onset* 'group of farm-buildings, farmstead'; see OED *onset* sb.², DOST *onset(t* n.² (from 1423), Middendorff:8. Note also the appearance of *onset* in L f.ns (such as *the Onsett* 1709 L:3·9, *y͞e onset* 1597 L:4·94), where it may denote an infield. Whether the OE instance involves a hermitage or a farm, the etymology is presumably similar, giving either 'solitary dwelling' or 'nucleated farmstead'.

~ **ān, setl**.
DOE *ān-setl*; MED –; EDD –; OED –.

ānstīg OE, *f.* 'path'. Gelling (PNLand:63–4) argues that the previously accepted specific sense of 'single-file path, narrow footpath', especially one that climbs a steep hill, rarely suits the topography, and proposes instead 'a short stretch of road used by at least four roads which converge on it at either end'. This may suit a number (though it does not seem to suit all) of the instances that survived as p.ns, but the word is also attested in OE charter boundaries, where Kitson (forthcoming:§6.41.2) asserts that it is topographically unsuitable for all the examples. Certainly it is difficult to square Gelling's suggestion with instances like *to bares anstigon* S:416 W (probably **bār** 'boar'), and *of horswege innan gatanstige* S:1556 Gl:1·190 (probably **gāt** 'goat'). As Kitson suggests, it may be that there were originally two OE terms, *ān-stīg (f.)* 'single path' of the sort that Gelling envisages, and *an-stig* 'steep path', directly related to *a-stīgan, on-stīgan* 'to climb (up or down)'. The latter term, on the evidence of recurring accusative *anstigo*, is neuter and generally used in the plural; its nominative singular may alternatively have been *anstīge*. There may also have been a weak *ǎnstīga*.

For an obscure OE gloss involving *anstiga(n)*, see **borg-stall**.
(*b*) Anstey 1086 D (East & West), 1086 Ha, 1086 Hrt, 1086 Lei, Anstie 1086 Sr, Ansty 1086 W, 1086 Wa, 1219 Do [Mills 1991], 1313 Sx, Ayngstree 1275 Wo.

~ **stīg, ?ān, ?astīgan**.
DOE *ān-stīga*; MED –; EDD –; OED –; DES *Anstee*.

appel-garth ME, 'orchard, apple orchard'. None of the examples has a trace of medial *d* from ON *apaldr*, and the element may therefore be a hybrid compound of OE **æppel** and ON **garðr**, cf. *Appleyard* YW (**æppel**, **geard**). Alternatively there may have been an ON *apal-garðr; cf. for the form without a suffix ON *apal-grár* 'apple-grey' and the *i*-mutated collective form **epli**.

(*b*) Applegarth 1154–63 YN, 1262 YE:102, 1279 YE:165, 1346 We:1·54, 1411 We:1·195, *Applegarth* 1561 YW, *Apulgarth* (f.n.) 1466 We:1·46.
(*c*) *Netherappelgarth* (f.n.) c.1260 YW:2·253 (**neoðera**).

~ **æppel, garðr.**

<small>MED *appel-garth* s.v. *appel* 7 (h); EDD *apple-garth*; OED *apple-garth* s.v. *apple* B.II; DOE *Applegarth*.</small>

apuldor OE, *f.* 'apple-tree'. A southern word, cf. **æppel-trēow**. In some names, as Appleford and Appuldurcombe Wt, *æppel-trēow* is occasionally exchanged, presumably reflecting the influence of standard English.

OE charters indicate that the weak feminine *apuldre* (e.g. *of þære haran apuldran* S:609 Do) was largely south-western, the strong feminine *apuldor* (e.g. *to þære apuldre* S:772 Bd) mostly more central and eastern. In a single boundary the word is masculine (*on þone longan apuldre* S:786 Wo). See Kitson 1990:202.

(*a*) Appuldurcombe 1189–1204 Wt [Mills 1996:23] (**cumb**), Aperfield 1242–3 K (**feld**), Appledore 1086 Co [OP], Appledore (*Apildorneford* 1330) D:166, Appleford 1086 Wt (**ford**), *Ableham* (*Apeldresham* c.1130 [13th]) Gl, Appledram 1100–35 Sx (**hām/hamm**).
(*b*) Appledore 1335 D:102, 1086 D:364, 1294 D:626, 968 S:1215 K. MELS:2 gives further instances from ME surnames in So.
(*c*) Appledore (*Surapla* 1086, *Sureapeldor* 1242) D:547 (**sūr**).

~ **æppel,** ON *apaldr.*

<small>DOE *apuldor*; MED *apelder*; EDD –; OED –.</small>

arable ME, *adj.* 'fit for ploughing, ploughed' appears relatively early in the f.n. Arable Sheephouse (*Arrable feild* 1626) Do:1·323. It becomes common in f.ns in the 19th century.

~ Lat *arabilis*, OFr *arable.*

<small>DML *arabilis*[1]; AND *arable*[2]; MED *arāble*; OED *arable*.</small>

arc OE, *f.* 'chest, bin' is preserved as northern dialect *ark* in, for example, the surname Arkwright. The word survived most commonly in the compound **eel-ark** 'a device for trapping or containing eels'; the following instances may also relate to fishing.

When borrowed early Lat *arca* appeared in OE as *earc* (OEG:§495).

(c) *le Gylharke* (f.n.) 1539 We:2·88 (**gil**), Middleark (*Mickle arke* 1652)
We:2·17 (**micel**).

~ Lat *arca*; **eel-ark.**

MED *ark(e*; EDD *ark* sb.[1]; OED *ark* sb.

arce-dīacon OE, *m.* 'archdeacon' appears in the Gloucester st.n.
Archdeakon St., referred to as *venella Archidiaconi* c.1250 and first
recorded with the English name *Arcedeakneslone* in c.1290. The
archdeacons of Gloucester had a house on the street's west side
(Gl:2·127).

~ Lat *archidiaconus*:

DOE *arce-dīacon*; MED *arche-dēken*; OED *archdeacon*; AND *arcedekene*; DML
archidiaconus; DES *Archdeacon*.

archer OFr (AN), 'archer'. The element cannot generally be distinguished
from the derived surname (Thuresson:161, DES), but in Stoke Orchard
(*Stoke le Archer* 1269) Gl, it is stated (Gl:2·93) that land was held by the
service to the king of supplying an archer equipped with bow and arrows
for 40 days a year.
(a) *Archerbryge* (f.n.) 1459 YW:7·153 (**brycg**), *Archerfelde* (f.n.) 1554
YW:1·219 (**feld**).

AFW *archier*; AND *archer*[1]; MED *archēr, -iēr* n.; OED *archer*; DES *Archer*.

*ardwo- Brit, 'height, hill' is found in Tollard 1086 W (***tullo-**). The base
of the noun is an adjective 'high'; in Irish the adjective is similarly used
as a noun in p.ns (LEIA). Adjective or noun may also appear in (The
Forest of) Arden 1088 [13th] Wa and Arden 1271 YE; these names could
be identical to Ardennes (France/Belgium). See Gelling 1974:74.

~ ***penno-ardwo-.**

GPC *ardd*; CPNE **arð*; cf. LEIA *ard*.

*are- Brit, *prep.* 'before, facing, beside' certainly appears in Orchard 939
[15th] S:445 Do:3·133 (***kaito-**), a name which is paralleled by several
Welsh places called Argoed '(land) facing the wood'. A late f.n. Argoedd
1838 Ch:4·29 is another example, probably transferred from Wales.
Further instances of the element may appear in Arlosh 1185 Cu:291
(***losko-**) and *Dollerline* 1598 Cu (***dolā**, R. Lyne). See CPNE:8.

GPC *ar*[2]; CPNE **ar*.

*arva ?pre-Celtic, of uncertain meaning. A r.n. that may belong to the
'Old European' linguistic stratum, cf. ***alaventa**. The name, perhaps from
a root IE **er-/*or-* 'to set in motion', is treated by Nicolaisen 1957:231,

Krahe 1964:45–6; cf. ERN:17, 311.
(*b*) R. Arrow (*arwan stream*) 11th Wo–Wa, R. Orwell (*into Arewan*
c.1060 ASC D s.a. 1016) Sf.
The same IE root is suggested for several other pre-Celtic elements in
English r.ns: **ara* in Oare Water 1086 So (see Nicolaisen 1957:228–9,
Krahe 1964:45; cf. ERN:305–6); **armīsa* in R. Erme 1086 D (see
Nicolaisen 1957:229, Krahe 1964:46; cf. ERN:149–50, DEPN); **arna* in
the lost R. Earn 762 [13th] S:261 So (see Nicolaisen 1957:230, Krahe
1964:46; cf. ERN:139–40).

arwe-smith ME, 'arrow-maker', probably as a surname.
(*a*) *Arousmithrode* (f.n.) 1304 YW:3·240 (***rod**[1]).
~ OE *arwe* 'arrow', **smið**.
DOE –; MED *arwe-smith* s.v. *arwe* 2; OED *arrow-smith* s.v. *arrow* IV, 2; DES
Arrowsmith.

askr ON, *m.* 'ash-tree' is combined with both ON and OE elements and
the word (or its sounds) have often replaced OE **æsc**, a process that seems
to be evidenced in Aske YN (*Has(s)e* 1086, *Aske* 1157). Several names
show alternation with the related ON collective noun **eski**, as, for instance,
Escrick (*Ascri* 1086, *Eskrik* 1169 etc.) YE (***ric**).
(*a*) Askern c.1170 YW (**ærn**), Asby c.1150 We (**bȳ**), Askham 1086 Nt
(**hām**), *le Askehurst* 1357 Ch:1·51 (**hyrst**), Askrigg 1086 YN (***ric**),
Ascow (f.n.) 1454 Ch:4·286 (**skógr**), Askwith 1086 YW (**viðr**).
(*b*) Askham 1232 We (dat.pl.).
(*c*) Matlask 1086 Nf (**mæðel**).
In Aspatria (*Aspatric* c.1160) Cu *askr* forms an inversion compound with
a Celtic pers.n.
~ **æsc**, **eski**.
ONP *askr*; DES *Aske*.

askre ME, 'newt', surviving in ModE dialect *asker*, *ask*. In areas of
Scandinavian influence, confusion is possible with ON **askr** (pl. *askar*).
(*a*) With second elements denoting streams in Asker Fleet (f.n.) 1764
YW:1·97 (**flēot**), Asker Syke (f.n.) 1651 Ru:86 (**sīc**).
~ probably related to OE *āðexe*.
MED *aske*; EDD *asker* sb.[1] (cf. *ask* sb.[2]); OED *asker* sb.[2] (cf. *ask* sb.[2]).

assa OE, *m.* 'ass, donkey'. There may have been a pers.n. of the same
form. On the probable identification of ASC D *Assandun* with Ashingdon
Ess, see Townend 1994–5.
(*a*) Assendon ?1.10th [11th] S:104 O (**denu**), Ashingdon c.1060 ASC D

s.a.1016 Ess (**dūn**), Asham 1135–54 Sx (**hām/hamm**).
~ perhaps OIr *asan* (see OEG:§565).

<small>DOE *assa*; MED *asse*; EDD –; OED *ass* sb.[1]; DES *Ass*.</small>

assise OFr, *f.* 'place, seat' in p.ns of French origin.
(*c*) *Belasize* 1154–89 YW, *Bellasize* 1212 YE, *Belsars* 1221 C (**bel**[2]), *Malasize* 1204–9 YW, *Malsis Hall* c.1510 YW (**mal**).

<small>AND *assise*; MED *assīse* n. (cf. sense 9); OED *assize* sb. (cf. sense 9).</small>

āst OE, *f.* 'oast, kiln'.
(*a*) *Ost End* 1216–72 Ess:427 (**ende**).
(*c*) *Brickhurst* 1620 K (**brike**), *Limehouse* 1367 Mx, *Lymhost* (f.n.) 1333 Sr:356, *Le Lymost* (f.n.) 1388 Brk:1·35 (**līm**), *Tilehurst* 1597 Sr, *le Tyleoste* (f.n.) 1548 Sr:356 (**tigel**).

<small>DOE *āst*; MED *ōst(e*; EDD *oast* sb.[1]; OED *oast*.</small>

āte OE, *f.* 'oats' is not common in OE records, but appears in *þæs bisceopes atlondes* S:1347 Wo (**land**) and perhaps in *on at leahe geate* S:786 He (**lēah, geat**) and *on athylle* S:115 Gl:1·218 (**hyll**; possibly *Oathill Slad* Gl:1·220, though BCS:229 and KCD:3·384 print the charter form as *achylle*.)
    The *Otenefurlong* Gl may preserve OE gen.pl. *ātena*, though an adj. **āten* 'oaten' is possible. A rare OE variant with *i*-umlaut, *ǣte*, is attested (DOE) but has not been identified in p.ns.
    The element sometimes becomes *Oak-*, especially when a second element begins with *l*-, as *Oakleaze* (*Oate Leaze* 1659) Gl:3·122 (**lǣs**).
(*a*) *Atecroft* (f.n.) c.1270–80 St:1·45 (**croft**), *Otfeld* (f.n.) c.1200 Gl:2·150 (**feld**), *Atefurlong* (f.n.) 13th Ch:4·114, *Otenefurlong* (f.n.) 1319 Gl:1·205 (**furlang**), *Oatlands* 1290 Sr (**land**), *Oteley* 1280 Sa (**lēah**), *Oats Royd* 1461 YW:3·88 (***rod*[1]), *Oteruding* (f.n.) 1268 Gl:4·100 [cf. 4·167] (***ryding**), *Oteslade* (surn.) 1327 So [MELS:144] (**slæd**), *Woodworth Green* (*Atwrthin* 1180–1220) Ch:3·306 (**worðign**).
    ~ **blak-ote, *pil-āte**.

<small>DOE *āte*; MED *ōte*; EDD *oat*; OED *oat* sb.</small>

atte, atten, atter ME. These forms represent a preposition with the definite article, 'at the'. As in OE, this was a common syntactical formula for p.ns (see **æt**), especially where the element that followed was still meaningful. The forms were commonly used for ME toponymic surnames of the type *Robert atte oke* 'Robert who lives near the oak' (MELS *passim*). *Atten* and *atter* are attested overwhelmingly before elements that begin with vowels, and usually survive in p.ns as initial *n-* or *r-* due to the wrong division of phrases: this process is clearly evidenced with *alret in Naldrett Sx, which is recorded as *Alrette* in 1279, *atten Alrette* in the 14th century and *atte Nalrette* in 1305.

It is tempting to try to distinguish patterns of usage for *atten* and *atter* on the basis of gender since, formally, *atten* derives from the masculine or neuter form of the definite article (OE *æt þæm*, early ME *at þem*) and *atter* from the feminine (OE *æt þære*, early ME *at þer*). Thus in the many examples of the p.n. Nash (Sa:1·218, Bk:71, Gl:1·179 etc.) *atten* appears with OE **æsc** *m.* In the common r.ns Ray and Rea *atter* is paired with OE **ēa** *f.* Here the OE generic term *ēa* 'river' has become a proper name, often replacing an existing r.n., as in Ray Bk–O, W (formerly *Worf*), Rea (*in þære ēa Nen* 11th S:1185) Sa–Wo (formerly *Neen*), Rea Brook Sa (formerly *Meole*). However, division of the forms according to gender is not clear-cut. 'Masculine' *atten* in particular seems to cross gender boundaries: it is frequently paired with the OE feminine **āc**, as in Noke (*Acam* 1086, Noke 1382) O and Noake (*Oke* 1320, *Noke* 1455) Gl. Nonetheless, although this example suggests that the choice between *atten* and *atter* before historically feminine words may sometimes have depended on other factors, it is tempting to see dialectal significance in some cases. For instance, Kitson shows that OE **ēg**, generally feminine, was masculine in part of the midlands as far south-west as Wiltshire (1990:193–5). Löfvenberg's surname material (MELS:56) shows that, as might be expected, *ēg* took *atter* in Sussex and Surrey, but that it almost always took *atten* in Somerset, which is a county close enough to Kitson's area to suggest that the ME evidence may be adding significant detail.

Traces of the preposition *æt* itself are rarely found in this construction, though it can probably be identified in Tawdbridge (*Taneldeford* 1246) La (**ald, ford**). Thurleigh 1086 Bd (**lēah**) seems to reflect ME *at þer*. In eastern Cornwall and the west of Devon, both *atte* and *atter* can come to resemble Cornish *tre*. Cf. Treway (home of Thomas *atte Weye* 1372) Co [CPNE:229] (**wēg**), Tredown (Richard *atter Doune* 1330) D:146 (**dūn**), Trehill (William *attar Hulle* 1339) D:200 (**hyll**) and Treleigh (John *atter Leghe* 1330) D (**lēah**). Note incidentally that all of the elements with which *atter* combines here were feminine in the OE period.

aumoner OFr (AN), *m.* 'almoner, one who distributes alms', often used as a surname. Cf. **almerie**.
(*a*) *le Aumeneresmede* c.1250 Sr:107 (**mēd**), *Aumenerridding* (f.n.) 13th YW:4·25 (*ryding), Ampers Wick 1539 Ess (**wīc**), Amery Court (*Aumeneresbleen* 1358) K (p.n.).
(*d*) Hinton Ampner 1544 Ha (the manor was held by, and paid the

expenses of, the almoner of St Swithin's, Winchester (Ha:93).

~ **ælmesse.**

AND *aumoner*; AFW *aumosnier*; MED *aumenēr* n.[1]; OED *almoner*[1]; DES *Aumonier.*

austr ON, *adv./adj.* '(to the) east' may have replaced OE *ēast* when combined with English elements, and is replaced by it in East Riding 1086 YE (**þriðjungr**). The ON comparative *eystri* 'more easterly' occurs in Asterby 1086 L (**bȳ**) [SSNEM:32]; the variant *austarr* apparently in *Austerwelles* (f.n.) c.1190 L:2·143 (**welle**).

(a) Austby 1246 YW (**bȳ**), *ovstdaleclif* (f.n.) e.13th L:3·130 (**dæl, clif**), *les Houstelanges* (f.n.) 1324 L:3·171 (**lang**[2]), Owston 1086 YW (**tūn**), Austhorpe 1086 YW (**þorp**), Austwick 1086 YW, Owstwick 1086 YE (**wīc**).

~ **ēast.**

ONP *austr*[3] adv.; MED cf. *ousten* adv.; EDD –; OED –.

auðn ON, *f.* and *n.* 'waste land, deserted land' might appear in Aunsby 1086 L, Owmby 1086 L (×2) and *Ounesbi* 1086 YN (**bȳ**), though the attested pers.n. *Auðunn* is a likely alternative (see SSNEM:33–4 and L:2·261). The related adjective *auðr* 'waste, deserted' may appear in Outhgill 1324 We (**gil**).

ONP *auðn*[1].

*averys ME, 'average, the pasturage of arable land after harvest' occurs in *Common Averys* 1436 YE:319 (**commun**), where it is clear that the reference is to a meadow after the hay has been cut. In Ambrose Holme (*Averencheholm* 1210–12, *Averisholm* 1340 etc.) Cu (**holmr**) a similar meaning is probable, though it is possible that here the reference is to land held in connection with a feudal service (MED *ăverăge*, OED *average* sb.[1]). The element is discussed more fully in Styles & Parsons forthcoming.

~ probably OE *eafor* 'draft horse'.

EDD *average* sb.; OED *average* sb.[3]

āwel OE, *m.* 'fork, hook' may be used in p.ns to describe to something hooked, forked or possibly pointed. It seems to occur twice with **cumb**, where reference might be to a forked or hook-shaped valley, or perhaps to one containing a river-fork. However, it is difficult to distinguish from *ǣwylle* 'spring, river source' (see **ǣwylm**).

(a) *Auliscomb* (f.n.) 13th [14th] Do:3·254, Awliscombe 1086 D (**cumb**).

DOE *āwel*; MED *oul*; EDD –; OED *awl.*

awkward ME, 'wrong, awry', perhaps 'wrongly placed' or 'difficult to manage' in *Awkerd Royde* (f.n.) 1585 YW:3·235 (***rod**¹) and Awkward Meadows (f.n.) 1777 YW:1·122 (**mēd**).

~ probably ON *ǫfugr* 'back-handed, reversed' and OE -*ward*, indicating direction. For another view, see Björkman:20.

MED *auk-ward* adj.; EDD *awkward* adj.; OED *awkward*.

Æ

æcen, ***ācen** OE, *adj.* 'oaken', in p.ns usually 'growing with oaks'. Several examples of the *i*-mutated *æcen* are problematic. Itchingwood 1312 Sr (**wudu**) is a fairly certain case. Edgcott 1086 Bk (**cot**) and Eachwick c.1160 Nb (**wīc**) evidence the expected assibilated consonant but consistently lack *-n*. Eggington 1195 Bd (**dūn**) and *Ekeney* 1242 Bk (**ēg**) have *-n* but do not develop assibilated consonants, perhaps by analogy with *āc* and **ācen*. Alternatively they may involve OE *ēacen* 'increased, huge', though this word seems to have been largely limited to verse and not to have survived into ME.

Unmutated **ācen* is represented by: Oakenbottom 1246 La (**botm**), Oakenden 1278 K (**denn**), Oakenpole 1220–4 K (**fald**), Oakenshaw 1133–53 YW:2·113, 1246 YW:3·17 (**sceaga**), *Akenside* 1332 Nb [NbDu:3] (**sīde**).

If *æcen* appears in Edgcott the meaning 'made of oak' is probable; the same meaning is possible with **ācen* in Oakengates 1414 Sa (**geat**), though the 'gate' of the latter is more likely to refer to a pass between hills (Sa:1·224).

~ **āc**.

DOE *æcen*; MED *ōken*; EDD *oaken*; OED *oaken*.

æcer OE, *m.* 'plot or strip of cultivated land', also 'acre, specific measure of ploughland', originally the unit a yoke of oxen could plough in a day. The general sense 'arable land' is found also in the compound *acre-land* (MED, OED); this may be represented by *Akerlond* (f.n.) 1262 Db:426 and Acreland 1189–93 YW:6·183, though there are other possibilities in the latter case (see Styles & Parsons forthcoming).

The OE element would generally be indistinguishable from ON *akr*. The examples given below are mostly drawn from 'major' names, and could be supplemented by many f.ns.

(*a*) *Akergarth* (f.n.) 1279 We:2·230 (**garðr**).

(*b*) Acre 1086 Nf, The Acres 1357 Ch:4·249.

(*c*) With an element denoting the crop: Benacre 1086 Sf, 843 S:293 K [KPN:184–5] (**bēan**), Wheatacre 1086 Nf (**hwǣte**), Lenacre 1200 K:566, Linacre 1189 Db:221, 1212 La, Linacres 1279 Nb [NbDu:135] (**līn**), Nepicar 1292 K (**nēp**).

With words for wild plants: Bessacarr a.1160 YW (*bēos), Dillicar 1208 We, 1379 YW:6·253 (dile), *Gorstiacra* 1156–60 [14th] Ch:2·182 (*gorstig), Weddicar c.1160 Cu (wēod).

With elements specifying soil quality: Chadacre 1046 [12th] Sf [ASWills:32] (cert), Hardacre 1538 K (heard), Lane Acres 1560 Ch:3·120 (hlǣne), Rivacre 1287 Ch:4·190 (rūh), Sandiacre 1086 Db (sandig), Stoneacre 1254 K (stān).

With elements (probably) denoting nearby features: Crossacres 1290 Ch:1·241 (cros), Uzzicar (*Huseker* c.1160) Cu (hūs), Marshacre 1378 Gl (mersc).

With elements denoting size and shape: *Oneacre* (f.n.) 1437 Sx:558 (ān), Crumacre 1200–20 YW (crumb), *Fyuacrewong* (f.n.) 1349 Ru:247 (fīf, vangr), Halnaker 1086 Sx (half), Longacre 1384 YW (lang¹), Muker 1274 YN (mjór), *le Seuenakres* (f.n.) 1286 Db:108 (seofon), *Scalacres* 1175–96 [14th] Lei (skál), Tenacre 1327 K (tēn).

With animal and bird names: *Gosacre* (f.n.) 1383 Sr:355 (gōs), *Oxacre* (f.n.) 1339 YE:319 (oxa), *Swinacre* (f.n.) 13th C:311 (swīn), Tarnacre c.1210 La (trani).

With personal names: Alsager 1086 Ch:3·2, *Dame Isabell' Acre* (f.n.) 1465 Ch:1·302, *Luuechild aker* (f.n.) 1199 Wa:321, *Steynulfaker* (f.n.) c.1250 Db:164, Susacres 1086 YW.

Interesting exceptional cases amongst f.ns include *Pottacres* 1566 Ru:88 (*pott, probably 'land on which ancient potsherds were littered'), *Spellacre* 1327–77 Nt:275 (spell 'speech', perhaps an old meeting-place), and *Smocaker* 1220 W:446, *Smochacre* c.1260 Gl:2·160, Smock Acre c.1280 O:417 (smoca 'smoke', referring to a household tax).

~ æcer-dīc, *æcer-hēafod, æcer-mann, æcern.

DOE *æcer*; MED *āker* n.¹; EDD *acre* sb.; OED *acre*; DML *acra*; AND *acre*; DES *Acres*.

æcer-dīc OE, *f.* 'acre ditch', perhaps 'the ditch marking the end of a ploughland' (DOE), is recorded early in OE charter bounds as *on þa æcer dik* S:605 Brk:735. The word is preserved in f.ns from the east midlands and is especially common in L. The predominance of spellings with final -*k* suggests the influence of Scandinavian pronunciation. See further L:3·109.

(*a*) Acre dike hedge (f.n.) 1577 L:2·51, *Akerdike Close* (f.n.) 1611 L:3·56.

(*b*) *ackerdicke* (f.n.) c.1233 L:2·176, Acre Ditch (f.n.) 1767 Db:165, *y* *acredikes* (f.n.) 1638 L:2·13, *le akerdic* (f.n.) 1154-89 L:3·170, *Akerdik* (f.n.) 1226 Nt:279, *le Akerdik* (f.n.) l.13th L:3·109, *Akerdyk* (f.n.) e.13th

L:3·118, *Akredich* (f.n.) 1210-15 L:4·20, *Hakerdik* (f.n.) a.1244 L:3·121.
(*c*) *the comon acredyk* (f.n.) 1550 L:3·167.

~ **æcer, dīc, dík.**
DOE *æcer-dīc*.

*æcer-hēafod OE, *m.* 'headland, area at the end of an acre-strip for turning the plough' is not attested as a true compound in OE, but similar phrases, with inflected first element, are found in OE charters: *bi þara acra heafdum* S:1337 Wa, *be þane akere heueden* S:502 Do (see DOE *æcer* sense 2b). In records of the ME period the element appears to be limited to the east midlands: besides the L examples noted here, the two instances in DML are from L and Nt. The compound occurs in f.ns and as a common noun (e.g. *duos Akirhefedes* 1318 L:4·45).
(*b*) *Acrheudes* (f.n.) 1342 L:4·87, *Akerheued* (f.n.) 1352 L:5·Great Grimsby, *akerheuede* (f.n.) 13th L:2·113, *Akerheuedes* (f.n.) c.1244–72 [14th] L:2·155.
(*c*) *Seeacrehede* (f.n.) 1457 L:5·Great Grimsby (surn.).

~ **æcer, hēafod.**
DOE –; MED –; EDD –; OED –; DML *acrahavedum*.

æcer-mann OE, *m.* 'peasant, ploughman', later a class of feudal tenant. This term or the derived ME surname is found in:
(*a*) *Akremannebreche* (f.n.) 13th Nth:261 (**brēc**), Acreland (*Hakermanislond* 1299) Nth, *Akermanslande* (f.n.) 1538 Brk:450 (**land**), *Acremanstrete* (st.n. Faringdon) 1551 Brk:367, Acremorestreet 1382 Hrt (**strēt**).

~ **æcer, mann**
DOE *æcer-mann*; MED *aker-man*; EDD –; OED *acreman*; DML *acremannus*, cf. *acremanlanda*; DES *Ackerman*.

æcern OE, *n.* 'acorn', perhaps also 'beech-nut, chestnut'. Possible medieval instances are Accrington a.1194 La (**tūn**) and Aconbury 1213 He (**burh**). The latter could instead involve OE *ācweorna* 'squirrel' though the spellings cited by DEPN (*Akornebir'* 1213, *Akornebury* 1218, *Okernebur'* 1241) are more consistent with forms of *æcern*, the development of which is affected by association with **āc** and **corn** (OED). Other instances that have been noted are late, as:
(*a*) Acorn Bank 1605 We (**banke**), Acorn Hill 1796 YW (**hyll**).

~ **æcer.**
DOE *æceren*; MED *ăkorn*; EDD *acorn* sb.; OED *acorn*.

ælmesse OE, *f.* 'alms, charity'. Specifically in the compounds *alms-house* 'house where lodging and maintenance were provided for the poor' (MED, OED), *alms-land*, 'land held in frank almoign (i.e. in perpetual tenure by gift of charity)' (OED). *Almesham* (f.n.) c.1230 Gl:2·143 (**hamm**) may have been a piece of land held in this way.

(*a*) *le Almesse crofte* (f.n.) 1540 YW:6·64 (**croft**), *the Almes howse* (f.n.) 1583 YW:4·133 (**hūs**), *Knollesalmeshous* (f.n.) 1406 YW:2·82 (pers.n., **hūs**), *Almeshowse Garth* (f.n.) 1602 L:2·287 (**hūs**, **garðr**), *Almaslande* (f.n.) 1536 YW:4·8 (**land**).

~ Lat *alimosina; cf: **aumoner**.

DOE *ælmesse*; MED *almes(se*; OED *alms*.

ælren, ***alren** OE, *adj.* 'of alder, growing with alders'.

The *i*-mutated *ælren* is found in one Anglo-Saxon charter from Wa (S:898), where it is combined several times with **stubb**, as 'alder stump' (*on þone ælrenan stob* etc.). In ME and later this form of the adjective, which would have developed to *elren by the end of the OE period (OEG:§193), could have been confused with **ellern** or, in Scandinavian-influenced areas, **elri**. But it may be evidenced in several Cheshire f.ns: *le Elrenegreuelond* 1307–27 Ch:3·129 (**græfe**, **land**), *le Helerenlond* 1334 Ch:2·71 (**land**), *Elerinscharde* 1280–1 Ch:4·162 (**sceard**).

Unmutated *alren is found in: *le Holrenbarwe* (f.n.) 13th Ch:3·184 (**bearu**), *le Ollerunbothe* (f.n.) 1466 Ch:5·xxix (**bōð**), Owler Carrs (*Ollerynekar* 1429) YW:1·237 (**kjarr**), *Olrinleg'* 1283 Ch:1·53 (**lēah**), *le Allereneschagh'* (f.n.) 1300–20 Ch:4·87, Ollerenshaw 1251 Db (**sceaga**).

~ **alor**.

DOE *alren* (citations indicate *ælren*); MED –; EDD –; OED *aldern*.

æmette OE, *f.* 'ant'.

(*a*) Antley a.1194 La (**lēah**).

~ **æmett-hyll**.

DOE *ǣmette*; MED *ampte*; EDD *emmet*; OED *ant, emmet*.

æmett-hyll OE, *m.* 'ant-hill'. The compound is recorded with this specific sense in OE, though an interpretation 'hill that swarms with ants' can presumably not be excluded from any name.

(*b*) *Amothile* (f.n.) 1292 YW:6·88, Ampthill 1086 Bd, *Ampthill* 1300 C.

~ **æmette**, **hyll**.

DOE *ǣmett-hyll*; MED *ampte-hil* s.v. *ampte* 1 (b); EDD *emmet-hill* s.v. *emmet* 2 (5); OED *ant-hill*.

æned OE, *f.* 'duck'. During the OE period the word generally developed to *ened* (OEG:§193d). ME spellings with *a-* are to be expected primarily in Ess and some adjoining counties (Jordan:§33, Ek 1975). Andwell Ha was originally *Enedewella*; however, the consistent initial *A-* of Anmer Nf (*Anemere* 1086) is surprising.

(*a*) *Suthenedebath* (f.n.) c.1300 Nt:275 (**bæð**, with **sūð**), Enborne 1086 Brk (**burna**), Endcliff 1216–72 Db (**clif**), Enford 934 [12th] s:427 W (**ford**), *Henedelake* (f.n.) l.12th Ch:2·182 (**lacu**), Enslet 1272 Db (***læcc**), Anmer 1086 Nf, Enmore 1086 So (**mere**[1]), Andwell 1100–35 Ha (**welle**).

DOE *ened*; MED *ĕnde* n.[2]; EDD –; OED *ende*.

æppel OE, *m.* 'apple', also applied to the fruit of other trees (DOE, MED, OED). The sense in some p.ns appears to be 'apple-tree'. Spellings in *Ep-* may represent the influence of ON **epli**, or of OE Kentish/Mercian dialect *eppel*.

(*a*) Appleby 1004 [?11th] s:906 Lei, Eppleby (*Aplebi* 1086) YN (**bȳ**), Apperknowle 1317 Db (**cnoll**), Appleford 892–9 [12th] s:355 Brk (**ford**), *Appleyard* 1297 YW, Mapple Yard 1208 YW (**geard**), Appleridge 1287 Gl (**hrycg**), Apley 1086 L, Appley 13th La (**lēah**), Appleshaw 1200 Ha (**sceaga**), *Apple Tor* 1216–72 Db (**torr**), Applethwaite 1256 We (**þveit**).

~ **appel-garth, apuldor, æppel-trēow, æppel-tūn, epli.**

DOE *æppel*; MED *appel*; EDD *apple* sb.[2]; OED *apple* sb.

æppel-trēow OE, *n.* (occasionally *f.*) 'apple-tree, fruit-tree'. OE charter bounds suggest that this was originally a northern equivalent to **apuldor**; the line between them ran through the midlands (Kitson 1995:80).

(*a*) *Apeltregarth* (f.n.) 1200 YW:7·152 (**garðr**), *Appeltreholm* (f.n.) 1232–5 We:2·230 (**holmr**), Apperley 1201 Nb, Apperley Bridge 1330 YW (**lēah**), *Apiltremedou* (f.n.) 14th Ru:254 (**mēd**), Appersett 1280 YN (**sǽtr**), Adder Wells (*Apeltrewell* 1285) Sx (**welle**), Appletreewick 1086 YW (**wīc**).

(*b*) Appletree 1086 Db, 1175 Nth, *le Appultr'* (f.n.) 13th Ch:4·209.

(*c*) Hareappletree 1323 La (**hār**[2]), *Merghapeltre* (f.n.) 1329 YW:7·152 (?1st el.).

~ **æppel, trēow.**

DOE *æppel-trēow*; MED *appel-trē*; EDD –; OED *apple-tree*.

æppel-tūn OE, *m.* 'orchard'. The compound has this specific sense in OE, but 'farm with an apple-tree' cannot perhaps be excluded from individual names (see **æppel**). On forms in *Nap-*, *Map-* see **atte**. MELS:3 and Carlsson:24 give further examples from surnames.

(*a*) *Napeltonecroft* (f.n.) Hrt:250 (**croft**).

(*b*) Appleton 942 [13th] s:480 Brk, 972–92 [11th] s:1453 YW, 1086 Ch:2·96, 1086 K:585, 1182 La, Mapleton 1313 K, Napleton 1182 Wo.

(c) *Wodeapelton* (f.n.) 1387 Hrt:250 (**wudu**), *Beaufizapelton* (f.n.) 1316 C:311 (pers.n.).

~ **æppel, tūn.**

DOE *æppel-tūn*; MED *appel-tun* s.v. *appel* 7 (t); EDD –; OED –; DES *Appleton*.

***æpset** OE, 'aspen wood'.

(b) *Epsette* (f.n.) 1350 Sr:359.

~ **æspe, -et.**

***ǽrgi** ON, *n.* 'shieling, pasture', perhaps specifically 'home-shieling, pasture near to the farm'. Thoroughly discussed by Higham 1977–8, Fellows-Jensen 1977–8 and Fellows-Jensen 1980. Following Matras, Fellows-Jensen establishes that *ǽrgi is the probable ON form of a word attested only in p.ns (previously it had been identified as *ærgin*, the form with suffixed definite article, and *erg*, the form used in a 16th-century Danish translation of a lost version of *Orkneyinga saga*). It represents a borrowing from Common Gaelic *áirge*. She indicates that in England there is a division between early spellings with initial *e* in northern La, Cu, We, YE, YN and northern YW, and those with initial *a* in southern La, Ch and southern YW. She notes that this line approximates to the dialect boundary between Northumbrian and Mercian OE, but concedes that the *a*-spellings remain difficult to account for. They may, just possibly, represent direct loans into Mercian OE from Gaelic.

(a) Arrathorne 1259 YN (**þorn**).

(b) Airy Holme 1086 YN:165, Argam 1086 YE, Arkholme 1086 La, Arram 1086 YE:79, Eryholme 1086 YN (all dat.pl.), Arrowe 1240–9 Ch:4·261.

(c) Berrier 1166 Cu (**berg**), Birker 1279 Cu (**birki**), Brettargh c.1178–90 La [Kenyon:63] (**Brettas**), Hewer 1292 Cu (**haugr**), Cleator c.1185 Cu (**klettr**), Moser 1196 We, Mosser 1203 Cu (**mos**), Salter c.1150 Cu:432 (**salt¹**), *Sever* 1297 We (**sef**), Stephney 1231 Cu (**stafn**), Stewnor c.1190 La (**stofn**), Tirril c.1189 We (**?tyri**), Winder 1170–80 We:2·211, 1193 YW, c.1200 Cu:406, 1225–45 La:197 (**wind¹**).

With pers.ns, the language of origin given where possible: Anglezark 1202 La (ON), Golcar 1086 YW (ON), Goosnargh 1086 La (Celtic), Grimsargh 1086 La (ON), Kellamergh 1201 La (ON), Mansergh 1086 We, *Starkerghs* 1086 YW.

OGNS *ærgin*.

ærn OE, *n.* 'building, house', in p.ns chiefly in the sense 'building used for a specific purpose', as it is also in many OE compounds such as *carc-*

ærn 'prison', *cweart-ærn* 'guard-house', *mæðel-ærn* 'meeting-house', *wīn-ærn* 'tavern'. Spellings in *-ren* (in *Stonrene* K, Waldron Sx) probably represent a metathesised form with *-e* from reduced stress in the second element of the compound (OEG:§193d, n.4).

(*c*) With elements referring to the purpose or contents of the building (cf. the further compounds listed below): *ate Children* (surn.) 1327 K [KPN:184] (**celde**), Colerne 1086 W (**col**), Cowarne 1086 He (**cū**), *the Dovearne* (f.n.) 1608 YW:1·174 (**dūfe**), *Ele arne* (f.n.) 1588 We:2·227 (**ēl¹**), Potterne 1086 W, 1280 Do:2·257 (***pott**), *Shyterne* (f.n.) 1299 D:689 (**scite**), Walkern 1086 Hrt (***walc**).

With other elements: Askern c.1170 YW (**askr**), Crewkerne 873–88 [11th] S:1507 So (***cryc**), Quither 1281 D (**cwēad**), Dilhorne 1086 St (***dylf**), *Newarne* 1279 Gl, Newerne 1086 Gl (**nīwe**), Postern 1329 Db (**post**), Stanion 1086 Nth, *Stonrene* 1247 K:574 (**stān**), Waldron 1086 Sx (**wald**).

~ **bæc-ærn, bed-ern, bere-ærn, brēow-ærn, *crocc-ærn, *eard-ærn, hord-ærn, salt-ærn, *tōt-ærn.**

DOE *ærn*; MED *-ern*; EDD –; OED *earn* sb.

*ærne-ford OE, *m.* 'riding-ford, ford that can or must be crossed on horseback' would be parallel to the recorded OE *ærne-weg* 'road fit to ride on, race-course', and to Radford O, which contains **rād**, 'riding'. It may appear in Arnford 1086 YW and Rackenford 1086 D. The latter is perhaps prefixed by **racu**, 'stream-bed'.

~ OE *ærnan* 'to gallop', **ford**.

æsc OE, *m.* 'ash-tree'. Common in OE boundary marks, usually with a descriptive element, as in *on þone holan æsc* S:360 Ha, *in smalan æsc* S:104 O, and also as a first element in *on æsc meres hammas* S:761 Brk:669. A metathesised form lies behind Axford 1184 W.

Spellings in *e-* that do not reflect Mercian and Kentish second fronting (OEG:§164, §288) may exhibit the raising before the palatal consonant noted in ME dialects from Nf to Nb (Kristensson 1967:46, Kristensson 1995:19). Examples include Esh 1153–95 Du [CDEPN], Esholt 1172 YW, Eshton 1086 YW (cf. YW:7·41) and the Nf surnames *del Esh* 1249, *atte Esshes* 1293 (Carlsson:39). Formally, influence from ON **eski** or the existence of an OE collective ***esce** would also be possible. On Nash and Rashwood see **atte**.

(*a*) With habitative generics: Ashbury 1086 Brk (**burh**), Ashampstead 1155–8 Brk (**hām-stede**), Ashton 873–88 [11th] S:1507 W:40, 955–7 [12th] S:664 Gl:3·62, Ashwicke 1287 Gl (**wīc**).

With topographical generics: Ashbourne 1086 Db (**burna**), Ashford
926 [14th] S:397 Db, 1086 Sa:1·19, 1155 Sa:1·19, Ayshford 958 [12th]
S:653 D (**ford**), Rashwood 1221 Wo (**hīd**), Aisholt 854 [12th] S:311 So
(**holt**), Ashop 1215 Db (**hop**), Astridge 14th Gl:3·326 (**hrycg**), Ashurst
c.1100 K:184 (**hyrst**), Ashley 1086 C, 1086 Gl:1·85, 1086 Ch:2·10, 1086
Ha (**lēah**), Ashleyhay 1294 Db (**lēah**, *ge-***hæg**), Ashover 1086 Db (**ofer**[2]),
Ashtead c.1150 Sr (**stede**), Ashwell 1086 Ru (**welle**), Ashwood 1232 St,
1285 Db (**wudu**).

(*b*) Ash 987 [14th] S:863 Db, 1086 D:32, 1086 D:92, 1086 D:133, 1086
D:448, c.1090 K:527, Ashe 1086 Ha, Nash 1210–12 Sa:1·218, 1182
[18th] Wo:146. In Ashton (*Asce* 1086, *Asshen* 1296) Nth:96 and Ashen
1086 Ess forms vary between sg. and dat.pl., and the latter has survived.
Note that simplex forms are particularly common in D.

(*c*) Frequently with pers.ns, as in Abnash 1243 Gl, Buttsash 1212 Ha,
Dodnash 1188 Sf, Franche 1086 Wo, Grumbald's Ash (*Grimboldstov*
1086) 1169 Gl, Hamnish 1086 He, Hutnage 1327 Gl, Kippax 1086 YW,
Prinknash 1121 Gl.

Status as a meeting-place is denoted in Molash 1226 K (**māl**), number
in Monyash 1086 (**manig**), and One Ash 1086 Db (**ān**) in the same parish.

~ **askr**, **æscen**, *****æscet**, **æsc-mann**, **eski**.
DOE *æsc*; MED *assh(e* n.[1]; EDD *ash* sb.[2]; OED *ash* sb.[1]; DES *Ash*.

æscen OE, *adj.* 'ashen', in p.ns usually 'growing with ash-trees'; the
meaning 'made of ash-wood' is also possible in *the Ashen causey* (f.n.)
c.1180 Gl:1·202 (**causee**).

(*a*) Ashington 1170 Nb [NbDu:6] (**denu**), Ashdon 1043–5 [14th] Ess
[ASWills:31], Ashendon 1086 Bk (**dūn**), *Aschinehalgh* (f.n.) 1249–65
Ch:2·322 (**halh**), Ashnott (*Heschenhirst* 1276) YW (**hyrst**).

~ **æsc**.
DOE *æscen* adj.; MED *asshen* adj.[1]; EDD *ashen* adj.; OED *ashen* a.[1]

*****æscet** OE, 'clump of ash-trees'. This cannot be distinguished from a
compound of **æsc** and **scēat**, and it is notable that only Ashford K agrees
with the markedly south-eastern distribution of other elements which
combine a tree-name with **-et**.

(*a*) Ashford (*Essetesford* 1046, 1086) K [KPN:7] (**ford**).

(*b*) Ashetts (f.n.) 1756 Gl:1·241, Eshott 1187 Nb, *Esshett* (f.n.) 1541
YW:7·152.

~ **æsc**, **-et**.

æsc-mann OE, *m.* 'sailor, pirate' became an OE pers.n., primarily
attested in East Anglia. The pers.n. is probable, but the original meaning

(perhaps as a nickname) possible, in the OE charter boundary *æt Æscmannes yre* S:781 Sf (?***yfre**) and Ashmanhaugh 1153–66 Nf:2·134 (**haga**[1]).

~ OE *æsc* '(Viking-)ship', **mann**.
  DOE *æsc-mann*; DES *Ashman*.

æspe OE, *f.* 'aspen-tree'. Forms with and without metathesis occur from the OE period onwards, as *Æpslea* (for Aspley Bd, S:772), but *in þa gratan æspan* S:142 Wo (**grēat**). Spellings in *a-* do not permit ON *ǫsp* to be distinguished; those in *e-* could reflect the influence of ON **espi**, or OE Kentish or Mercian dialect (there is a tendency for *æ* to become *e* also in Du and Nb). A strong feminine OE *æsp* is also recorded.
(*a*) *Apescrosse·furlong* (f.n.) 1649 Ru:279 (**cros**, **furlang**, possibly referring to a boundary marker of the Bishop of Lincoln's land), Aspall 1086 Sf (**halh**), Aspul 1212 La (**hyll**), Apsley c.1210 [14th] Bk, Aspley 969 [11th] S:772 Bd, 1086 St:1·36, 1108 [14th] Nt, Espley 1242 Nb (**lēah**).
(*b*) Apps 1086 Sr:96, Apse 1086 Wt [Mills 1996:23], Asps 1194 Wa. MELS:3–4 gives further examples from ME surnames.

~ ***æpset**, ***æspen**, **espi**.
  DOE *æsp*; MED *aspe*; EDD *aps, asp, aspen*; OED *asp*[1], *aspen*; DES *Apps*.

***æspen** OE, *adj.* 'of aspen, growing with aspen-trees' cannot be distinguished from inflected forms of **æspe** (especially gen.pl. *æspena*).
(*a*) *le Espenefeld* (f.n.) 1329 Ch:4·21 (**feld**), *le Aspenehurste* (f.n.) 1301–3 Ch:3·5 (**hyrst**), Aspenshaw 1216–72 Db (**sceaga**), Aspinwall 1246 La (**welle**).
  MED cf. *aspen* s.v. *aspe* 2; EDD *apsen* s.v. *aps*; OED *aspen*.

æt OE, *prep.* with dative, 'at' was the common preposition of location in p.ns (see **atte**), and seems sometimes to have become an integral part of the OE name. Bede sometimes preserves the Latin equivalent *ad* in situations where the normal syntax demands a simple nominative, and the OE translator usually translates his forms quite literally: *in loco qui dicitur Adbaruae, id est Ad Nemus* (iv.3), OE *in þære stowe þe is nemned Æt Bearwe* for Barrow upon Humber L (**bearu**). Cf. charter forms of Sedgeberrow Wo and Bishop's Cleeve Gl: *viculus qui nuncupatur æt Segcesbearuue* 778 [11th] S:113, *ad monasterium quod proprie nuncupatur æt Clife* 768–79 [11th] S:141. It may be significant that early examples seem to be limited to names involving topographical rather than habitative elements.
  Traces of *æt* are preserved in the addition of an initial *T-* to the early

form of Tiddingford Bk, *æt Yttingaforda* 10th ASC A s.a.905; of Enborne Brk:294 (**æned, burna**), *Tanebvrne* 1086; and of Itchell Ha, which is *on icæles æwilmas* 973–4 [12th] S:820, but *Ticelle* 1086. The loss of initial *T*- in other p.ns suggests the colloquial use of *æt* with them: Acton (*Tacatone* 1086) Do:1·34 (*****tacca**, **tūn**), Adlestrop (*Titlestrope* ?714 [16th] S:1250, *Tedestrop* 1086) Gl (pers.n., **þrop**), Arracott (*Tadiecote* 1327) D (**tādige, cot**), Elstree (*Tiðulfes treow* ?785 [12th] S:124) Hrt. Both types can be attributed to the wrong division of phrases.

  ~ **atte, atten, atter.**
   DOE *æt*; MED *at* prep.; EDD *at* prep.; OED *at* prep.

æðling OE, *m*. 'prince, nobleman'.
(*a*) Athelney 10th ASC A s.a.878 So (**ēg**), Adlingfleet 1086 YW (**flēot**), *Athelingstrete* (2 st.ns London) c.1213 now Watling Street, 1244 now Addle Hill Ldn:81 (**strēt**), Allington 1086 Do, 1086 L, 1086 W:311, Athelington 1219 Sf (**tūn**), Ellenthorpe 1086 YN (**þorp**).

  ~ OE *æðele* 'noble'.
   DOE *æþeling*; MED *ǣðeling*; OED *atheling*; DML *adelingus*.

æwylm OE, *m*. 'spring, source' is common in charter bounds, which show that the forms of this, and the closely related variant *ǣwyll*, are complex. Beside *ǣwylm*, strong *m*., there is also *ǣwylma*, weak *m*. Beside *ǣwyll*, strong *m*., there is *ǣwylle*, strong *n*.

  Cole 1985 studies the use of the element, showing that it is most common on the chalklands of southern England, and that it denotes springs or groups thereof feeding both minor brooks and larger rivers.
(*a*) Aldon 1086 Sa:1·15 (**dūn**), *Ewelynge* (f.n.) 1342 YW:2·148 (**eng**), Alton 1086 W:317, 1086 Ha, Carshalton 1086 Sr (**tūn**; the last with later addition of **cærse** 'cress'). The OE charter form *æt Aweltune* 873–88 [11th] S:1507 is identified with Carshalton by Sr:41.
(*b*) Awell 1526 Sx, The Evils (f.n.) 16th Brk:530, Ewell 1066 Sr, 1212 Ess, ?10th [13th] S:140 (cf. ASCh:4·14) K:560, 1198 K:160, Ewelme 1086 O, Ewen 12th S:436 Gl (source of R. Thames), Newelm 1296 Sx (for initial *N*- see **atte**).
(*c*) Sometimes prefixed by the name of the resulting river or stream: Clyst William (*Clistewelm* 1238) D (R. Clyst), Toller Whelme (*on Tollor æwylman* 1035 [12th] S:975) Do (R. Toller).

  ~ probably *ǣ*-, *āweallan* 'to well up, gush forth', but there may sometimes have been association with **ēa**, 'river'; **welle, welm.**
   DOE *ǣ-wyll, ǣ-wylm*; MED –; EDD –; OED –; DES *Ewell*.

B

*badde OE, *adj.* 'bad, worthless, evil'. Coates 1988 argues that this form is likely to be the etymon of ME *badde*, attested from 1203 (MED), and that it probably appears in the recurring OE name **(æt þære) baddan byrig* (**burh**). This is represented by Badbury (*æt Baddanbyrig* 10th ASC A s.a.900) Do, Badbury (*Baddeburi* 955 [14th] S:568) W, Badby S:495 Nth and others; see Brk:362. Outside this recurring name, however, the element is rare. Uncertain possibilities include Badley 1200 Sf and Baddeley 1227 St. An OE pers.n. *Badda* is attested (Redin:44) and may be derived from the element. Another derived pers.n. could be **Bæddi*, which seems to appear in Badsey Wo and Badsworth YW; see Coates 1988:98.

Later instances of the element have rarely been noted, but Bad Lane (f.n.) 1601 L:1·200 is apparently an example.

~ uncertain. Coates suggests that OE *bæddel* 'hermaphrodite' is derived from OE **badde*, rather than the source of it, as OED suggests.

DOE −; MED *badde* adj.; EDD *bad* adj.; OED *bad* a.

*bagga OE, 'bag'; apparently in p.ns more often referring to an animal, probably the badger. The sense 'badger' is suggested on the grounds that a word of this form is frequently combined with non-habitative elements, chiefly denoting woods and hills. The OE word may have been used figuratively, as Sw *bagge* 'wether, ram' and MDu *bagghe* 'small pig' seem to have been, for 'a creature resembling a bag'. Bawdrip (*Bagetrepe* 1086) So contains **træppe** 'snare' and may refer to something which could be snared or trapped, whilst the commonly associated elements denoting 'wood', as in Bagley 1086 So, c.1090 Sa, 1148 YW:1·53, Baguley 1086 Ch:2·12 (**lēah**), Bagshaw 1251 Db, 1379 YW (**sceaga**) or 'hill', as in Bageridge 1250 Do, Baggridge 1314 So (**hrycg**), Bag Hill 1159–70 YW:2·78 (**hyll**), Bagnor 1086 Brk (**ōra¹**), Bagtor 1086 D (**torr**) etc., might suggest a wild animal; cf. also Bagpath 1174 Gl:2·239 (**pæð**). The various conditions tend to imply an animal living in woods or on slopes, capable of being snared, and probably of a shape that could be described as 'bag-like', presumably with the meaning 'fat'. *Bagga* is also well attested in OE charter bounds, such as *to baggan leage* S:378 Ha, *to bacga slæde* S:179 Gl:2·19, where it often has the spelling *bacga*. For discussion of the forms see Kitson 1993:72–4, concluding that 'it is hard to believe that any of the charter instances is not the animal "badger"', and see also OEG:§64, arguing that the distinction between the spellings *cg* and *gg* in OE is inconsistent. It may well be that the word *badger* itself (see ***bagger**) is ultimately to be derived from OE **bagga*, although if so its form has been altered, possibly influenced by *badge* 'device, emblem' in allusion to the white markings on the animal's head.

However, in several p.ns the sense 'badger' is inappropriate. A word of the same form recurs, for example, in st.ns of the type *Bag Lane* (Derby) c.1220 Db, *Bagge Lone* (Congleton) 1264 Ch:2·296, *Baggelon* (Chester) 1264 Ch:5·66, where it appears to denote a blind alley; cf. with the same sense Ger *Sackgasse*, Sw *säckgata, säckgränd*, Fr *cul-de-sac* (Ch:5·66). In such urban contexts, however, **bagga* would be especially difficult to distinguish from ***bagge** 'beggar'. The term may also have been used topographically, to denote a feature in the landscape resembling a bag in some way, as has been suggested for the f.ns *Baggeplok* c.1320 Ch:4·73 (***plocc**), *pastur' voc' le Bagge* c.1560 Gl:3·12 and *Bagg acre* 1636 Gl:3·13. The rare OE pers.n. *Bacga* (Redin:83) or the ON *Baggi* would be indistinguishable from the common noun, and may lie behind some p.ns like Bagworth 1086 Lei (**worð**). Other possibilities that may be relevant include dialect *bag* 'long-tailed titmouse' or a verb with the sense 'to cut crops close to the ground with a bagging hook' (EDD).

~ ME *bagge* is often derived from ON *baggi* (cf. also OFr *bague* 'bundle'), but the p.n. evidence and the existence of a Dutch cognate tends to suggest a native origin.

DOE –; MED *bagge* n.[1]; EDD *bag* sb.; OED *bag* sb.

baggard ME, 'one who carries a pack, a migrant craftsman, a beggar' is found also as a surname, e.g. *Nigellus Baggard* c.1195 (MED). It appears in *Beggars Lane* (st.n. Middlewich; *Bagardelone* 1487) Ch:2·242.

~ ME *bagge* (see ***bagga**) and the OFr suffix *-ard*. Cf. ***bagge**, **baggere** and **begger** (especially the etymological note).

MED *baggard*; OED –.

*bagge ME, 'beggar' may appear in Bag House 1640 Db (**hūs**), for which the sense 'tumbledown cottages such as beggars might inhabit' has been suggested. It might be found with a similar sense in st.ns of the type Bag Lane, but ***bagga** is an alternative for these names (examples are given there). Similarly, in combination with OE **rāw** 'row (of buildings)', both **bagga* and **baggere** (where examples are given) are possible alternatives. Cu:259 makes the interesting suggestion that *Baggeraw* may be a ME term like the recurring *Rattenraw* 'rat-infested row', used of a row of dilapidated buildings fit only for beggars to inhabit. On the other hand, independent evidence for the existence of this ME **bagge* 'beggar' is lacking.

~ ***bagga, baggard, baggere**.
Cf. DES *Bagg*.

*bagger ME, 'badger' would be the ME etymon of ModE *badger*, which is not independently evidenced until 1523 (OED); cf. ***bagga**. The word could not be distinguished from **baggere** 'hawker', but topographical generics render it likely in:
(*a*) Badsberry (*Baggerburgh* 1346, *Badgerburgh* 1430) La [Kenyon:85] (***burg**), Badgerholes (*Baggerheld* 1415) Db (**helde**), Bagger Wood 1344 YW (**wudu**).
MED −; EDD −; OED *badger* sb.[2]

baggere ME, 'itinerant seller of grain and other commodities, hawker' also denoted 'maker of bags or pouches'. It is attested, in either or both senses, as a ME surname (Fransson:94–5). It is formally indistinguishable from ***bagger** 'badger', but is more likely than that in some contexts. *Beggergate* (st.n. York; *Bagergate* 1243) YE:282, *Bageresgate* (st.n. Lincoln) a.1252 [14th] L:1·49 (**gata**), *le Bagourhouses* (f.n.) 1309 YW:1·266 are clear instances, and parallel to them may well be a group of names with **rāw** 'row (of buildings)', as Baggara 1589 Cu, Baggra (*Bagrawe* 1399) Cu, Baggrow (*Baggerawe* 1332) Cu, Bagraw 1385 Nb. In this combination, however, *baggere* cannot confidently be distinguished from ***bagge** 'beggar' or ***bagga** 'bag', perhaps in the sense 'dead-end'.
~ ***bagga**, cf. **baggard, *bagge**.
MED *bagger*; EDD *badger* sb.[1]; OED *badger* sb.[1]; DES *Badger*.

baiard OFr (AN), 'a bay horse'. ME *baiard*, derived from the adj. *bai* 'red-brown, bay' was originally applied to horses of this colour. However, following its use in medieval romances as the proper name of a horse owned by Charlemagne, the term was commonly given as a mock-heroic name to horses of any colour, as in the phrase *blind as Bayard* 'blind as an old nag' (OED, MED). This sense survives in the dialect expression 'Bayard of ten toes', equivalent to 'Shanks' pony' (EDD). The word is recorded as a ME pers.n. (DES). ME *baiard* was also used of a type of hand-barrow (MED *baiard*[2], OED *bayard* sb.[2]; cf. AFW *baiart*, DML *baiardum*), a sense which might be relevant to some names. Notable occurrences of the word in p.ns. are *Bayard's Green* 1194 Nth, a tournament ground on the O–Nth border licensed by Richard I (O:238,

xxvii) and Bayswater Mx:132, which is recorded in 1380 as *aqua vocata Bayard's Watering Place* (cf. Bayswater 1676 O:5). Byergates 1601 YW:5·87 (**gata**) probably contains this element, but the Fr surname *Biard* may be involved, here as elsewhere.

(*a*) *Bayardacker* (f.n.) 1361 YW:3·240 (**æcer**), Bayard's Cove 1351 D:321 (**cofa**), *Bayard Furlong* (f.n.) 1777 O:167 (**furlang**), *Bayerdes leyes* (f.n.) 1552 O:338 (**lēah**).

(*b*) Use of the element as a simplex may be implied by *both the bayards* (f.n.) 1609 Sx:236, perhaps referring to two fields with the same name.

AND *baiard*; MED *baiard*[1]; EDD *bayard*; OED *bayard* a. & sb.[1]; DES *Bayard*.

baie OFr, *f.* 'bay, inlet of the sea'. This word does not appear in French until the 14th century (TLF *baie*[1]), and is attested in ME literary texts from c.1400. It is rarely noted in early-recorded p.ns, but is found in Robin Hood's Bay 1532 YN, and perhaps *Boltbay* 1451 D:307 (**bolt**). Formally, it cannot be distinguished from several other elements that come into ME as *bay* (see **bay**).

AND *bai*[2]; MED *bai* n.[3]; EDD –; OED *bay* sb.[2]; DML *baia*[1].

baille OFr, *m./f.* 'bailey, palisade or wall of a castle courtyard' can be difficult to distinguish from *baillie* 'bailiff' or 'bailiwick' (see **baillif**). A significant group of names in *baille* are referred to early in Latin and French documents but are not named in the vernacular until comparatively late. The Baile (st.n. York) is first recorded in French as *le Veuz Baille*, while the English name of Bail Dyke, first recorded with the Latinised form *ballium* as *fossato de muro ballii mei Lincolnie* 1155–8 [14th], does not appear until as late as 1613. The earliest known reference to *The Upper Bailey*, Chester Castle, is *Ballium circa castrum Cestriae* c.1246; only in 1777 does the element appear in a vernacular context, as *the upper 'ballium'* (sic), where *ballium* is clearly still considered a foreign word.

Where names refer to a particular fortified building, this is indicated in the list below.

(*a*) Bail Dyke (bdg.n. Lincoln) 1613 L:1·7 (**dīc**; Lincoln Castle), Bailgate (bdg.n. Lincoln; *a porta vocat Bailyat* 1307) L:1·7 (**geat**; Lincoln Castle), *Baylhouse* (surn.) 1327 L [METT:48], *lez baylhouselandes* (f.n.) 1558 L:2·191 (**hūs**).

(*b*) The Bailey (bdg.n. London) c.1166 Ldn:188 (later Old Bailey), *le Bayl de Skipse* 1260 YE:82 (Skipsea Brough), Bailey Fd (f.n.) 1610 Ch:3·276 (Peel Hall), *le Baillie* (bdg.n. Oakham) 1329 Ru:110 (Oakham Castle), The Bail (bdg.n. Lincoln) 1185 L:1·6 (Lincoln Castle), The Baile (st.n. York) 1296 YE (one of two castles erected by William I), *Upper Bailey* (bdg.n. Chester) 1777 Ch:5·42 (Chester Castle), *le Baile* c.1225 YW:4·29.

AND *baile*[1]; AFW *baile*; MED *baille* n.[2]; EDD *bailey*; OED *bailey*; DML *baillium*; DES *Bail, Bailey.*

baillif OFr, *m.* 'bailiff' was used in the ME period of various administrative and judicial officials, including magistrates, town councillors and the feudal lord's agents in the management of his estates. The variant *baillie* is well-attested in ME, and forms with -*f*- and without often alternate in spellings of a single name. Bailey Hills YW is *Bayliffe Hill* 1593, *Baley Hill* 1621; the field in Macclesfield Ch called *the Bayliffe butts* in 1620 was earlier *Baillebut* (1471), and is perhaps identical with *terra Thome le Bailly* c.1330, named from Thomas de Macclesfield, bailiff of the town c.1280–1300 (Ch:1·124).

As the above discussion suggests, the derived surname is attested (MED, Thuresson:136–7) and may appear in p.ns. Moreover, where *f*-spellings do not appear, the element is formally indistinguishable from the related OFr noun *baillie* 'delegated office (especially that of bailiff)', which developed the sense 'district, domain or bailiwick' in ME (see **bailli-wik**). This usage of *baillie* explains the apparent occurrence of Bailey as a generic, both in simplex p.ns and in combination with surnames. An example of the latter is Blaize Bailey Gl, which is first recorded as *balliua de Bleyth* around 1270, and preserves the family name of Alexander *Bleyt*, who held the bailiwick in the 13th century. Note also *la Westbayly* 1402 Do:1·3, which is *the West-baillywike* 1541.

Confusion is also possible with OFr **baille** 'bailey, the wall surrounding a castle or city' (cf. the ME variants *bailli, bali*; MED *baille* n.[2]).

(*a*) *le Bailicroft* (f.n.) 1310 YW:1·68, *Bailycroft* (f.n.) 1352 YW:2·58 (**croft**), Bailey Flat 1591 Db (**flat**), Bailey Ridding 1363 Ch:1·67 (***ryding**), Bailiff Bridge (*Bailibrigge* 1374) YW (**brycg**).

(*b*) Bailey 1275 Cu, 1655 Gl, Bailey Ridge (*La Baillie* 1351) Do:3·344, Bailie Gate (*Le Bailly* 1412) Do:2·47, *campo voc' le Bayly* (f.n.) 1290 Gl:3·180.

(*c*) With surnames in Badcock's Bailey 1633 Gl, Blaize Bailey c.1270 Gl, and Lea Bailey 1194 Gl.

~ **bailli-wik**.

AND *baillif*; AFW *baillif*; MED *baillif*; EDD *bailie*; OED *bailie, bailiff*; DML *baillivus*; DES *Bailleff, Bailey.*

bailli-wik ME, 'district or place under the jurisdiction of a bailiff'. For the synonomous use of OFr *baillie* see **baillif**. In the Do and Gl instances, below, the term is used of forest areas, referring to the forest of Purbeck and the forest of Dean respectively.

(*b*) *Baliwych* 1324 YW:6·59.

(*c*) *the West-baillywike, the Est-baillywike* 1541 Do:1·3 (**west, ēast**), Blakeney Bailey (*baliue de Blakeney* c.1270, *Baillifwik of Blakeney* 1486) Gl:3·251.

~ **baillif, wīc.**

MED *baillif-wĭk*; OED *bailiffwick, bailiwick*; DML *baillivicus.*

bak-side ME, 'property behind a dwelling'; also apparently 'land on the edge, or in a remote part, of an area'. It would be formally indistinguishable from a 'true' compound of **bæc** and **sīde**, which could mean 'side of a ridge', 'hillside'.

(*a*) Backside Close 1771 (f.n.) YW:3·251, *Backside end* (f.n.) 1614 Do:3·292.

(*b*) *claus', curtill' vocat' le Backeside* 1563 (f.n.) Do:3·378, *The Backsid* (st.n. Nottingham) 1576 Nt:19 (referring to a small thoroughfare on the city's boundary), Back o' th' Edge (f.n.; *the backside of Taxall Edge* 1611) Ch:1·175, Backside 1640 Cu, 1673 We, The Backside or Cow Pasture (f.n.) 1696 Ch:2·142, *the backsides* (f.n.) 1611 Ch:1·130, *pastur' vocat' Backsyde of Wyldboreclough* (f.n.) 1626 Ch:1·163, *uno parcella terr' vocat' a backesyde* (f.n.) 1584 Do:1·166.

(*c*) With the name of the owner: *Bryan Franklines backside* (f.n.) 1640 Ru:254, *George Bates's Backside* (f.n.) 1726 Ru:77.

~ **bæc, sīde.**

MED *bak-sīde*; EDD *backside*; OED *backside.*

bál ON, *n.* 'fire'. In northern dialect *bale* is used of beacons and signal fires; *bale-hill* is recorded with the sense 'hill where lead has been smelted' (cf. ***bole**).

(*a*) *Balgreuemor* c.1260–70 Ch:2·314 (**græfe, mōr**), Belly Pasture (f.n.; *Balehougete* 12th) YW:6·96 (**haugr, geat**), Bale Hill 1588 We:2·109, 1688 We:2·61 (**hyll**).

(*c*) Tag Bale Hill (*Tagg Bail* 1717) YW (***tagga**).

~ **bēl.**

ONP *bál*; MED *bāl(e* n.²; EDD *bale* sb.¹; OED *bale* sb.²

balca OE, *m.* 'ridge, bank'. The headform is uncertain: the weak noun appears only in inflected forms, e.g. *on þan ufer ende balcan* S:920, and might as well be feminine or neuter *balce*; a strong form *balc* is also attested. In p.ns this element would be formally indistinguishable from ON *balkr* 'partition', and the extension of the word's sense to 'beam' in the

ME period may owe something to this. However, the word is most commonly used in f.ns in its technical sense, of the ridge of unploughed land that marked the boundary between adjacent strips of the common field (see Rackham 1986:166). The element is commonly combined with *ge-mǣre* 'boundary', e.g. in the f.ns *Mearebalke* 16th C:311, *le mere bawke* 1525 Hrt:250 and *le Meerbalkes* 1549 YE:319. That balks sometimes formed the boundaries of larger land units is suggested by names like *Seaton balke* (f.n.) 1602 Ru:288, which was also known as *seton meare* (*ge-*mǣre) in the early 17th century, and lies on Morcott's border with the parish of Seaton. Likewise, *le Prosessyonbalke* (f.n.) 1458 C:311 appears to connect the balk with the beating of parish bounds. The f.n. *Sheere balke*, meanwhile, occurs in several parishes on Hertfordshire's borders and refers to the county boundary (**scīr**[1]). Use of such uncultivated ridges as paths is probably referred to in *Weybalke* (f.n.) 1372–1480 C:311 (**weg**) and *Merygangebalke* (f.n.) 1422–71 Nt:275 (?**ge-mǣre, gang**). All of the instances below are f.ns with the exception of Balk YN.

(*a*) *Balkendes* c.1250 YN:325 (**ende**).

(*b*) Balk 1192–9 YN, *le Balke* (f.n.) 13th YW:1·280, *le Balke* 1315 Nt:275.

(*c*) With elements referring to size or shape: *Broadbaucke* 1649 Nt:275, *le Brodebalks* 1312 C:311 (**brād**), *Endlessebalk* 1591 C:311 (**ende-lēas**), Long Bork 1443 YW:7·154, *Longebalke* 1220 Wa:321, *le longebalkes* 1480 C:311 (**lang**[1]), *Lungechampnysbalk* 1323 C:311 (**lang**[1], pers.n.).

With elements specifying location: *Austbalca* 1202 YN:325 (**austr**), *Nestthesutherrestbalke* l.12th YE:319 ('next to the most southerly balk').

With elements denoting topographical features: *Byrybalke* 1393 C:311 (**burh**), *Haloughbalk* 1480 C:311 (**halh**), *Lound balke furlong* 1632 Ru:242 (**lundr, furlang**), *Wodebalke* 15th Db:715 (**wudu**).

With elements denoting vegetation: *Claverbalke* 1437 Nth:260 (**clǣfre**), *Crabtree balke* 1626 Nt:275 (**crab-tre**), *Crabbtree Balke furlong* 1652 Ru:29 (**crab-tre, furlang**), *Þornbalke* 13th C:311 (**þorn**).

With elements denoting man-made structures: *Limekilne balke* c.1700 Ru:265 (**lim-kilne**), *the milne balke* 1598 Ru:183 (**myln**), *le Temple balke* 1216–72 Wa (**templ**).

With personal names: *Beebies Baulk* 1619 Ru:72, *Bettes Baulke* 1633 Ru:28, *Malkenbalke* 15th Db:715, *Peppers Balk* 1798 Ru:236.

With words for local functionaries (or the derived surnames): *Constables baulk* 1762 Ru:286 (**conestable**), *Le Foresterbalke* 14th YW:1·139 (**forester**), *the Judges balke* 1688 Ru:219 (**juge**), *Lawemannes*

balke 1237 Nth:260 (**lah-man**), *the Parsons Balke* 1696 Ru:219 (**persone**).
With other descriptive elements: *le comen balke* 1562 C:311 (**commun**), *Rowe balk* 1638 W:422 (**rūh**).
DOE *balc*; MED *balk(e*; EDD *balk* sb.¹; OED *balk* sb.¹; DML *balcus*.

*balg OE, *adj.* 'rounded, bulging, smooth' has been proposed on the strength of ME *balgh* 'bulging', which is applied to a hill at *Sir Gawain* 2172 *balʒ berʒ*. The OE element has been thought to appear in Balham Sr and Bardon Hill Wa, which can be identified with the OE charter forms *to bælgenham* 957 [12th] S:645 (**hām/hamm**) and *balgandun* 669–709 [11th] s.64 (**dūn**) respectively. On the other hand, Udolph 1994:20–1 argues for a connection between the English element and the Low German noun *balge* 'ditch, tidal channel' which appears in Continental names.
An element of the same form is also possible in the following cases, though note that instances without a trace of medial *-i-* or *-g-* are particularly uncertain, and might be referred to **ball*. The headword given here would be Anglian—Kentish and West Saxon would have **bealg*.
(a) Balladen (*Baleden* 1522, *Balyden* 1525) La (**denu**), Balham (f.n.) 1448 Gl:1·43 (**hamm**), Balshagh (f.n.) 1333 Ch:2·203, *Balghschae* 1296 La:7, Boscar (*Balschawe* 1142) YN (**sceaga**), *Balitroumer'* (f.n.) 1346 St:1·182 (**trog, mere**¹).
~ **belg**.
DOE –; MED *balgh*; EDD –; OED *balgh*.

*ball OE, 'ball'. The sense in p.ns varies. ModE *ball* is recorded in So dialect as meaning 'rounded hill, hillock' (EDD), a meaning identified also in D p.ns (D:211). The application may have been more widespread; it is certainly a known use of ON *bǫllr*, from which *ball* cannot be formally distinguished and which may enter into northern and eastern English p.ns. ModE *ball* is also known from W as 'a mound of earth set up as a boundary mark' (cf. W:422, IPN:159), and that is likely to be represented in minor names of the south-west and perhaps elsewhere. In Ball Green 1499 YW and *Balgrene* (f.n.) c.1260 YW:2·147 (**grēne**²) the reference may be to a ball-game, cf. **bowling-alley**. Bow Broom (*Ballebrom* 1224) YW:1·115 perhaps contains **balled**; in any case this, and other names in *Ball-*, could involve the senses 'ball-shaped' or 'bare' discussed under that headword. There is also an ON pers.n. *Balli*, from which the noun(s) could not generally be distinguished.
The element is discussed in MELS:5–6, where examples are given of the simplex in surnames, such as Joh. atte Balle 1327 So, Ric. atte Balle

1386 Wo. Note also Alfwin Attebal 1165–6 Nf (Carlsson:24). A parallel toponymic surname Baller is identified by Fransson:194, e.g. Adam le Baller 1243 So.

Ball-game may appear early in *de Balgameshull'* 1313 K:287 (**hyll**).

(*a*) *Ballefeld* 1472 Ch:4·41 (**feld**), Ballgrove 1612 YW (**grǣfe**), *Balland* (f.n.) 1606 Ru:173, *Ballelonde* (f.n.) 1442 YW:1·242, *Ballands* (f.n.) 1633 Ru:129 (**land**), *Balrum* (f.n.) 1240 YW:5·124 (**rūm**[1]).

(*c*) *Knyghtebal* (f.n.) 1216–72 W:422 (**cniht**), *le Northball* (f.n.) 1429 D:689 (**norð**), Sandy Balls 1488 Ha [cited at W:422] (**sandig**), Cabus (*Kaibal* 1200–10) La, Cakebole 1270 Wo, *Loverdesballe* (f.n.) 1232 W:422 (pers.ns), Thrushelball 1529–32 D (r.n.).

~ the word is not recorded in OE, though ON *bǫllr*, OHG *ballo* and the OE derivative **balluc** point to its existence. Cf. also **balled**.

DOE –; MED *bal*; EDD *ball* sb.[1]; OED *ball* sb.[1]; DES *Ball*.

balled ME, *adj.* 'bald, rounded like a ball'. The etymology of this word is not clear. Originally it may have implied 'rounded like a ball', from ***ball**, or 'marked with a white blaze on the head' (as 'bald coot'), involving a 'ball' of different (probably Celtic) origin (OED *ball* sb.[3]). Both senses are evidenced, and either could have given rise to 'bald, hairless, bare'. Alternatively, *balled* may be borrowed from ON already with the sense 'hairless, bare' (cf. ODan *bældet* 'bald-headed' cited by Björkman:229). Perhaps a complex, mixed origin is most likely. The matter is of relevance with regard to the p.n. instances, which take the word back earlier than other certain records by a century. In p.ns the most common application is to trees and, particularly, bushes. The meaning is generally supposed to be 'rounded', and this is clearly supported by the parallel example of *Ballocþorn* (see **balluc**). On the other hand, 'bare, leafless' would also be possible (as in *As You Like It* IV, iii, 106: 'An old oake, whose . . . high top bald with drie antiquitie'); it might also be noted that *Baldstaffmore* 1251 C:212, an early alternative name of Byall Fen, probably contains *balled* with **stæf** 'staff, pole', which is unlikely to be rounded, but might be either bare and smooth, or marked with a notch or 'blaze'. Further, there is the possibility of confusion with a probable ***bolled** 'pollarded' (cf. particularly the early spelling of Balbush, below), which would be of yet another origin.

The instance of a simplex name is baffling.

(*a*) *Baldbirch* (f.n.) 1674 St:1·98 (**birce**), Balbush (f.n.; *Le Boldbusk* 1371) YW:5·191, *Balledbusc* (f.n.) 13th YW:4·240, *Le Balledbuske* (f.n.) 13th Cu:233, *Balledebusk* (f.n.) 1471 YW:6·97 (***busc/*buskr**), *Baldhill* (f.n.) 1669–78 Gl:2·255 (**hyll**), *Balledthorn* (f.n.) 12th YW:4·251 (**þorn**),

With the compliments of Betsy Springer

English Place-Name Society
Department of English Studies, Nottingham University, University Park, Nottingham NG7 2RD
☎Direct Line 0115 9515919

Bawtry 1199 [13th] YW, *le Bawtree Carr* (f.n.) 1699 YW:2·248 (**trēow**; these two instances are probable, but less certain because of the loss of final -*d* before *t*-).
(*b*) *le Ballede* (f.n.) c.1260 Db:535.
MED *balled*; OED *bald* a.; DES *Bald*.

balluc OE, *m.* 'testicle' is probably used in some topographical sense in Bullock Low (*Balloklaw* 1415) Db (**hlāw**). Alternatively, this could perhaps be an elliptical compound involving one of the species of orchid known as ballock-grass, ballock-wort etc. (OED s.v. *ballock*). Presumably the rounded shape is alluded to in *Ballocþorn* (f.n.) 1275 Db:342 (**þorn**). Note the term's use as a byname for a moneyer of Cnut, MATADAN BALLVC (Smart 1992:89). The headform is Anglian; West Saxon pl. *beallucas* is also attested.
~ *ball.
DOE *bealluc*; MED *ballok*; OED *ballock*; DES *Ballock*.

balme OFr, *m./f.* 'balm, a scented herb, mint' probably appears in *Balmecroft* (f.n.) 1208 YW:4·52 (**croft**), the Balme Ing (f.n.) 1798 YW:3·70 (**eng**), *Balmefyld* (f.n.) 1498 St:1·163 (**feld**), Balm Flatt (f.n.) 1546 YW:1·155 (**flat**). Though several of these p.ns have been connected with OFr *baume* 'hollow' (YW:7·155; cf. TLF *baume*[2]), there seems to be no evidence for the use of this word in English; the term given here, which is known in ME, is therefore probably to be preferred.
~ Lat *balsamum*.
AND *basme*; AFW *basme*; MED *baume*; EDD *balm* sb.; OED *balm* sb.

balne ME, 'bath', perhaps also 'place for bathing'. This term, borrowed from Lat *balneum*, is attested from the late 15th century referring specifically to a vessel containing hot water used in alchemy (MED, OED). Although this is the name not only of a parish, but is also applied to a larger district (YW:2·1–2), it is unlikely to be of pre-English origin, since it recurs independently several times elsewhere in the county, as Balne Beck 1469 YW:7·120, *Bawn Beck* 1817 YW:3·221 (**bekkr**), Bawn (f.n.) It may, however, appear as a rather earlier borrowing in Balne 1167 YW. 1814 YW:2·194. The sense may be 'pool' or 'bathing place' (cf. **bæð**). It is discussed at length at YW:2·14–15 and YW:7·xvii.
~ Lat *balneum*. The word does not seem to have come through Fr, since OFr *bain* descends from Vulgar Lat *baneum.
MED *balne*; EDD –; OED *balne*; DES *Balne*.

bān OE, *n*. 'bone' is not easy to distinguish in ME p.ns from **bón** 'favour, benevolence'. Insley 1996 also suggests that there may have been an OE *bān cognate with ON **beinn** 'straight, direct', and that either this or *bān* 'bone' may appear in Bonhunt 1086 Ess **(funta)**. *Bān* 'bone' may also be found in the following.

(*a*) Bonehills c.1250 Db **(hyll)**, Bumpitt 1254 K **(pytt)**.
(*c*) Holy Bones 1349 Lei:124 **(hālig)**.
~ **bon-fir**.
DOE *bān*; MED *bōn* n.[1]; EDD *bone* sb.; OED *bone* sb.

bana OE, *m*. 'killer' seems to appear in a group of names connected with springs or streams, where it may refer to those that are dangerous or poisoned (cf. EDD, and MED *bāne* sense 2b 'poison' from a.1398). Combination with **welle** is particularly common, and can be taken back to OE charter forms of Banwell So—*æt Bananwylle* S:373, S:806. An early name for *Holding Brook* Ch (*Banalsiche* c.1200) may represent the same compound contracted, with later addition of *sīc* 'stream' (Ch:1·29). MELS:6 suggests that the surname *atte Banse* 1333 So represents a variant in which *bana* is combined with **sǣ**.

An unattested OE pers.n. *Bana has been adduced for many p.ns (Gelling 1984:31, Hough 1995), while the name of some of these places might conceivably be due to association with a murderer—'watercourse in which a murderer had drowned himself or murderers were drowned' according to MELS:6—but the interpretation given above seems a less fanciful explanation of the recurring compound.

(*a*) Banewells (f.n.) 1848 YW:4·99, Bannall's Fm (*Banewelle* 1305) Wo:56 (this instance is possibly transferred as a surname from Banwell So), Bannawell 1320 D, Bannel (f.n.; *Banewelle* 1326) Nth:280, Banwell 893 [11th] So [Asser] **(welle)**, ?*Bonwellfelde* (f.n.) YW:4·59 **(welle, feld)**.
DOE *bana*; MED *bāne*; EDD *bane* sb.; OED *bane* sb.[1]

baner OFr (AN), *f*. 'banner, standard' has been identified in the Westmorland p.ns *Banerhowe* 1256 **(haugr)**, Banner Rigg 1677 and Banner Riggs 1857 **(hrycg)**—see We:1·194. Alternative explanations have been offered for these names, involving ON *bannari 'challenger' and ME *baneur* 'standard-bearer'. However, both the pattern of compounding with generics denoting hills and the additional example of John Bell's Banner 1614 We (pers.n.), a lofty peak and boundary marker, suggest that these names might rather apply *baner* 'flag' to a landmark (We:1·194). Alternatively it might be relevant that the dialect term *bannering* is used in Shropshire dialect for the custom of beating the parish bounds, which involved the carrying of flags (EDD).

AND *baner*; AFW *baniere*; MED *banēr(e*; EDD –; OED *banner* sb.[1]; DML *banera*.

banke ODan, *m*. 'ridge, hill, slope, bank, artificial embankment'. ME *banke* seems to be derived directly from the ODan form. An OE cognate *banca* is attested in the compound *hōh-banca*, 'heel-bench, couch', but the p.n. distribution does not suggest it was used topographically (though cf. **benc**). In OWN the cognate form was *bakki*, developed by nasal assimilation (cf. **brekka, slakki**). This may appear in some English p.ns (though it would generally be indistinguishable from **bæc**), but the distribution of ME *banke* suggests that the unassimilated form was taken up by speakers of all backgrounds (SSNNW:81–2, 316–18).

Banke is common in the minor and f.ns of northern and eastern counties, with many examples noted especially in the comprehensively studied YW and Ch. Outside the north and east it is rare before the 14th century; *Northbanke* (f.n.) 1216–72 W:422 is a notable early instance.

Beside *bakki/banke* is an *i*-mutated unassimilated ON **benkr*, represented by OIcel *bekkr*, Sw *bänk*, Norw *benk* 'bench'. Either this, or a Scandinavianised form of OE *benc*, accounts for the alternation with *banke* in Ninebanks Nb: *Ninebenkes* 1228, *Nine bankes* 1296 and *Nynbenkys* 1479 [NbDu:150]. Cf. also MED *benk*, EDD *benk, bink* sb.[1], OED *benk, bink*.

(*a*) Bank Head 1472 Db (**hēafod**), Bankwood 1684 Nt (**wudu**).

(*b*) Bank 1251 La:137, 1293 Cu:447, *Bank* (f.n.) 1327 L:2·283, Banks 1256 Cu:70, *le Bonks* (f.n.) 1349 Ch:3·232.

(*c*) Bedern Bank (st.n. Ripon) 1369 YW (**bed-ern**), Beck Bank c.1325 YE:206—cf. *Becbanck* (surn.) 1301 Y [METT:48]—(**bekkr**), *Aikebanc* (f.n.) 1170 YW:7·154, Aikbank 1292 We (**eik**), Ellerbeck (*Ellerbank* c.1215) Cu:424 (**elri**), Gale Bank 1293 YN (**geil**), Whinbank 1292 Cu (***hvin**), Thornbank c.1230 Cu (**þorn**), *Wyndybonke* (f.n.) 1366 Ch:1·267, Windy Bank c.1300 La (**windig**), *Alysandrebanke* (f.n.) c.1330 Ch:1·124 (pers.n.), *Lirlyngbankes* (f.n.) 1395 C:312 (pers.n.), Arthington Bank 1312 YW:4·194 (p.n.), Roebanks 1272 Cu (r.n.), Laver Banks 1512 YW (r.n.).

~ **benc**.

ONP *bakki*[1]; MED *bank(e* n.[1]; EDD *bank* sb.[1]; OED *bank* sb.[1]; DES *Bankes, Banker*.

banne-note ME, 'a nut', probably 'walnut'. *Bannut* 'walnut' is recorded in the west of England from Cheshire to Somerset (EDD, OED). In p.ns it is almost always combined with **trēow**; it has been noted without that element only in Bannots hill (f.n.) 1841 Gl:3·66.

(a) *Bannuttree close* (f.n.) 1609 Gl:1·125 (**clos**), Baynut Tree Yd (f.n.) 1612 Sa:2·130 (**geard**), Bannuttree Orchard (f.n.) 1775 Gl:2·88 (**orceard**).

(b) *the Bannettree* (f.n.) 1647 Gl:2·85.

~ *ban, banne*, of unknown meaning, **hnutu**.

MED *banne-nŏte tre*; EDD *bannut*; OED *bannut*.

bār OE, *m*. 'boar' clearly appears in p.ns in the compound **wild-bor**, but is otherwise often difficult to isolate. When shortened to *Bar-* in compound p.ns, it can be hard to distinguish from **bær, bere, bǣr** and **bearu**. When there is a genitival *-s* the word is possibly being used as a pers.n., though such a use is not well-attested (Redin:17, Feilitzen:192).

(a) Barsham 1086 Nf, 1086 Sf (**hām**), Boars Hill a.1170 [13th] Brk, Boarzell a.1123 Sx (**hyll**), Barwell 1086 Lei (**welle**), Husbands Bosworth 1086 Lei (**worð**).

~ **wild-bor**.

DOE *bār*; MED *bōr*; EDD *boar*; OED *boar*; DES *Boar*.

barat OFr, *m*. 'strife, conflict, grief' may appear in *Barettfelde* (f.n.) 1476 Ch:1·239 in the sense 'disputed' or 'troublesome field', or perhaps 'field where conflict(s) took place'. The surname Barratt may derive from this word, and is recorded from the 12th century (DES).

AFW *barat*; AND *barat*; MED *barat(e*; EDD –; OED *barrat*; DES *Barrat*.

barbecane OFr, *f*. 'outer fortification of a city or castle' was also used in the ME period of a fortified gate or bridge.

(a) *Barbycandyke* 1469 YW:5·112 (**dīc**).

(b) *la Barbecane* c.1240 Wo:389, Barbican (st.n London) 1279, *Barbican* 13th YW:4·11, *Barbican* (st.n. Exeter) 1397 D:21, Barbecan Road (st.n. Barnstaple; *Le Barbigan* 1329–30) D:26 [& Cu:3·lxviii].

~ perhaps ultimately from Arabic or Persian.

AFW *barbacane*; AND *barbecane*; DML *barbacana*; MED *barbicǎn*; OED *barbican*.

barbour OFr, *m*. 'barber, petty surgeon, dentist' is recorded as a ME surname from the 13th century (Fransson:188, DES), and appears in *le Barberslone* (st.n. Chester) 1440 Ch:5·34 (**lane**).

AND *barbur*; AFW *barbier*; MED *barbŏur*; EDD –; OED *barber*; DES *Barber*.

bar-gate ME, 'barrier, city-gate'. The compound is tautologous; see **barre**. Some instances have *yate* derived regularly from OE *geat*; others have the form *gate* which became standard, and shows the influence of the

OE plural *gatu* and/or of ON pronunciation. Those with *gate* in Danelaw cities may alternatively contain ON **gata**, giving 'street by the barrier'—Nt:14 interprets *Barregate* in this way. Barrass Gate Cu (and Barrasgate 1545 Dumfries [Cu:145]) contains a plural or variant form; see **barre**.

(*b*) *Barezete* (surn.) 1327 So [MELS:6], Bargate (st.n. Lincoln; *atte Baryate* 1280–90) L:1·13, *Bargate* (surn.) 1275 Wo [MELS:6], *Bargates* (f.n.) 1231 YW:4·233, *Barrass Gate* 1711 Cu:145, *Barregate* (st.n. Nottingham) 1242 Nt:14, (surn.) 1327 Nf [Carlsson:25], Barryate 1567–73 Ch:5·61.

(*c*) *Estbarreʒate* (st.n. Oakham) 1494 Ru:115 (ēast), *Le Westbarreyate* (st.n. Oakham) 1373 Ru:115 (**west**).

~ **barre, geat**.

MED see *Attebargate* s.v. *barre* sense 1(b); OED *bar-gate* s.v. *bar* sb.[1] sense 30; DES *Bargate*.

barge OFr, *f.* 'sailing vessel; river craft, ferry' probably lies behind *Le Barge* (f.n.) 1363 Ḃrk:538 in the parish of Wallingford, on the Thames. Other examples might include *Milne Barge* (f.n.) 1551–2 Brk:183 and Hr and Lr Barge (f.n.) 1839 Do:3·25 (perhaps with reference to a ferry). However, The Bargeway 1840 Brk:498 leads up to the Berkshire downs and Brk:850 records the local use of *barge* in the sense 'farm waggon'. Another formal possibility would be dialect *barge* 'something large, large, protuberant' recorded from Devon to Shropshire (EDD *barge* sb.[2] & adj.).

AFW *barge*; AND *barge*; DML *bargia*[1]; MED *bărǧe*; OED *barge* sb; DES *Barge*.

baril OFr, *m.* 'barrel, tub' seems to appear in *Nicollesbarrell* (f.n.) 1593 Gl:4·101 (pers.n.). In Barrelwell 1685 Ch:5·78 (**welle**), reference may be to a well with a barrel (cf. **bolla**), or to one with tub-like construction. It is recorded as a surname from the ME period, either for 'cooper' or with the sense 'tubby' (DES).

AFW *baril*; AND *baril*; MED *barel*; EDD *barrel*; OED *barrel* sb.; DES *Barrell*.

bark ME, 'bark', generally referring to its use in tanning. The word probably entered English directly from ON *bǫrkr*, *m.*; if so, its appearance in an 11th-century OE recipe, *nim . . . eft gewæxen barc* 'take "grown-again" bark' (Cockayne:1·378), is an early instance of the loan. Barkbooth We is presumably equivalent to a **bark-hous**; note also *Barkinbotherake* (f.n.) 1357 YW:3·187, with ME *barking* 'tanning'.

(*a*) Barkbooth 1535 We (bōð), Barkhill 1585 YW:3·232 (**hyll**).

~ **barkere, bark-hous**; cf. ***berkarie***.

DOE *barc*; OGNS *börkr*; MED *bark*; EDD *bark* sb.[1]; OED *bark* sb.[1]; DES *Bark*.

barkere ME, 'tanner'. The element cannot usually be distinguished from the occupational surname derived from it, though Barker Gate, Nottingham, was *vicus tannatorum* 1308, and *le Barkerriding* YW was granted by one *Johannes le Tannur*. For Barkin (*Barkerkin* 1278) We:1·24, it has been suggested that *Barkar*, gen.sg. of an ON pers.n. *Bǫrkr*, is an alternative; this would also be possible elsewhere, though it is not particularly likely. A more serious ambiguity arises from the existence of ME *berkere* (< OFr (AN) *bercher*) 'shepherd', which is well attested in surnames (MED *bercher*, Thuresson:63). From at least the 14th century, in the north, *bark-* and *berk-* would have fallen together in speech and writing (Jordan:§67), so that certainty is impossible in many of the examples given here. The 13th-century *Berkergate* in York looks like *berkere*, though just possibly it postdates the coalescence. Fransson:121 observes that *Barkere* as a surname has a largely Anglian distribution.
(*a*) Barkerend 1577 YW (**ende**), *le Barchersefflat* (f.n.) 1333 Ch:2·71 (**flat**), Barker Gate (st.n. Nottingham; *Barkergate* c.1375) Nt:14, *Berkergate* (st.n. York) 1240 YE:300 (**gata**), *Barkerhill* (st.n. York) 1373 YE:300 (**hyll**), Barker St. (st.n. Nantwich; *le Barkereslone* 1421) Ch:3·32 (**lane**), *le Barkerriding* (f.n.) 13th YW:4·35 (**rydding**), *le Barkereswad'* (f.n.) c.1180 YW:5·93 (**vað**).
~ **bark**.
MED *barker*; EDD *barker* sb.[1]; OED *barker* sb.[2]; DES *Barker*.

bark-hous ME, 'tan-house'. Besides the following earlier examples, numerous instances have been noted in late minor names in YW, We and Ch. Cf. also Barkbooth (see **bark**).
(*a*) *barkehowse fyld* (f.n.) 1525 Ch:4·18 (**feld**), *le Barkhousyord* (f.n.) 1404 Ch:4·41 (**geard**), *Barkhowse meadowe* (f.n.) 1609 (cf. *the Tanne howse* 1578 same parish) Ch:3·17 (**mēd**).
(*b*) *Barchous* (surn.) 1316 Nb [METT:48], *le Barkehowse* (f.n.) 1541 YW:1·277, *Barkehowse* 1597 YW:6·230, *the Barkhowse* (f.n.) 1519 Db:420. Löfvenberg 1946:90 notes 'one tanning house called "Barkhouse"' 1396 Nt, and Ch:1·124 records *unum Barkhous* in 1350, though here the term is being used as a common noun and not a name.
~ **bark, hūs**.
MED *bark-hous* s.v. *bark* sense 3; OED *bark-house* s.v. *bark* sb.[1] sense 10; DES *Barkhouse*.

barn ON, *n*. 'child, offspring' may appear in the genitive plural in Danelaw p.ns of the type Barnby. Parker (1984–5) lists the material, arguing that the names may refer to estates held jointly by a number of heirs, without being physically divided between them. Alternatively, it has been suggested (SSNY:14, SSNEM:20–1) that a *Barnaby* is a secondary settlement established by the children of tenants or land-owners at the edges of their parents' estate, a sense first proposed for Swedish names containing *Barna-* (Sahlgren 1945). It was previously thought that the Danelaw names contained a Scandinavian pers.n. Note that the cognate OE *bearn*, in its Northumbrian form *barn*, would be indistinguishable.

(*a*) Barnbow 1185–93 YW (**bú**), Barnburgh 1086 YW (**burh**), Barmby c.1050 [12th] YE:249, Barnby 1086 Nt:67, 1086 Sf, 1086 YN:36, 1086 YW:1·17 (**bý**).

OGNS *barn*; MED *bǎrn*; EDD *bairn*; OED *bairn*; DES *Barne*.

baron OFr, *m.* 'baron, noble, manorial lord'. Note that Cu and We were divided into baronies, often rendered by Lat *baronia* in early documents, as *baronia de Westmeriland* 1236 We:2·1. The English borrowing is not noted before *barony of Leddall* 1460 Cu:3, *the Barony of Kendale* c.1540 We:1·22.

(*a*) *Baron cross* (st.n. Appleby) 1684 We:2·92 (**cros**), *le Baron medewe* (f.n.) 1338 St:1·118 (**mēd**), Baronwood 1485 Cu (**wudu**).

AFW *baron*; AND *baron*; DML *baro²*; MED *barŏun*; OED *baron*; DES *Baron*.

barro- Brit, 'top, summit, hill' seems to appear in Great Barr St, which is *Barre* 1086, and probably to be identified with *æt bearre* 957 [12th] S:574. It may well also occur in Baslow Bar (*Basselawe Barre* 1307–27) Db, though here there is a complication. In this name Brit ***barro-*** has been equated with Db dialect *bar* 'horseway up a steep hill', said in the late 18th century to be the source of 'Bakewell Bar, Beely Bar, Baslow Bar, Rowsley Bar, etc.' (Db:40–1). Yet EDD includes the same quotation s.v. *bargh*, which it notes more widely across northern England, and derives from OE **berg** 'hill'. One of the EDD citations is a 1678 commentary on a Yorks. proverb: 'Bargh, in the Northern dialect, is properly a horse-way up a steep hill; though here it be taken for the hill itself'. If *bargh* (also spelled *barf*) and *bar* are indeed variant developments of the same term, as this implies, it would not be straightforward to relate this to a base ***barro-***. On the other hand, the earliest form of Baslow Bar certainly tells against an origin in **berg** for this name, at least. The other 18th-century Db names mentioned above have not been separately collected as p.ns, but Brit ***barro-*** and/or dialect *bar* may also appear in the county in Barr Hall (*Barr* 1565).

The Brit element has also been suggested for Barhill 1394 Ch:4·48 (**hyll**), though as a first element it would be difficult to distinguish from

bār and some other elements.

A Goidelic cognate (cf. Irish *barr*) may enter into the Scandinavian island name *Barrey* (**ey**) found in the Hebrides (Barra), in Shetland (where the name is lost), and in Barrow-in-Furness (*Barrai* 1190) La (see La:204). The PrW development of Brit **barro-* would have been *barr.

~ ***barrāko-**.

GPC *bar²*, CPNE *bar*; cf. LEIA *barr*.

*barrāko- Brit, *adj.* 'hilly' appears in Barrock Fell (*Barrok'* 1272) Cu and in the county-name Berkshire 893 [11th; Asser], where it was earlier applied to a wood (Brk:1–2). The equivalent name Barrog is twice recorded in Wales (*ibid.*). The PrW development of the element would have been *barrǭg; see JEPNS:1·44.

~ ***barro-, -āko-**.

barre OFr, *f.* 'bar, barrier, obstruction' appears in Chester Bar Ch, where it denotes the harbour bar across the mouth of the Dee estuary, and in the C names Barlees and Bar Pastures where it probably refers to some obstruction in the stream that runs alongside these lands (C:282). In *Le Barredich* Brk and *le Barredyk'* Ru, the element appears to be used of defensive earthworks around the towns of Windsor and Oakham respectively, while *Barrdyke* YW refers to the moat which surrounded Doncaster in place of a wall. The term was more commonly applied in ME, however, to the barricade blocking an entrance to a walled city and thus by extension to the city-gate. This sense is preserved in *The Swine Bar*, the name of Nottingham's east gate and Bootham Bar, one of the four city-gates of York. See also **bar-gate**. Places whose names contain the element in this sense are often recorded early in Latin documents with MLat *barra*: the street in Chesterfield Db now known as West Barrs is first mentioned in the 14th century in the phrase *ad barram de Cesterfeld* and does not appear as *the West Barrs* until 1563, while the east gate of Oakham Ru, referred to in the st.n. *Estbarreȝate* in 1494, is first alluded to almost 200 years earlier as *atte Barre orientale* (1305).

In Swanleybar, *Sternesbarre* and *Nevilesbarre* reference is probably to the gates of a forest rather than a city (Hrt:66), and *Dalston-Barrs* Cu were gates 'placed to prevent straying from the common on the north side of Dalston' (cf. nearby *Barwis house*).

Several names like Barras c.1210 Cu:70, *le Barreys Heth* 1466 Ch:5·xxvii, and *the Barhasse feild* (f.n.) 1593 Ch:4·19, are probably to be connected with another, related word (cf. OED *barrace* 'outwork before a fortress, jousting lists', EDD *barras* 'enclosure for contests').

However, these would often be difficult to distinguish in form and sense from the plural of *barre*.

(*a*) *Le Barredich* (f.n.) 1216–72 Brk:34 (**dīc**), *Bardyke* (f.n.) 1507 YW:1·33, *le Barredyk'* 1377 Ru:115 (**dík**), *Barwis house* 1593 Cu:131 (**hūs**).

(*b*) Barrs St. (st.n Bristol; *les Barres* 1389) Gl:3·86.

(*c*) *The Swine Bar* (st.n. Nottingham) 1408 Nt:21 (**swīn**), *Nevilesbarre* 1467–8 Hrt:66, *Sternesbarre* 1467–8 Hrt:66 (?pers.ns), Chester Bar c.1536 Ch:4·304, *Dalston-Barrs* 1547–53 Cu:131, Swanleybar 1467 Hrt:66 (p.ns), Bootham Bar (st.n. York) l.12th YE (st.n.).

~ **bar-gate**.

AFW *barre*; AND *barre*; DML *barra*; MED *barre*; EDD –; OED *bar* sb.[1]; DES *Barr, Barrer*.

báss ON, *m.* 'cowshed', probably surviving as Yorkshire dialect *beace*, *beeas*: see EDD *boose* and YN:134. South of the Ribble-Humber line, from the 13th century onwards, *báss* would be indistinguishable from the cognate OE **bōs* (Jordan:§44).

(*a*) Baysbrown 1216–72 We (**brún**[2] or pers.n.), Baysdale 1189–1204 YN (**dalr**).

OGNS *báss*.

bastard OFr, *adj./sb.* 'bastard' could have several senses in p.ns. When applied to land it may be derogatory, used of fields of abnormal shape or low yield. However, note the use in various counties of *bastard-crop* and *bastard-fallow*, apparently involving crops fitted into the pattern of rotation out of turn (EDD). For *Bastard Hedge* Gl, cf. 'An ill-thriven tree or shrub' (EDD). Note also that the word was used as a surname, and *Bastardescroft* Brk may be connected with *Will. Bastard'* 13th (Brk:181).

(*a*) *Bastarde close* (f.n.) 1627 Ru:77 (**clos**), *Bastardescroft* (f.n.) e.14th Brk:181 (**croft**), *Bastard Hedge* (f.n.) 1540 Gl:2·227 (**hege**), *North Bastard Ley* (f.n.) c.1745 Ru:262 (**norð, lēah**).

AFW *bastart*; AND *bastard*; DML *bastardus*; MED *bastărd* n., adj.; EDD *bastard* sb. & adj.; OED *bastard* sb. & a.; DES *Bastard*.

bastel OFr, *m.* 'castle tower' appears in *the Bastile Room* (f.n.) 1537 Ch:1·298 (**rūm**[1]), a parcel of land in the Market Place, Stockport, apparently alluding to the site of the castle at Castle Hill. It might also be noted that EDD *bastile* records a widespread dialect sense 'workhouse'.

AFW *bäastel*; AND *bastile*; DML *bastilla*; MED *bāstĕl*; EDD *bastile, bastle*; OED *bastille* sb.

bat ModE, 'river island, land liable to flooding' is recorded in northern dialects (EDD), and appears in minor names: The Batts 1680 YW:5·200 is a wooded slope on the bank of the Ure, near an island in the river, while *Benty batts* (f.n.) 1687 We:2·30 has as its first element OE **beonet** 'bent-grass'. Derivations from ModE *bat* 'stratum of shale in a coal seam' have been suggested for these names (We:2·232), but the former interpretation is probably to be preferred.

EDD *bat* sb.⁴; OED –.

batable ME, *adj.* 'debatable, disputed' appears in early forms of Debateable Land Cu (*the Batable landez or Threpelandez* 1449), applied to disputed territory between England and Scotland (the alternative name contains OE **þrēap** 'dispute'). Similarly, the present participle *bating*, 'debating', is found in Batenbush 1536 Cu (***busc**), known to have been a place where Scottish and English borderers met for discussion and negotiation (Cu:99).

~ OFr *debat* 'dispute', *batre* 'to beat'.

MED *bātāble*, *bāting* ger.²; AND *batable*; EDD *bateable*; OED *batable*.

bataille OFr, *f.* 'battle'. Battle Sx is named from the abbey founded to commemorate the Battle of Hastings. *Batylham* 1527 Gl:2·67 (**hamm**) may well refer to the Battle of Tewkesbury, 1471 (the names of the area also include a *Blodyforlong* 1498 and a Bloody Meadow 1830). Battlefield Sa probably refers to the Battle of Shrewsbury, 1403, and appears to contain *bataille* by popular etymology: the name is first recorded as *Hayteleyfeld* in 1406, becoming *Bateleyfield* 1410 and *Batelfeld* 1419 (Sa:1·32).

Other references may similarly be to battlefields, and some may recall legal battles (Field:15, OED *battle* sb. sense 2). Note also the word's use as a surname, presumably denoting a soldier (DES).

An unrelated Scots and north-country term *battel*, adj. 'rich with grass, fertile' (EDD, OED) has been proposed as an alternative in the We instances.

(*a*) Battlebarrow 1450 We (**berg**), *Bateylcroft* (f.n.) 1265–81 Ch:5·74 (**croft**), Battledores (f.n.) 1697 Ch:1·300 (**dāl**), *le Batayleflat* (f.n.) 1351 Db:583 (**flat**), Battail Holme 1352 Cu (**holmr**), *Battell hill* (f.n.) 1540 Gl:2·73, Battle Hill 1558–1603 We (**hyll**), *Battleplace* 1275 L:1·14 (**place**), *Batelstones* (f.n.) 1499 YW:3·156 (**stān**), *Battle Street* (st.n. Cirencester) 14th Gl:1·62 (**strēt**), *Battailwonge* 1343–7 Lei:359 (**wang**). (*b*) Battle 1086 (*abbas de Bello* 1082) Sx.

AFW *bataille*; AND *bataille*; MED *batail(le*; OED *battle* sb.; DES *Battle*.

baun ON, *f.* 'bean'.

(*a*) *Bounecroft* (f.n.) 1300 We:1·57 (**croft**), *Baunedale* (f.n.) c.1200 L:2·44 (**deill**), *Bauneflat* (f.n.) 13th YW:4·246 (**flat**), *Boungarth* (st.n. Lincoln) 1263 L:1·17 (**garðr**), *Lytil bounyerd* (f.n.) 1373 YW:3·25 (**geard**), *Bouneholm* (f.n.) 13th YW:4·252 (**holmr**), *Bounlandes* (f.n.) 1312 L:2·216, *Baunllandwro* (f.n.) n.d. YE:319 (**land, vrá**).

~ **bēan**.

OGNS *baun.*

bay ME, 'dam, weir'. In *Baylake* and Bay Meadow W, the reference is to a dam in the River Og. Löfvenberg 1946:82 points out that the earliest form of Bay Meadow, *Baihedemede* 1503, contains an otherwise unrecorded *bay-head*, parallel to the OED's *dam-head* and *weir-head* 'which both mean about the same thing as *dam* and *weir*'.

The element may appear in Bay Gate 1592 YW:6·197 (**gata**), though a derivation from **baie** or OFr *bäee* 'opening, recess in a wall, stall in a barn' is also possible (see MED *bai* n.[4]). The noun would also be difficult to separate from the OFr/ME adjective *bai* 'bay coloured, red-brown'.

(*a*) *Baylake* 1547 W:303 (**lake**), Bay Meadow (f.n.) 1503 W:498 (**mēd**).

(*c*) *la Millebay* (f.n.) 1282 Gl:3·97 (**myln**).

~ uncertain; Löfvenberg 1946:82–6 argues for an OE origin.

MED *bai* n.[4]; AND *bai*[4]; DML *baia*[2]; EDD *bay* sb.[2]; OED *bay* sb.[5]

bæc OE, *n.* and *f.* 'back' is used topographically of a ridge. The element is difficult to identify. ME spellings of the type *Bak-*, *-bak* could equally belong to OWN *bakki* (see **banke**) or to one of the possible forms of **bæce** 'stream, valley'. In addition, it has been suggested that *bæc* may have had an early locative case **bæci*, which would produce a later OE **bece*, with palatalised *ċ*. This is identical with another of the possible forms of **bæce**: both would give ME spellings of the type *-beche* (PNLand:125). Some progress towards identification might be made with the dialectal information offered by OE charter bounds, which suggest that *bæc* is feminine in the south-east (where *bæce* is neuter), and neuter in the western Thames Valley (where *bæce* is rare). See Kitson 1990:199. In general, however, topography must be the deciding factor. For example, in Brk Gelling firmly associates four instances in OE charters with surviving features, three linear earthworks and a strip linchet (Brk:770). She also identifies a low tongue of land at Bashall YW, a broad ridge at Backford Ch, and high ridges near Beckhampton W and at Bacup L and Backwell So (PNLand:125). There is a marked ridge at Backbarrow La according to La:198.

Gelling argues that several names in the fens of C, Hu and L (most of them are listed below) more probably derive from the palatalised locative **bece* than from *bæce*. Topographically these would be used of slight elevations in the fens (PNLand:126–7); Chisbridge Bk may be a further example, referring to a ridge of gravel. As Kitson points out (1990:199 n. 18), this locative **bece* could well then be the origin of ModE *beach*.

More problematic is Gelling's further suggestion that the regular dative *bæce* could also develop a palatalised *ċ*, producing ME forms of the type *-bache* (PNLand:126). This is not impossible (cf. Hogg:§7.16 n.3), but it conflicts with usual phonological developments (OEG:§§426–35, Hogg: §7.16). Nonetheless, since the topography apparently suits *bæc* better than *bæce*—to which the names are generally attributed—Burbage W, Lei, Db and Debach Sf are tentatively listed here.

In Brokenback a.1244 L:3·115 and Broken Back (f.n.) 1621 L:4·162 (**brocen**) there is perhaps a connection with ME *broken-bakked* 'hunchbacked' (MED s.v. *brēken* sense 2b). The former name seems to refer to a round barrow, the latter to the sloping shape of the field. Other similar instances, however—Broken Back c.1577 L:4·100, Broken Back 1845 Ch:1·317, *Break backke* (also *an acr' called Broak backe*) 1595 L:4·127—do not appear to be topographically appropriate, and may be a derogatory nickname for back-breaking land (see Field:28 for further examples).

(*a*) Backbarrow 1537 La (**berg**), Backford 1150 Ch:4·172 (**ford**), Beckhampton 1086 W (**hām-tūn**), Bacup c.1200 La (**hop**), Bashall 1086 YW (**scelf**), Backwell 1086 So (**welle**).

(*b*) *Atteback* (surn.) 1303–4 Nf [Carlsson:24], Bake 1257–80 Co (St Germans parish) [OP], 1354 Co (Pelynt parish) [OP], Landbeach (*Bech* 1086) C.

(*c*) Ashbeach 1199 Hu [& Hrt:xxxvii] (**æsc**), Burbage 961 [12th] S:688 W, 1086 Lei, 1417 Db:52 (**burh**), Chisbridge 1175 Bk (?**cis*), Holbeach 1086 L (**hol²**), Pinchbeck 1086 L (?**pinca*), Debach 1086 Sf, Wisbech 1086 C:291 (r.ns).

The word came to be used with adjectival sense, 'lying behind, at the back' (cf. the adverbial OE *on bæc* 'to the back'). This usage appears relatively early in Back St. (st.n. Thornbury) 1474 Gl:3·14 and Back Wallgate (*the Backstreete* 1620; st.n. Chester) Ch:1·115. It becomes common in the 19th century, particularly in 'the Back Lane', which is early recorded in Back Lane 1690 (st.n. Bridlington) YE:lix. Two Bristol st.ns, *The Back* 1323 Gl:3·86 and *St Augustine's Back* 1382 Gl:3·90, are said to denote places at the back of town, or 'backing' onto the R. Avon, a use of the noun which is distinct from its earlier topographical application and links with the adjectival.

DOE *bæc*[1]; MED *bak* n.; EDD *back* sbs[1-3]; OED *back* sb.[1], *back* a., *back-*; DOE *Back*.

bæc-ærn OE, *n.* 'bakery' appears in *Bacherne* (surn.) 1327 Nf [Carlsson:24] and perhaps Bachern (n.d.) Gl:4·100.

~ OE *bacan* 'to bake', **ærn**, cf. **bæc-hūs**.

DOE *bæc-ern*; MED *bak-ern*; EDD –; OED –.

bæce OE, *m.* 'stream, stream valley'. Gelling (PNLand:12) suggests that it may be used specifically of 'a small stream flowing in a fairly well marked, but not dramatic, valley'.

The OE term is attested almost exclusively in charter boundaries. A number of variant forms are found. *Bæc* would be the regular cognate of Ger *Bach*, though unlike the German word it is neuter (e.g. *on þ[æt] heow bæc* S:619 Ha, if the abbreviation is correctly expanded). Masculine *bece* is an *i*-stem, cognate with OSax *beki* (e.g. *andlang ðæs beces* S:994 Ha). *Bec* (e.g. *in on þ[æt] bec* S:738 O) is a mixed form. So too is *bæce* (e.g. *in þone suðeran holan bæce* S:579 Wo). This variant is adopted here as the headword since it is the antecedent of forms in ME *Bache-, -bache*, which are particularly numerous amongst the surviving names; moreover *ba(t)ch* persisted in dialect with various senses (see the EDD, but note that several of the examples cited there represent p.ns interpreted rather than a clear survival in independent speech). Kitson 1990:199 states that the distinction in gender of the OE forms is dialectal, with neuter predominant in the south-east, masculine in the west midlands.

The origin of the variant *bæce* is not easy to explain, but Ekwall (1963:22) argues that it arose by the blending of *a*-stem and *i*-stem forms, with subsequent levelling through the paradigm of *bece*, a solution which has the merit of accounting for the assibilated consonant that evidently developed. Certainly it appears easier to attribute ME spellings of the type *bache* to *bæce* than to **bæc** 'back, ridge' (though cf. what is said there regarding Burbage etc.). ME spellings of the type *Beche-*, as first element, should also involve *bæce* (in the variant *bece*) rather than *bæc*, though here confusion with **bēce** 'beech-tree' is possible. Other possible spellings, as *bak, bek*, or *-beche*, cannot formally be distinguished from *bæc*; *bek* could also belong to the ON cognate **bekkr**.

In p.ns the element is most common in the midlands, especially the west midlands; it is relatively rare in the south and south-west, and practically absent from the north (PNLand:12). Its frequency in the minor names of Sa, He, Ch, Wo and Gl indicates its survival in the dialects of these counties.

Gelling (PNLand:125–7) argues that some names usually attributed to *bæce* belong to *bæc*; they are discussed and listed there.

The element is discussed at length, and many examples given—though not all of them are convincingly distinguished from *bæc*—in Ekwall 1963 and Ekwall 1965. Further instances from surnames are listed by MELS:4–5.

(*a*) Batchcott 1212 Sa, Badge Court 1221 Wo (**cot**), Beighton 1002–4 [12th] Db [ASWills:17], Betchton 1154–89 [17th] Ch:3·18 (**tūn**).

(*b*) Bache 1119 [12th] Ch:4·144, 1086 He, 13th Sa.

(*c*) Colebatch 1208–9 Sa:1·94 (?**col**), *Catesbache* 1278 Ch:3·206 (**cot**), Comberbach 1178 Ch:2·111 (***Cumbre**), Eastbach c.1275 Gl:3·212 (**ēast**), Haselbech 1086 Nth, Hazlebadge 1086 Db (**hæsel**), Howbeach 1282 Gl:3·222 (**hōl²**), Welbatch 1086 Sa (**hwēol**), Sandbach 1086 Ch:2·269 (**sand**), Pulverbatch 1086 Sa:1·245 (?1st el.), Cottesbach 1086 Lei, Evesbatch 1086 He (pers.ns).

~ **bekkr**.

DOE *bæc²*; MED *bach* n.¹, *bek* n.¹; EDD *bach(e, beck* sb.¹; OED *bache, beck* sb.¹; DOE *Bach, Bacher*.

bæcere OE, *m.* 'baker' has been noted less commonly in p.ns than the historically feminine form **bæcestre**. From the evidence of their use as surnames, Fransson:61 found that there was a regional distinction: *bæcere* was largely limited to the south and east, *bæcestre* to the 'Anglian counties'. The scarcity in p.ns may therefore be due to the relative under-representation of southern areas by detailed modern surveys.

In *Baxter Row* (st.n. Chester; Ch:5·23) original *bæcere* (*le Bakersrawe* 1293) was replaced by *bæcestre* (*le Baxterrowe* 1330 etc.).

(*a*) Baker St. (st.n. Gloucester) 1589 Gl:2·127.

~ OE *bacan* 'to bake'; **bæc-ærn, bæcestre, bæc-hūs, bæc-stān.**

DOE *bæcere*; MED *bǎkere*; OED *baker*; DOE *Baker*.

bæcestre OE, *f.* 'baker'. Originally the word was applied to women, but ME *bakestre, baxter* was used of both sexes, perhaps especially in midland and northern counties. Cf. **bæcere**. The term was commonly used as a surname (Fransson:61), which may be the immediate source of some p.ns.

(*a*) the element appears in the parish name Baxterley c.1170 Wa (**lēah**), but survives most commonly in st.ns: *Baxtergate* (Lincoln) 1191 L:1·50, Baxter Gate (Loughborough) 1386 Lei:375, (Hedon) 1401 YE, (Doncaster; *in vico pistorum* l.13th, *Bakster Gate* 1456) YW:1·30 (**gata**),

Baxter's Row (Carlisle) 1380 Cu (**rāw**), *Baker Street* (Worcester; *Baxterstrete* 1302) Wo:21 (**strēt**).
~ OE *bacan* 'to bake'; **bæcere**.
DOE *bæcestre*; MED *baxter*; EDD *baxter*; OED *baxter*; DOE *Baxter*.

bæc-hūs OE, *n.* 'bakehouse, bakery' is common in minor names. Note that potentially there could be confusion with EDD *backhouse* sb.[1] 'back room, scullery', recorded by OED s.v. *back-* sense 5, from 1710.
OE *bæc-hūs* is attested only in a 13th-century copy of a pre-Conquest text (DOE).
(*a*) *Bachouscroft* 1375 Hrt:224, *le Bakehousecroft* (f.n.) 1514 Ch:2·300 (**croft**), *Bakehoushille* (f.n.) 13th YW:1·74 (**hyll**), *ye Backehouse land* (f.n.) 1612 Ru:192 (**land**), *Bachouse Lane* (st.n. Norfolk) 1330 Nf:1·147, Bakehouse Lane (st.n. Leicester; *de la Baghus* 1278) Lei:116, *Bakhouslane* (st.n. Beverley) 1439 YE (**lane**).
(*b*) Bacchus 1824 Gl, *atte bachus* (surn.) 1290 Nf [Carlsson:24], *Bakehous* (f.n.) 1429 YW:1·134, *le Bakehous(e)* (f.n.) 1487 Ch:2·171, *le Bakehouse* (bdg.n. Northwich) 1506 Ch:2·193, *le Bakhous* (f.n.) 1354 Ch:1·240, *Bakhouse* (surn.) 1309 Sx [MELS:5].
(*c*) *le Comyn Bakhous* (bdg.n. Kendal) 1474 We:1·119 (**commun**), *St Giles Bakehouse* (bdg.n. Chester) 1313 Ch:5·33 (hospital n.), *The King's Bake-house* (bdg.n. Macclesfield) 1819 had remained a bakehouse since the first reference to it as *furnus burgi* c.1260 (Ch:1·117).
~ OE *bacan* 'to bake', **hūs**; cf. **bæc-ærn**.
DOE *bæc-hūs*; MED *bāk(e-hŏus*; EDD *backhouse* sb.[2]; OED *bakehouse*; DOE *Backhouse*.

bæc-stān OE, *m.* 'baking-stone, flat stone for baking on' is first attested independently in a 12th-century gloss added to an OE manuscript (DOE, MED). It is much more common in the ME period in p.ns, which usually seem to denote places where such stones were obtained. The element has a markedly northern distribution, as also in modern dialect; ON **steinn** occasionally replaces *stān*.
(*a*) Backstone Beck 1314 YN, Backstone Gill (*Bacstenebec* 1198) YW:5·204 (**bekkr**), *Bakestainberghe* (f.n.) 1239 YW:6·127 (**berg**), *Bacstanberks* (f.n.) 1230–50 YN:325 (?**brēc**), Bakestone Cliffe 1379 YW (**clif**), *Bakstandaleflat* (f.n.) 1407 YN:325 (**dalr, flat**), Baxenden a.1194 La (**denu**), Baxton Gill 1292 Cu (**gil**), *bacestaingrave* (f.n.) c.1170 YN:325 (?***grafa**), *Blackstone Hall* (*Bakestanhou* 1227) Nt (**haugr**), Baxton Holme 1186–1200 We (**holmr**), *Backstonerigg* 1322 Nb [NbDu:9] (**hryggr**), *Bakestaneshull* (f.n.) c.1206 [17th] Ch:2·70 (**hyll**), *Bakestonwel*

(f.n.) 13th YW:1·153 (**welle**).

(*b*) *Bakestan* (f.n.) 13th YW:6·154, *Bakestanes* (f.n.) l.12th YW:2·52.

~ OE *bacan* 'to bake', **stān**.

<small>DOE *bæc-stān*; MED *bāk(e-stōn*; EDD *backstone* sb.[1]; OED *bakestone*.</small>

bær OE, *adj.* 'bare, without vegetation' appears in an OE charter as *æt ðere baran fyrhðe* S:820 Ha (**fyrhð**), but in ME spellings can hardly be distinguished on formal grounds from **bær, bār, bearu, bere**. It is revealed by context in the modern derogatory f.ns Bare Arse, Bare Bones, Bare Knuckles etc. (Field:13). Likely medieval examples include Barville (*de Berefeld* 1270, *Barefeld'* 1313) K:584 (**feld**), *Bareroyd* (f.n.) 1411 YW:7·153 (***rod**[1]), *the Baresteades* (f.n.) 1611 Ch:1·157 (**stede**).

<small>DOE *bær*; MED *bār*; EDD *bare* adj.; OED *bare* a., adv., sb.; DES *Bare*.</small>

bǣr OE *f.*, 'pasture', especially 'woodland-pasture for swine'. In OE charters the term—sometimes in compounds such as *den-bǣr, weald-bǣr, wudu-bǣr*—is used for the area of pasture that belongs to an estate: *pascua porcorum que nostra lingua Saxhonica denbera nominamus* S:332 K, *Ðis is seo bær ðer to hyrð* S:377 Ha, *þis sind þære wudu bære land gemæru* S:934 Brk:767. In ME spellings the element cannot be distinguished from **bearu** in southern England (and it does not seem to have been suggested in northern p.ns). Names like Beer D, Bere Do, could contain either. They are given under **bearu**, though since there was a royal forest at Bere Regis Do it perhaps belongs here (Do:1·273, PNLand:190). The context similarly suggests that *bǣr* is likely in Bere 1168 Ha, the name of two forests (Ha:32), unless they are forests which grew from the small beginnings presumably appropriate to *bearu* 'grove, small wood'. *Wodebere* (f.n.) 1275–6 Brk:36 is another likely case, equivalent to the OE compound noted above; Bear Wood (*Bissopesbir'* 1256) Brk:126 (**biscop**) may be a further instance. MELS:9 offers additional examples in surnames from Sx, Sr and So; formally any of these could belong to *bearu*, but since secure attestations of that element have not been found in south-eastern England, the Sx and Sr instances, especially, may well contain *bǣr*.

~ OHG *bara*.

<small>DOE *bǣr*[3]; MED –; EDD –; OED –; DOE *Bear*.</small>

bǣrlic OE, 'barley' is attested in OE only in *to bærlice crofte* S:737 Bk; it is presumably a late side-form of **bere**, perhaps in origin an adjective. Certainly it seems to appear in fewer early p.ns than **bere**.

(*a*) Barley Croft (f.n.) 1305 Ch:2·104 (**croft**), *Barliceflat* (f.n.) 1283 YW:7·154 (**flat**), *Barlichforlange* (f.n.) 13th Gl:2·170 (**furlang**), *le*

Barlehelme (f.n.) 1466 Ch:5·xviii (**helm**), Barley Hole 1515 YW (**hol**¹), Barley Hill 1391 Lei:277, *Barlichhul* (f.n.) 1200 Nth:265, *Barlychhulle* (f.n.) 1319 Gl:1·107 (**hyll**), *les Barlilandes* (f.n.) 12th YW:4·239 (**land**), *Barleymarket Yard* (st.n. Norwich) 1282 Nf:1·86 (**market**, **geard**), Barleythorpe 1286 Ru (**þorp**), Barlichway 1174 Wa (**weg**).

~ **bere**.

DOE *bærlic* noun; MED *barlī*; EDD *barley* sb.; OED *barley*; DES *Barley*.

bær-mann OE, *m*. 'porter' also has the sense 'waiter' in ME. It appears as a ME surname from 1279 (*Rad. Bareman*, Thuresson 1950:96). The Anglian equivalent of the headword may have been **bēr-mann*, but the initial vowel length is uncertain.

(*a*) *Baremanelane* (st.n. London) 1285 (**lane**), *Bermonnestrete* (st.n. London) c.1225 (**strēt**).

~ OE *bær* 'bier', *beran* 'to carry'.

DOE *bắr-mann*; MED *bēr(e)-man*; EDD –; OED *berman*¹; DES *Barman*.

bærnet OE, *n*. 'burning', in p.ns presumably 'piece of land cleared by burning'. It can be difficult to distinguish from past participle forms like *brant*, *barnt*; see **brend**. Löfvenberg (MELS:12) notes several instances in local surnames in Sx, Sr, as *de la Bernet* c.1200, *atte Bernette* 1296 etc.; following Bülbring he suggests an OE form *bǣrnet* with lengthening to account for the common ME *e*-spellings.

(*a*) *Barnetseyson* ?14th K:513 (**seisine**).

(*b*) Barnet 1064–77 [14th] Hrt, 1235 Mx:99 (note that the Mx and Hrt instances were originally a single place), Barnetts 1283 K, Burnett 1086 So.

~ OE *bærnan* 'to burn'; **brend**.

DOE *bærnet*; MED *bernet*; EDD –; OED *bernet*; DES *Barnet*.

bærning OE, *f*. 'burning', presumably 'land cleared by burning'.

(*a*) *Brenniningges* (f.n.) 13th YW:7·154 (?**eng**).

(*b*) *Brening* 1207 Ess.

~ **bærnet**, **brend**

DOE *bærning*; cf. MED *brenninge*; OED *burning* vbl.sb.

bæst OE, 'bast, the fibrous inner bark of the lime-tree used for rope-making'. One OE gloss suggests it may also have been used of the lime-tree itself; see DOE, and cf. ME *bast-tre*. Bassenhally 1246 C (**halh**) may contain the OE adjective *bæsten* 'made of bast' in the unrecorded sense 'growing with lime-trees'.

(*a*) Barston 1319 C (**tūn**), Bastwick 1086 Nf, Woodbastwick 1086 Nf

(**wīc**), *Bastewood* (f.n.) 1524 We:1·75 (**wudu**). Perhaps also in *Baststret* (st.n. Bristol) 1350 Gl:3·86 (**strēt**).
(*b*) *Bast* (f.n.) 1379 Db:178.
   DOE *bæst*; MED *bast* n.[1]; EDD *bast*; OED *bast* sb.[1]

bæð OE, *n.* 'bath'. The term is applied to the Roman constructions around the hot springs of Bath So—*æt þæm hatum baðum* 'at the hot baths' 864 [11th] S:210—and the reference is similarly to the Roman spa at Buxton in Bathamgate Db ('the road to *Bathum'). At Morebath D there are chalybeate springs. Elsewhere 'pool, pond' is meant, as in *Suthenedebath* (f.n.) c.1300 Nt:275 (**æned**), and at Balking Brk, where a series of triangular pools beside the R. Ock (earlier the *Lācing) were probably built for use in cleaning wool (Cole 1993–4). 'Bathing-place' may well be the meaning in other names, such as Bathley Nt, which is on the R. Trent. For the difficult recurrent minor name Digbeth see PNLand:13–14.
   For *Bathesteres Lane* (st.n. London) 1246–7, Ekwall suggests either a ME *bathestere 'bath-keeper' or a word *bath-stairs* meaning 'steps or landing-stage from which people could bathe' (Ldn:111–12).
(*a*) Bathamgate 1400 Db (**gata**), Bathampton 1086 W (**hām-tūn**), Bampton 1084 D (**-hǣma-tūn**), Bale (*Bathele* 1086) Nf, Bathley 1086 Nt (**lēah**), Bathpool 1474 Co [OP] (**pōl**), Balking c.870 [13th] S:539 Brk (r.n.).
(*b*) Bath 796 [11th] S:148 So, Bathe Barton 1281 D.
(*c*) Moorbath 1086 Do, Morebath 1086 D (**mōr**).
   DOE *bæþ*; MED *bath*; OED *bath* sb.[1]; DES *Bath*.

beak ModE, 'land cleared for ploughing'. *Beak* is used dialectally of the bladed agricultural tool, the mattock. From this derives a verb, 'to beak', with a specialised sense of 'to clear land for ploughing' by using such a tool (and then by burning the rubbish); from the verb, in turn, comes the noun 'beak' (also 'bake') applied to land cleared in this way. The EDD notes the simplex *beak* in this sense only in W, and the sole early-recorded example that has been noted comes from this county: *messuage called Beak* 1631 W:155. Field:15–16 gives later examples from a wider area of southern England (though a topographical 'pointed piece of land' would be a possible formal alternative in any individual case). See also W:450–1 and ***burn-bake**, which is closely related in origin and usage.
   ~ ModE *beak* is generally derived from OFr *bec*. Connections with Germanic words are not clear. It may be that ***bica** is related. And in the present case there is a strong temptation—despite the vowel-length—to see a link also with OE *becca* 'pick-axe, mattock' which survived as *beck* in Hrt and Sx. The apparent relationship with ***bete** is also

difficult to explain.
EDD *beak* sb.[1]; OED –.

bēam OE, *m*. 'tree; beam, piece of timber; post'. Sometimes the reference is clearly to a tree, as in the hollow trees of Holbeam D, K and in compounds such as **hnut-bēam**, but often it is hard to decide which meaning applies. Instances of Bampton could be farmsteads that are timber-built or that are distinguished by trees, just as the OE boundary clause *on beam weg* S:1556 Gl:1·189 might refer to a wooded lane or a wooden walkway. Likewise, Bamford and Banford (cf. also OE *beamford* S:345 So) could refer either to fords marked by trees or posts, or to river-crossings making use of tree-trunks. Here, however, there is reason to lean towards the latter interpretation. Dagenham Beam Bridge (*pontem voc. Dagenham Beem* 1299) Ess, Beam Bridge (*le Beem* 1272–1307, *le Bembrugg* 1302–6) Ch, and Beam Bridge (cf. *Stephen de la Beme* 1199–1216) Ess suggest that the element sometimes—perhaps rather often—had the specific sense of 'beam laid across a stream to form a footbridge'. This meaning may well also be relevant to Benfleet Ess and to the OE charter *on beam broc* Do S:534 (ASCh:5·16). See further MELS:7–8 (with instances of *ate Beme* etc. as a surname) and ERN:27.

OE *bēam*, ME *bēm* had other applications, including 'the Cross of crucifixion' and a variety of senses generally involving the concepts 'long' and 'straight', as 'shaft of light', 'gallows', 'vein of ore', 'balance for weighing'; some such specific senses could conceivably be relevant to p.ns. It might finally be observed that the meaning 'tree' is rare in ME and probably became archaic during the OE period; it would not therefore be expected in late-formed names. Note that Kitson 1995:78–9 suggests that simplex *bēam* 'tree' was in dialectal opposition to **trēow** in OE boundaries, with *bēam* already recessive, and limited to parts of the south and south-east.

(*a*) Benfleet 10th ASC A s.a.893 Ess (**flēot**), Bamford 1086 Db:39, 1282 La, Banford (f.n.) 1208–29 Ch:3·265 (**ford**), Bampton 1069 O, c.1160 We, 1227 Cu:143, Bempton 1086 YE (**tūn**).
(*b*) Beam Bridge (*le Beem* 1272–1307) Ch:3·153, (*la Beme* 1199–1216) Ess:92.
(*c*) Bladbean 1226 K (**blōd**), Holbeam 1086 D, 1240 K (**hol**[2]), *Snodbeam* 1240 K (**snād**), Dagenham Beam Bridge (*Dagenham Beem* 1299) Ess:92 (p.n.).

~ **cwic-bēam, hnut-bēam, *horn-bēme.**
DOE *bēam*; MED *bēm*; EDD *beam*; OED *beam* sb.[1]

bēan OE, *f.* 'bean', referring both to broad-beans and to the coarser horse-beans given to animals. The element is attested in OE charter bounds, as *on bean broc* S:413 Brk:697, *to bean stede* S:528 Sr, *on þæt bean furlang* S:713 Brk:691 etc., and is frequent in later names. Medial *-e-* in ME spellings may indicate length in the first vowel or represent the reflex of gen.pl. *bēana*; alternatively the adjective **bēanen** may sometimes be involved. Southern names (e.g. Binste(a)d Ha, Sx, Wt) seem sometimes to reflect a ME development of *ēa* > *īe* > *ī* (MELS:8). In *benaker / bouneaker* (f.n.) l.12th [14th] L:2·143 (**æcer**) *bēan* alternates with the ON cognate **baun**.

Note that in ME spellings the element could not be distinguished except by context from **bēn** 'request, favour', which developed the specific sense of feudal 'boon work'.

(*a*) Benacre 843 S:293 K [KPN:185], 1086 Sf, *Benacre* (f.n.) 1283–4 Brk:239 (**æcer**), *Bancroft* (f.n.) c.1261 Ch:2·54, *Bencroft* (f.n.) 13th Gl:2·50 (**croft**), Bincombe 987 [13th] S:1217 Do:1·197 (**cumb**), Bendish 1086 Hrt, Bendysh 1068 [14th] Ess (**edisc**), *Benithe* (surn.) 1358 Sx [MELS:9] (**ēgeð**), Beynhurst 1086 Brk (**ersc**), Bamfurlong 1327 La:102 [& METT:48], *Benefurlonge* (f.n.) 12th Gl:2·50 (**furlang**), Banham 1086 Nf, Beenham 1142–84 Brk:150 (**hām/hamm**), *Benhull* (f.n.) 1374 Gl:1·223 (**hyll**), *Attebenelandes* (f.n.) 1255 Gl:1·249 (**atte, land**), Beanleach 1364 Ch:1·256 (***læcc**), Beanley c.1150 Nb (**lēah**), Benroyd 13th YW (***rod**[1]), Banstead 1086 Sr, Binstead 1086 Ha, 1086 Wt, Binsted 1086 Sx (**stede**), Benwray 1292 Cu (**vrá**), *Benewell'* (f.n.) 13th Brk:187 (**welle**). For further f.n. examples, see Field:16.

(*d*) As an affix, sometimes rendered by Latin *faba*, in Barton in Fabis (*in le Benes* commonly from 1388) Nt, Barton in the Beans (from 1591) Lei:534, Thornton le Beans YN (from 1534).

~ **baun, bēanen.**

DOE *bēan*; MED *bēn(e* n.[1]; EDD *bean* sb.[1]; OED *bean*.

bēanen OE, *adj.* 'of beans, growing with beans'. This adjective could lie behind some of the names given under **bēan**, especially those with medial *-e-* in ME spellings. The full form seems to be preserved in Benhall (*Benenhala*, beside *Benehala* 1086) Sf (**halh**) and *Myddulbenyndone* (f.n.) 1388 Gl:1·50 (**middel, dūn**). A weak plural of **bēan**, marginally attested according to DOE, would be a formal alternative.

~ **bēan.**

DOE *bēanen*; MED *bēnen*; EDD –; OED –.

*bearde OE, *f.* 'battle-axe' is proposed on the basis of cognates by Arngart (1978:15–17; 1980), in order to explain a curious recurring compound with the second element **stapol** 'post': Barnstaple 979 D, Barstable Hundred 1089 Ess:140, *Berdestapel* 1260 Bd:298, *Berdestapelesholme* 13th Hrt:296, and probably Bastow Hill (*Berstalhell* 1362, *Berstapelfeld* 1479) Hrt:296. Arngart takes the compound as 'battle-axe post', parallel to 'spear tree, spear post' in the names Gartree and Garstang (see **geirr**), which are thought to have represented Viking meeting-places. He argues that since the Langobards had a *gairethinx* 'spear meeting', just as the Vikings had their *vápnatak* 'taking of weapons', so the early Saxons could have had assemblies characterised by the use or brandishing of weapons. Alternatively, to develop Arngart's suggestion along different lines, a *beardan-stapol 'axe post', might perhaps have been a chopping block or, if this is too commonplace an item to have given rise to a few distinct names, possibly an executioner's block.

There have been many previous explanations of the Barnstaple group. A pers.n. *Bearda is possible—and probably occurs in Bardney 731 L [Bede] (ēg)—but is hardly likely in the recurring compound. OE *beard* 'beard', in some extended sense, can probably be discounted since the OE forms of Barnstaple D indicate a weak noun. Zachrisson 1934:248 proposed a weak *bearde as a side-form of *beard*, with the sense 'edge' that is the usual meaning of ON *barð*. 'Post of the edge', or 'boundary post' is not an unreasonable suggestion for a recurring compound (though Zachrisson himself proposes 'post on a ridge'); it may be an unlikely feature to have given its name to a hundred, however.

~ OS *barda*, OHG *barta*, ON *barða* '(battle)-axe'.

DOE −; MED −; EDD −; OED −.

bearu OE, *m.* 'grove, small wood'. This element presents several problems of identification, especially in ME and later spellings—the various developments are detailed in the following paragraphs. Nonetheless, the probable instances, supported by the OE charter material, suggest that the term had a restricted distribution: it occurs most commonly in the south-west, is absent from a large area of central and southern England, but is found again in the east midlands and counties further north—it is fairly frequent, for instance, in Ch and YW (see PNLand:189–90, Hallqvist 1948:135–52, Kitson 1995:81,83). Gelling (PNLand:189–90) suggests that **bearu** may be used specifically of small and isolated woods, perhaps less extensively coppiced than a **grāf**.

The treatment of OE *ea* in ME varied according to dialect (Hallqvist 1948). Development from the OE nom.sg. *bearu* might be expected to give, in the north and midlands, ME **bare* (probably reflected in Bare La), and in the south, ME **be(a)re* (which possibly appears in instances of Beer D, though see further below). Often, however, development was from dat.sg. *bearwe*. In the north and midlands this gave *bar(e)we*, in parts of the south *ber(e)we*. Since **berg** 'hill' similarly developed *ber(e)we* from its oblique cases there are problems of identification: in the north and midlands *bar(e)we* and *ber(e)we* are distinct, but only until c.1300 (Jordan:§67); in parts of the south the words could never be formally distinguished in ME. In the south-west, however, it has been shown that OE *bearu* did not have *-w-* in oblique cases, but a dat.sg. *beara* (D:107–8, Hallqvist 1948:135–52). Either dat. or nom.sg. forms therefore give ME spellings in *bere*, which cannot be confused with **berg**; on the other hand, these spellings cannot be distinguished from **bǣr** '(woodland) pasture'.

Various additional factors complicate this picture. It is difficult to give precise chronological and geographical limits to some of the vague terminology that has been used. Moreover, there are clearly exceptions; notably that beside the many *e*-spellings, *a*-spellings are nonetheless fairly common in southern names—this may have to do with the local origins of ME scribes or with the advance of a standard derived principally from the midlands. Another significant point is that *bearu* is rarely attested outside p.ns after the OE period, and appears no longer to have been a living term for most ME speakers. We have therefore to reckon with the likelihood of contamination from similar-sounding common elements such as **berg** and **burh**.

One further ambiguity should be mentioned: where dat.sg. *bearwe* is proposed as a first element (a structure which implies an earlier simple p.n. 'at the wood', to which another element has later been added), it cannot be formally distinguished in ME from either OE *bearg* 'barrow-pig, castrated pig' or from OE *bearwe* 'barrow, cart'.

(*a*) Bar Bridge (*Berewebrugge* c.1220) Gl (**brycg**), *Barrowdish* 1265–91 Ch:2·307 (**edisc**), Barrasford 1242 Nb, Barrowford 1296 La (**ford**).

(*b*) Bare 1086 La, Barrow 731 L:2·15 [Bede], ?958 [14th] S:667 Ch:3·261, 1086 Db:429, 1086 Lei:275, c.1200 Sa:1·30, 1209 Gl:2·76, 1284 YW:1·120, Beer 1086 D:32, 1086 D:620, Bere 1086 Do:1·273.

(*c*) Ogbeare 1262 Co [Svensson:60] (**āc**), Ollerbarrow 1406 Ch:2·24 (**alor**), Catsbury 1266 Gl (**catt**), Crebor 1166 D, Pencrebar 1221 Co [Svensson:84] (**crǣwe**), Harebarrow c.1220 Ch:1·101, Harrowbarrow 1280 Co [Svensson:86] (**hār²** or **hara**), Rockbeare 1086 D (**hrōc**), Whitbarrow 1538 Ch:2·40 (**hwīt**), Haselbury 1086 So, 1201 Do:2·100, Hazlebarrow a.1290 Db (**hæsel**), Hollin Bar 1461 YW (**holegn**),

Larkbeare 1086 D:571 (**lāwerce**), Mooresbarrow c.1215 Ch:2·251 (**mōr**), Shebbear 1050–73 D (**sceaft**), *Sherbarrow* l.12th YW (**scīr**²), Timsbury 1086 So (**timber**), Sedgeberrow 778 [11th] S:113 Wo (?pers.n.).

DOE *bearu*; MED *bĕr(e* n.⁵, *berwe*; EDD *barrow* sb.⁴; OED *berwe*; DES *Barrow, Bear.*

bēatere OE, *m.* 'beater' was used in ME for members of several trades, e.g. 'boxer', 'spice grinder', 'fuller' and 'metal-worker' (MED; cf. Fransson:102). The sense 'street-walker, nightwatchman' is recorded from the 16th century (OED) and a ME homonym was also used of a 'mender' (MED *bēter* n.²; cf. OE *dǣd-bētere* 'penitent'). Any of the senses may be relevant to *Beater St.* (st.n. Winchcombe) e.13th Gl:2·30.

The parallel OFr *batour* 'fuller', 'metal-worker' (Fransson:102) may appear in *battersdall* (f.n.) L:3·154 (?**deill**).

~ OE *bēatan* 'to beat'.

DOE *bēatere*; MED *bēter* n.¹, *bĕter* n.²; EDD *beater*; OED *beater*; DES *Beater*.

bēaw OE, *m.* or *n.* 'gadfly' would be difficult to distinguish in p.ns from a (possibly derived) pers.n. *Bēaw*, especially allowing for the possibility that such an element may have been compounded in the gen.sg. (cf. Parsons & Styles 1995–6:19–20). There is a further uncertainty, because Kristensson (METT:20) adduces a local surname *atte Bewe* 1327 Gl, which suggests a word of similar form with generic sense. Following Wallenberg (KPN:52–3), Kristensson speculates that there may have been an OE noun **bēaw*, related to *bīwan* 'to polish', and meaning 'something bright'. Note that Beauxfield K lies in Bewsborough Hundred, so that a single instance of *bēaw* (or *Bēaw*) may account for these cases.

(*a*) Bewsborough 1086 K (**berg**), Bowcombe 1219–20 D [& C:liii] (**cumb**), Bawsey 1086 Nf (**ēg**), Beauxfield ?10th [13th] S:140 (cf. ASCh:4·14) K (**feld**), Beaford 1086 D, Beauford 13th C (**ford**), Beausale 1086 Wa (**halh**), Bewley 1257 W (**lēah**).

DOE *bēaw*; MED –; EDD –; OED –.

bēce OE, *f.* 'beech-tree'. The element can sometimes be hard to distinguish from forms of **bæc** and **bæce**.

Fransson:194 & 203 notes instances of ME topographical surnames *Bechere* 1359 Sx and *Becheman* 1332 Sr.

(*a*) Bitchfield 1242 Nb (**feld**), Beech Hill 1384 Brk:149 (**hyll**), Betton 1086 (×2) Sa:1·45–6 (**tūn**), Beckwith (*bec wudu* 972–92 [11th] S:1453) YW (**wudu**).

(*b*) Beech 1285 St, Beach 1327 Gl.

(*c*) Cowbeech (*Coppetebeche* 1261) Sx (**copped**), Longbeech 1226 K (**lang**[1]).

~ **bēcen**, ***bēcet**, **bōc**[1], ***bōcen**.

DOE *bēce*; MED *bẹ̄che*; EDD –; OED *beech*; DES *Beech*.

bēcen OE, *adj.* 'of beech', in p.ns presumably 'growing with beech-trees'; also apparently used as a substantive. Inflected forms of **bēce** might alternatively be involved.

(*a*) Beechen Hill 1282 Gl:3·220 (**hyll**).

(*b*) Beachin 1258 Ch:4·86.

~ **bēce**, **bōc**[1], ***bōcen**.

DOE *bēcen*; MED *bẹ̄chen*; EDD *beechen*; OED *beechen*.

*bēcet OE, 'beech copse'.

(*b*) Becchette 1332 Sx:239, Bechette 1350 Sr:359.

~ **bēce**, **bōc**[1], **-et**.

MED *bechet* s.v. *bẹ̄che* 2.

bēcun OE, *n.* 'sign, signal' occurs commonly in the p.n. Beacon Hill, referring to the place where a beacon-fire was made for signalling purposes. Beacon Hill L:4·114 records the interesting sequence *le Fyre bombe* 1416 (**fir-bombe**), *le firebeacon* 1556, *Firebeaconhill* 1595. This use of *bēcun* may date from the OE period (DOE *bēacen* sense 5, Forsberg 1970:65–9), though the element has not been securely identified in this sense in early-recorded p.ns (cf. **ād**). In Beckney 1086 Ess the recorded pers.n. *Becca* (Redin:85) is a likely alternative. In Beaconsfield Bk, where *bēcun* is more certainly involved, the reference is unknown, and it should be noted that the OE term had a range of meanings, including 'cross' and 'memorial stone'. In Beacon Field (f.n.) 1703 L:4·111 [see also L:4·47] it appears probable that the 'beacon' was a round barrow which marked the meeting—place of Haverstoe Wapentake.

The head-form used here is Anglian, with smoothing (OEG:§222); West Saxon preserves earlier *-ēa-*.

(*a*) Beaconsfield 1184 Bk:214 (**feld**), Beacon Hill 1450 Ess:59, 1633 Brk:447, 1707 Cu:136, 1713 D:651, 1771 (*le Bekyn super altitudine montis* 1553) YW:3·90, 1773 W:362, 1781 Wa:144, 1797 Ch:3·230.

(*b*) Beacon 1469 D:643, Beacon End (*le Bekyn* 1414) Ess:400, Beacon Hill (*la Bekne* 1374) Sx, *the Bekene* (f.n.) 1373 Nt:275.

(*c*) Beacon Hill (*le firebeacon* 1556) L:4·114, Firebeacon 1400 D:78, 1571 D:545 (**fȳr**).

DOE *bēacen*, *ge·bēacen*; MED *bẹ̄ken* n.; OED *beacon* sb.

bedd OE, *n*. 'bed, plot of land for growing plants'. The element is attested in this sense in OE charters, e.g. *of ðæm æscbedde* S:219 Wo (**æsc**), *of ðam riscbedde* S:618 O (**risc**), *on þe withibed* S:466 W (**wīðig**), *to þæm wiðin bedde* S:898 Wa:321 (***wīðign**). It has been suggested for early forms of Ribbesford Wo with **ribbe** 'ribwort' (*æt Ribbedforda* 1014–16 [18th] S:1459).

(*a*) *Bedsycke* (f.n.) 1566 Ru:86 (**sīc**).

(*c*) With the names of plants: Brackenbed 1462 YW (***brakni**), *le leuer bedde* (f.n.) 13th W:423 (**lēfer**), *Leekebeddes* (f.n.) 1611 Nt:275, *le lekbeddes* (f.n.) 1384 Ch:1·130, *Lekesbedde* (f.n.) 1349 (**lēac**) C:312, *Myntbedd* (f.n.) 1484 Ess:574 (**minte**), *Netelbedde* (f.n.) c.1220–30 Brk:381, *Nettelbedd* (f.n.) 1591 W:423, Nettlebed 1246–7 O, *Nettlebeds* (f.n.) 1400 Gl:1·137 (**netel**), *Netlebeddesmor* (f.n.) 13th Wa:321 (**netel, mōr**), *Russebed* (f.n.) 1226 Nth:260, *le Rysshebed* (f.n.) 1379 Wa:321 (**risc**).

With the names of trees and bushes, especially the willow: *Ahssebed* (f.n.) 1311 C:312 (**æsc**), Hollybed 1216–72 Wo:214, *Holyebedde* (f.n.) 1535 Gl:3·149 (**holegn**), *Slaghyornebed* [*sic*] (f.n.) 1415 Db:375 (**slāhþorn**), *Willobeddes* (f.n.) 1530 Db:716, *Willowbedd* (f.n.) 1681 We:2·232 (***wilig**), *Wethybedd* (f.n.) 1540 Gl:4·101, *Whetheybed* (f.n.) 1458 Mx:195, *Withiebed* (f.n.) 1326 Sr:356, *Wythebed* (f.n.) 1380 Mx:195, *Wythibed* (f.n.) 1150 Wa:321, *Wythibeddes* (f.n.) 1230 C:312 (**wīðig**), *Wythinbeddes* (f.n.) 1317 Db:716 (***wīðign**).

With elements that seem to refer to the nature or quality of the earth: Honeybed 1564 W (**hunig**), Sandbed 1622 We, *Sandbed* (f.n.) 1222 YW:2·125 (**sand**), *Sandbedwey* (f.n.) 1290 Wa:321 (**sand, weg**), Spoonbed 1327 Gl (**spōn**), *Tigelbeddburne* (f.n.) 13th Sr:356 (**tigel, burna**).

With other elements: *Trostelbedde* (f.n.) c.1250 Brk:442 (?**þrostle**), *Ernoldesbed* (f.n.) 1415 Nth:260 (pers.n.).

DOE *bedd*; MED *bed* n.¹; EDD –; OED *bed* sb.; DES *Bedd*.

bed-ern ME, 'prayer-house, chapel' is preserved in the Ripon st.n. Bedern Bank, where it refers to the common residence of six vicars, founded in 1304 (YW:5·165). A lane once called *The Bedern* in Beverley was named from the premises of the Provost and College of the Minster (YE:196), and a street of the same name housed York Minster's vicars choral (YE:282). Confusion with OE *bēod-ærn* 'refectory' would formally be possible.

(*a*) Bedern Bank (st.n. Ripon) 1369 YW (**banke**).

(*b*) The Bedern (st.n. York) 1275 YE, *The Bedern* (st.n. Beverley) 1280

YE, *Bedern Lane* (st.n. Lincoln; *De bederna canonicorum Linc'* c.1160) L:1·51.

~ OE *(ge)bed* 'prayer', **ærn**; cf. **bed-hūs**.

MED *bēd(e-ern* s.v. *bēd(e* 2b.; EDD –; OED –; DML *bederna*.

bed-hūs OE, *n.* 'prayer-house, chapel' occurs in several minor names. In ME this word was sometimes used of an almshouse, while ModE dialect *beadhouse* had the additional sense 'workhouse': these applications may be relevant to some p.ns.

(*a*) *Bedhusland* (f.n.) 1226 YW:4·221 (**land**), *Bedehouse Lane* (st.n. Lincoln) 1527 L:1·51 (**lane**), *Beadhouse peice* (f.n.) c.1700 Ru:263 (**pece**).

(*b*) *le Beadhouse* (bdg.n. Oakham) 1622 Ru:112 (the chapel of the Hospital of St John), *the Bedehouse* (f.n.) 1542 YW:4·66, *le Beydhous* (f.n.) 1454 YW:4·119.

~ OE *(ge)bed* 'prayer', **hūs**; cf. **bed-ern**, **bettws**.

DOE *bed-hūs, ge·bed-hūs*; MED *bēd(e-hous* s.v. *bēd(e* 2b.; EDD *bead-house* s.v. *bead* v.[1] 2(1); OED *bead-house* s.v. *bead* 3.

bedlem ME, 'mental hospital', generally derogatively as 'lunatic asylum, madhouse', is ultimately derived from ME *Bedlem* 'Bethlehem'. This word was used in the ME period as a proper name for the Hospital of St Mary of Bethlehem, London (MED), which became a mental institution some time before 1402 (OED sense 1); the wider application to any mental institution is evidenced from the 16th century (OED sense 2). The use can be seen in the *Bethel* or *Bedlam* Hospital in Norwich, which gave its name to Bethel Street (st.n. Norwich) 1745 Nf:1·89 (note that *Bethel* is a distinct biblical name 'house of God', but that the two interchange commonly in this name). *Bedlam* was subsequently used as a term for an inmate of an asylum or one fit for such a place; this sense may also be relevant to the derogatory use of the term for unproductive fields 'land which only a madman would cultivate'. Patients discharged from the London hospital were licensed to beg, hence the extended sense 'a beggar' (OED sense 5), and some p.ns may reflect this use of the word (cf. Field:17).

(*a*) Bedlam holme (f.n.; *Le Bedlum holme* 1605) Cu:251 (**holmr**).

(*b*) Bedlam 1714 C:236, Bedlam (*Bedlam pieces* 1717) Gl:2·112, Bedlam (f.n.) 1779 Gl:1·260, Bedlands (*Bedlem* 1631) We:2·147 (though later some spellings suggest an identification with a local family name *Beathome*), New Bedlam (f.n.; *Bedlome* 1539) YW:4·194.

MED *Bedlẹ̆m*; EDD *bedlam* sb.[1]; OED *bedlam*.

ge-bed-mann OE, *m.* 'one who prays, cleric' appears in p.ns with reference to lands owned by the church or a monastery. *Bedeman's Berg* 1177 Ess (**berg**) was the site of an early hermitage, and each of the examples listed below was owned by a monastic foundation.

(*a*) Bedmangore 1278 K (**gāra**; owned by Boxley Abbey, Kent), Bedmonton 1254 K (**tūn**; owned by St Augustine's Abbey, Canterbury).

~ OE *(ge)bed* 'prayer', **mann**.

DOE *ge·bed-mann*; MED *bēde-man*; EDD *bedman*; OED *beadsman*; DML *bedemannus*; DES *Beadman*.

bed-rīp OE, *n.* 'labour exacted at harvest time' was a service whereby tenants were obliged to reap their landlord's corn for a day at his request. Its use as a generic in f.ns suggests that the word was also applied to land upon which this service was performed, though this sense does not seem to be attested outside p.ns (cf. **averys*, as discussed in Styles & Parsons forthcoming).

(*a*) *Bedrepfelde* (f.n.) 1509–47 Ess:574 (**feld**).

(*b*) *Bederepe* (f.n.) 1297 Ess:574.

(*c*) *Gretebedryp* (f.n.) 1373 Sx:562 (**grēat**).

~ OE *(ge)bed* 'prayer, request', OE *rīp* 'harvest, reaping'.

DOE *bed-rīp*; MED *bed-rĭp(e*; EDD *bedrip*; OED *bedrip*; DML *bederipa*.

*beg OE, 'berry' is recorded outside p.ns only in OE compounds: cf. *beg-bēam* 'mulberry-tree, bramble-bush', *heorot-beg* 'a berry (of some kind)'. Though the origin of the OE word is obscure, its ME reflex would be *bey*, *bay*, indistinguishable from OFr *baie* 'berry' (from Lat *baca*), and the two words may have fallen together in ME *bai*. The element is difficult to distinguish from **bēg** and the OE pers.n. *Bēage* (Redin:113). It is possible in:

(*a*) Baydon 1146 W (**dūn**), Bayfield 1247 K (**feld**), Bailey 1204 La (**lēah**).

~ ***begen, beger**.

DOE –; MED *bai(e*; EDD –; OED *bay* sb.[1].

bēg OE, *m.* 'ring' perhaps occurs in an OE boundary, *on þat withi begh* S:573 Do:1·33, where the combination with **wīðig** 'willow' attracts attention. It fuels the suspicion that some of the instances of Willoughby and Wilby, common in the east midlands and East Anglia, may refer to circles of willow-trees, originally combining **wilig* with *bēg* and only later confused with **bȳ** (cf. SSNEM:78, PNLand:221). The spellings of some instances tend to give support to this possibility: Wilby Sf is *Wilebey*, *Wilebi* 1086, Willoughby Wa is *on wiliabys* [?for *wiliabyg*] 956 [11th] S:623 (see ASCh:2·14) but *Wilebei* (beside *Wilebere*, *-bene*, *-bec*) 1086. On the other hand, note that *on þat withi begh* comes in a spurious charter, and may well be an error: it is recapitulated *of þanne wiþi bedde* (**bedd**; see ASCh:5·20).

Elsewhere the element would be readily confused as a first element with ***beg** and the OE pers.n. *Bēage*. Nonetheless it is probable in Beal 1086 YW (**halh**), which seems to refer to land in a bend of the R. Aire. Bewholme 1086 YE is a dative plural name (*Begun* 1086, *Begum* 12th) perhaps also denoting bends in streams.

The headform used here is the Anglian equivalent of WS *bēag*. Note that in ME spellings *bē(a)g* could not be distinguished from a related ON noun **bjúgr* (beside the attested ON adjective *bjúgr* 'bent, crooked'), which seems to refer to river-bends in several Scandinavian p.ns (YE:78).

~ ***bēgel, boga.**

DOE *bēag*; MED *bei*; EDD *bee* sb.[2]; OED *bee*[2]; DES *Bay*.

*bēgel OE, 'bend, loop', cognate with MLG *bögel*, Norw *bøygel*, is likely to be the etymon of ME *beil* 'ring, arch, handle' (cf. Björkman:66). It may be found in Baylham 1086 Sf (**hām/hamm**), where it probably refers to a bend in the R. Gipping, and Baildon c.1030 YW (**dūn**), where any of several referents would be possible (cf. YW:4·158–9). The headword used here represents an Anglian form, the West Saxon equivalent would be **bīegel*. If the 11th-century forms of Baildon—*on Bægeltune, on Bældune*—can be trusted, this name might rather preserve a variant **bǣgel*, without *i*-mutation and with Anglian smoothing.

~ **bēg.**

DOE –; MED *beil(e*; EDD *bail* sb.[1]; OED *bail* sb.[2]

*begen OE, *adj.* 'growing with berries' would be difficult to distinguish from **bēan** and the genitive singular of the OE pers.n. *Bēage*. It is possible in:

(*a*) Bengrove (*Bayngrove* 1287) Gl:2·46 (**grāf**), Baynham 1405 Gl:2·207, 1635 Gl:3·220 (**hamm**), Binegar 1176 So (**hangra**).

~ ***beg.**

DOE –; MED –; EDD –; OED –.

begeondan OE, *prep.* 'beyond' appears to alternate with **behindan** in Indicombe D (*Byendecoumbe* 1314, *Hyndecomb* 1330, *Yundecomb* 1333), and like this latter element, often displays loss of the unstressed syllable *be-* in compound p.ns. The element is probable, for example, in Indio (*Yondeyoe* 1544) D, a farm directly across the river from Bovey Tracey and from that standpoint 'beyond the water' (**ēa**). It is attested in ME local surnames (cf. Walterus *Biyendebrok* 1327 St, cited in MED) and is particularly common in Devon p.ns (see D:1·xxxvii): Henwood (*Indewood* 1650) D:260 was associated with Thomas *Byundewode* in 1333 (**wudu**), Yendamore D:100 with William *Beyundemyre* in 1333 (**mýrr**) and Yonderlake D:383 with William *Byundelake* (**lacu**).

(*a*) Yarnbrook (*Yondebrok* 1367) W (**brōc**), Hendicott (*Ʒondecote* c.1262) D, Yendacott (*Yendecoth'* 1242, *Jondecot* 1254) D, Yondercott (*Yundecote* 1289) D (**cot**), Indicombe 1314 D (**cumb**).

~ **bī.**

DOE *be-geondan, geondan*; MED *biyŏnd(e*; EDD *beyond*; OED *beyond*.

beger OE, ?*n*. 'berry' is recorded in OE glossaries and in the compound *wınbeger* 'grape'. It is probable in the following cases; for a further instance in a similar name see **berige**.

(*a*) Bairstow 1284 YW:3·141, *Bairstow* 1408 YW:3·90 (**stōw**).

~ ***beg, berige, blá-ber.**

DOE *beger*; MED –; EDD –; OED –.

begger ME, 'beggar' appears in Beggar's Wife Bridge YW in combination with **vað** 'ford, river-crossing', a site which beggars may have used to take advantage of passing travellers. Other names may also denote beggars or mendicants: OED (*beggar* sb. sense 8) includes *Beggar's Bush*, a recurring f.n., as a literal 'bush under which a beggar finds shelter'. In other cases, however, the term may denote poor or unproductive land (cf. EDD *beggar* v. 'to impoverish land, exhaust soil of nutrients'). In the Cheshire name *Beggersburghe* 'beggar's manor', a farm belonging to one Thomas Wright of Eccleston (Ch:4·152), its use is clearly ironic, as probably elsewhere. For further examples see Field:17–18.

(*a*) *Beggersburghe* (f.n.) 17th Ch:4·152 (**burh**), Beggar Croft (f.n.) 1615 Hrt:275 (**croft**), Beggars Dean (f.n.) 1597 Hrt:265 (**denu**), *le Beggersgreve* (f.n.) 1466 Ch:5·xxviii (**grǣfe**), *Beggargrene* (f.n.) 1260 YW:7·156 (**grēne**²), *Beggarestey* (f.n.) c.1363 Gl:2·38 (**stīg**), *Beggaston* (f.n.) 1539 [17th] Ch:4·123 (**tūn**), *Beggarthorn* 1629 L:2·77 (**þorn**), Beggar's Wife Bridge (*Beggerwathe* 1580) YW (**vað**), *Beggereswelle* (f.n.) c.1248 Gl:3·96 (**welle**).

(*d*) Beggearn Huish (*Beggerhywys* 1276) So.

~ of uncertain origin. Perhaps OFr *begart, begard* 'beghard, member of a medieval lay brotherhood of mendicants' (OED *beg* v.). Cf. **baggard.**

DOE –; MED *begger(e*; EDD *beggar* sb.; OED *beggar* sb.; DES *Beggar*.

beggerie ME, 'the practice of begging, poverty' seems to be applied to land that reduces its tenants to poverty rather than to a place where beggars live. Dialect *beggary* (EDD sb.[1]) is used specifically of poor or neglected land. The element occurs in later f.ns from Db, D and Lei (cf. Field:17–18), though as a first element it would be difficult to separate from the dialect plant-name *beggary* (EDD sb.[2]).

(*b*) Beggary 1227 Bd.

~ **begger**.
MED *beggerīe*; EDD *beggary* sb.[1]; OED *beggary*.

behindan OE, *prep.* 'behind, at the back of' is found in *Behindeby* (*vico que vocatur Behindeby* 13th) L (**bȳ**), where it appears to have the sense '(the place) behind, at the back of the town' (Great Grimsby). Note also *Bihindeburc* c.1216–44 L:3·28 (**burh**), apparently identical with the Latinised *Retro Borg* 1231–40 (which shows the influence of ON **borg**[1]). In the name Hindharton 1299 D a reduced form *hind* (cf. OE *hindan*) is compounded with *Herton*, an alternative name for the nearby village of Hartland.

~ **bī**.
DOE *be-hindan*; MED *bihĭnde(n*; EDD *behint, behintan*; OED *behind*.

beinn ON, *adj.* 'straight, direct'. The adjective had an extended sense 'helpful, hospitable', and ME *bain* has senses such as 'willing, accommodating' derived from this. Northern dialect has further related meanings, such as 'convenient, near'. Various shades of meaning are therefore possible in p.ns, but it may be relevant to note that it is commonly applied to roads, indicating 'the best way' (EDD). Used with topographical features it perhaps implies a convenient path or short-cut; in r.ns it probably denotes 'the straight (or most convenient) one'. For other suggestions see We:1·209, ERN:24.

Bainbridge 1219 YN is named from the R. Bain.

(*a*) Baneriggs 1374 We (**hryggr**), ?Bannest 1560 Cu (**hyrst**).

(*b*) R. Bain 1140–50 L, 1153 YN.

OGNS *beinn* adj.; MED *bain* adj.; EDD *bain*; OED *bain* a. & adv.

bein-viðr ON, *m.* a kind of tree, probably holly. This form, construed as 'bone-tree', is the most likely, though other forms and etymologies, involving **beinn** 'straight' and **víðir** 'willow', have been suggested. Apparent cognates in the Scandinavian languages are used of more than one species; for 'holly' see Lindkvist 1912:24 & n.1, who gives local information on Bainley YN. In English and Scots usage it becomes practically impossible to separate such terms as *bindweed, bendwith, bindwith, bindwood, bennie-weed, benweed, binweed*, which are used of a wide variety of species (OED, EDD, SND). Outside p.ns, where all the cited examples have early forms similar to *bainwith*, the only likely instance of the 'pure' ON word is *benewyth tre*/*benwyttre* in the 15th-century *Promptorium Parvulorum*: unfortunately no Latin equivalent is there offered (Mayhew 1908:30, Way 1843–65:1·31).

(*a*) Bannerdale (*Baynwytdale* 1256) We (**dalr**), Bennethead (*Baynwytheued* 1285) Cu (**hēafod**), Bainley (*Bainwithlith* c.1200) YN (**hlið**[1]), *Baynwythrig* (f.n.) 1220–46 We:1·107 (**hryggr**).

~ **viðr.**

OGNS *beinviðr*; MED *benewith-trẹ̄*; cf. OED *bendwith*.

beit ON, *f*. 'pasture' is probable in the following names, though difficult formally to separate from *bate* 'dispute' (see **batable**).

(*a*) the *Baytefield* 1559 Ch:2·103 (**feld**), Bate End (*Batehayne* 1426) YW:3·97 (***hegn**).

~ **beiting, bite.**

OGNS *beit*; EDD *bait* sb.[1]; OED *bait* sb.[1]; cf. MED *bait* n.

beiting ON, *f*. 'pasture' appears in Baitings 1309 YW, which is known to have provided summer pasture for cattle (YW:3·63), and *Baitingstid* (f.n.) 1154–89 We:1·130 (**stede**). The forms are distinguished from *bating* 'debating' (see **batable**) by their early *-ai-*, *-ay-* spellings.

~ **beit.**

OGNS *beiting*; cf. MED *baiting* sense 2; EDD *bait* vb.[1]; OED *baiting* vbl.sb. sense 2.

bekkr ON, *m*. 'stream' is widely used in northern and eastern England. Fellows-Jensen (1986:66–9) argues that when combined with other ON elements it may often be indicative of specifically Danish influence (though note *Boutherbeck* (f.n.) 1663 Cu:355, apparently with OWN *búð*; see **bōð**). Clearly the word later came to be adopted into ME dialect, and it is also often compounded with OE elements. Once in English, *beck* remained regional but spread beyond areas of direct Scandinavian influence: in Durham, for instance, there are no purely Scandinavian *beck* names (Watts 1988–9:27), whereas in Cheshire, surprisingly, there are no certain instances at all.

The frequency of *bekkr* names suggests that they must have replaced many earlier English names in **burna, brōc, bǣce** etc. The process is evidenced in Holbeck Nt:176, which was *on holan broc* 956 [14th] S:659 (**hol**[2], **brōc**) but *Holebek* from c.1180, while in Skirbeck 1086 L, it is suspected that ON **skírr** and *bekkr* replace OE **scīr**[2] and *bǣce* (DEPN, SSNEM:160). This replacement of, or influence on, the related OE *bǣce* may be particularly common (cf. Fellows-Jensen 1986:60).

The problems of assigning priority to the forms of one language or another are well demonstrated in the records of Henmore Brook Db:8–9. This was *Askebek'* c.1200, apparently involving ON **askr** and **bekkr**; in 1276 it was *acque de Esseb'ne vocatus Scalebrok*, with OE **æsc** and **burna**, and an alternative name combining ON **skáli** with OE **brōc**; in 1306, however, *Assebecke* appears to contain OE **æsc** and ON **bekkr**.

(*a*) Becca 1189 YW (**haga**[1]), Beckermonds 1241 YW, *Beckermote* (f.n.) 1175 YW:5·206 (**mōt**; with gen.sg. *bekkjar*—see SSNNW:103), Becksitch 1389 Db (**sīc**).

(*b*) The Beck c.1230 Nt:1, *la Bek* (f.n.) 1342 C:312; cf. Beverley Beck, below.

(*c*) Combined with adjectives: Blea Beck 12th, 1280, 1325 We (**blár**), Black Beck 13th YW (**blæc**), *Blind Beck* 1190–1210 We (**blind**), Bloody Beck 1268 YN (**blōdig/blōd**), Caldbeck 11th [13th] Cu:275 (**cald**), Drybeck 1230–40 We:1·40 (**drȳge**), *Fulbek* (f.n.) 1400 Nth:260 (**fūl**), Whitbeck c.1160 Cu:447 (**hwīt**), *Mickelbek* (f.n.) c.1200 We:2·124 (**mikill**), Skirpenbeck 1086 YE (?**skarpr**), Skyer Beck (*Skyrbeck* 1154–89) YN (**skírr**), Swarthbeck 1278 We:2·217 (**sweart**), Firbeck (*Thirbeck* 1325) Db (**þyrre**).

Combined with topographical nouns: *Fall Beck* 1154–89 We (**ge*-**fall**), Gill Beck 1209 YW:4·178 (**gil**), Hell Gill Beck (*Helebec* 1201) YN, Hillbeck c.1170 We (**hella**), Lythe Beck 1109–14 YN (**hlíð**), Holbeck 1109–40 YW:3·216, 1181–90 YW:7·129, 1154–63 YN, 1630 Ru, Howebeck 1201 We (**hol**[2]), Keld Beck 13th YN (**kelda**), Kex Beck 12th YW:7·130 (**kjóss**), Mud Beck c.1240 YW (**mudde**), Sandbeck 1148 YW:1·137 (**sand**), Tarn Beck 1256 Cu (**tjǫrn**).

Combined with tree-names: Birk Beck 1279 We (**birki**), Ellerbeck 1086 YN:212, Eller Beck 1154–89 YN:233, 1227 Cu, c.1233 Cu, 1246 La, 1257 YW:7·127 (**elri**), *Heselbec* (f.n.) 1231 Nt:275 (**hesli**), Linbeck c.1280 Cu:424, Line Beck 1315 Cu:20 (**lind**), Maplebeck 1086 Nt (**mapul*), *Thornbek* (f.n.) 1341 Nt:275 (**þorn**).

Combined with other nouns: Bustabeck (*Biscopbek'* 1285) Cu (**biscop**), Bow Beck (*Bollebec* c.1125) YW (**bol**), Brocka Beck (*Brocholebec* 1109–14) YN (**brocc-hol**), Bier Beck 1154–89 YW (**bȳre**), Eel Beck 1189–99 YW (**ēl**[1]), Grise Beck 1331 Cu, Grizebeck 13th La (**gríss**), Rais Beck c.1270 We:1·12 (**hreysi**), Capplebeck c.1300 Cu (**kapall**), Kirk Beck c.1200 YW:6·189 (**kirkja**), Mill Beck 1220–46 We:1·11, 1371 YE:9 (**myln**), Scale Beck 1292 We:1·13 (**skáli**), Trout Beck 1179 We:1·14 (**truht**).

Combined with pers.ns (examples are fairly rare): *Anlavbek* 1327 Nf [ERN:30], Artlebeck c.1200 La, *Mildred becke* (f.n.) 1586 C:312, Snary Beck (*Becsnari* c.1203) Cu.

Combined with p.ns (examples are frequent): Bannisdale Beck 1195 We:1·138, *Beckfarlam* 1387 Cu:14, Beverley Beck (*le Bek* 1345, *Beverley Beck* from 1536) YE, Blencarn Beck (cf. *Becblenekar* 1201) Cu:5, Boredale Beck 1337 We:2·218, Cave Beck 1370 YE, Crossdale Beck 1230 Cu, Crambeck 13th YN, Scampston Beck (*la Bec de Scameston'* 13th) YE, Sutherland Beck 1335 YN:79.

Occasionally *bekkr* has been added to an early name of the river: Alwent Beck (*Alewent* 1235–6) Du [ERN:10], Dover Beck (*Douerbec* 1154–89) Nt:3, Tyne Beck 1199–1216 YW:7·140.

(*d*) As an affix in Barnoldby le Beck 1662 L:4·54.

~ **bæce.**

OGNS *bekkr*; MED *bek* n.¹; EDD *beck* sb.¹; OED *beck* sb.¹; DES *Beck.*

*bel¹ OE, of uncertain meaning, is suggested by Ekwall 1936:159–63 as a cognate for ON *bil*, 'interval, space'. He tentatively suggests that it may have been used in English p.ns to refer to a clearing in a forest or a piece of dry land in a fen. The latter sense would suit *Bele*, a feature in L fenland noted from 1327 as a local surname by Kristensson (METT: 18–19); there are now further examples from fenland parishes, as *Attebele* (f.n.) 1287 L:4·40, *attebel* (f.n.) 1304 L:4·20, *atte Bele* (f.n.) 1332 L:4·175 (all with **atte**). The sense 'glade' could fit the topography of Belton 1222 Lei (**tūn**), which lies on raised ground between brooks in a formerly wooded area (Lei:344), and nearby Beltoft 1086 L (**toft**); it may also be suitable for that of Belton 1066–87 Ru (**tūn**), once within the bounds of Leighfield Forest. However, the element would generally be indistinguishable from **bēl** 'fire'.

bel² OFr, *adj.* 'beautiful' is common in p.ns with other French elements; the number of recurring compounds suggests that such names were generally modelled on existing ones, either in England or France. Sometimes the names are given to replace English ones: *æt Fulanpettæ* 1000–2 S:1486 'foul pit' was not a good advertisement for the place, and it became Beaumont (*Bealmont* 1180) Ess:327; while Belgrave Lei, began as *Merdegrave* 1086 'marten grove' (**mearð**), but was altered by c.1131, presumably because it offended the sensibilities of French speakers.

Both *bel* and the later form *beau* occur in early forms of many names. Spelling and/or pronunciation is sometimes anglicised to *biu, bew.*

(*a*) *Belasize* 1189 YW, Bellasize 1212 YE, Belsars 1221 C (**assise**),

Beachy Head 1274 Sx:427, Beauchief c.1175 Db (**chef**), Beaudesert 1293 St, 1175 Wa (**desert**), Beaufront 1356 Nb (**front**), *þe Beaue Laughen* (f.n.) 1611 Ch:1·192 (**launde**), Beaulieu (*de Bello Loco* 1205, *Beulu* c.1300) Ha (**lieu**), Beaumanor 1265 Lei (**manoir**), Beamy's Castle (*Beaumys* 1265) Brk, Beamish 1288 Du (**mes**), Beaumont 1203 Ru, 1276 Le, 1450 YW:3·172, Belmont 1194 YN, 1257 [13th] YW:5·113 (**mont**), Bear Park (*Beaurepayre* 1267) Du, *Beaurepair* c.1215 Gl, Beaurepaire 1272 Ha, *Beaurepaire* 1301 YW, Belper 1231 Db (**repaire**).

AFW *bel* adj.; AND *bel*; MED *bĕl, beau*; OED *bel* a., *beau* a. & sb.; DES *Beal, Bell*.

bēl OE, *m.* 'fire' is independently recorded in the sense 'funeral pyre', and several names may reflect this use: Beald 1109–31 C is *Bele super Dedhil* c.1195 (**dēad, hyll**), while Belstead 1086 Ess, which may preserve the compound *bæl-stede* 'cremation site' attested at *Beowulf* 3097, is close to the site of a cremation burial at Broomfield (JEPNS:2·44). The derivation of Belstead has been contested, however, on the grounds that OE *ǣ²* (represented by southern *ǣ*, Anglian *ē*) became ME *ā* in Essex (Ekwall 1957:139); in turn this throws some doubt on the same interpretation given to the apparently identical Belstead 1086 Sf. Moreover, Beald C has been considered topographically appropriate to **bel¹* (L:4·41).

The meaning 'signal fire, beacon' is possible—cf. the ON cognate **bál**—in places with suitable topography, such as Baycliff 1212 La (**clif**, 100ft above sea-level on the coast), Belas Knap (*Belknap* 1361) Gl (**cnæpp** 'hill-top') and Bell Hagg (*Belhaye* 1567) YW (**haga¹**, in a prominent place on a hillside).

Belwood c.1184 L (**wudu**) might be related to the *bæl-wudu* 'wood for a funeral pyre' of *Beowulf* 3110; both this name and Belgrave c.1290 Ch:4·149 (**græfe**) could be interpeted as 'wood serving a fire', i.e. from which firewood was obtained.

Clearly most of these suggestions are uncertain: **bel¹* '(?) clearing', **belle** 'bell' or pers.ns ON *Beli*, OE **Bella*, could provide alternative derivations for many of the names.

Other instances of an element *Bĕl-* include:
(*a*) Belahaye (f.n.) 1161 Gl:2·173, Belaugh (*Belaga* 1086) Nf, *the Beleawe* (f.n.) 1475 Ch:3·176, Belhagh (f.n.) 13th YW:4·244, Bylaugh (*Belega* 1086) Nf (all with **haga¹**), Belriding syche (f.n.) 1348 Ch:3·234 (***ryding, sīc**), Belton 1086 Sf (**tūn**).

~ **bál**.

DOE *bǣl*; MED –; EDD –; OED –.

belg OE, *m.* 'bag' developed the sense 'belly' in ME. It seems to appear with **denu** in Ballidon (*Belidene* 1086) Db, where the description ' valley with a bag-shaped embrasure' fits well with the topography (PNLand:98). The same word also became ModE *bellows*, which seems to appear in *bellows fyld* (f.n.) 1557 Ch:3·307.

~ **balg.*

DOE *belg*; MED *belī*; EDD –; OED *belly* sb.; DES *Bellow*.

belle OE, *f.* 'bell' probably has the sense 'bell-shaped' in Belstone D and Bell Busk YW. In f.ns it often denotes land endowed for the maintenance of church bells, and the proceeds of the fields called *The Bellstring land* 1608 YW.1·172, *Belstringelunde* 1559 YW.1·134, Belstring Flatt 1633 YW:7·156 and Bellropes c.1320 Nth:281 would have paid specifically for bell-ropes (see further Field:18). Fields adjoining churchyards may be the sites where the bells were cast (Fellows-Jensen forthcoming).

As a generic it appears to have the transferred sense of 'bell-shaped hill, knoll' preserved in Scots dialect *bell* (SND *bell* n.[3], EDD), which is likely in Yeavering Bell Nb, a hill of almost 1200 ft. There are hills at both Kimble Bk and Belchalwell Do. Cf. also the form **belling(e)*, discussed under **billing*. The element can be difficult to distinguish in p.ns from **bel*[1], *bel*[2] and *bēl*.

(*a*) *Belacre* (f.n.) 1229 Sr:397 (**æcer**), Bell Busk 1585 YW (**buskr*), *Bellcrofte* (f.n.) 1494 Hrt:269 (**croft**), Bell Cross 1663 YW:1·66 (**cros**), *Belflats close* 1693 YW:6·40 (**flat, clos**), *Bellands* (f.n.) 1410 YW:7·156 (**land**), Belstone 1086 D (**stān**).

(*b*) Belchalwell (*Bell'* 1207) Do:3·180, Bell Hill (*Belle* 1220–46) We.

(*c*) Barebell 1612 YW (**bær**), Kimble 903 [10th] S:367 Bk (**cyne-**).

~ **bell-hūs, bell-yetere.**

DOE *belle*; MED *belle* n.[1]; EDD *bell* sb.[1]; OED *bell* sb.[1]; DES *Bell*.

*bellerica MLat, 'dyehouse, tanhouse' is discussed in detail by Coates 1982–3. *Bellericus* is attested from the 13th century in English Latin sources, and survives in early ModE *belleric*; in both cases it appears to denote the fruit of the Indian tree Terminalia bellerica. This fruit was a source of tannin, which could be used in the tanning process and in producing permanent black dye. **Bellerica* was presumably, therefore, applied to sites where dyeing or tanning took place. This solution was earlier suggested by J. Harvey in McGarvie 1974–9.

(*b*) Bellerica 1535 So, *Billerica* 1278 K, (f.n.) 1549 W:482 [& McGarvie 1974–9:354], Billericay 1274 Ess [& W:xxxvii].

MED –; EDD –; cf. OED *belleric*, DML *belliricus*.

bell-hūs OE, *n.* 'bell-house, belfry' could not always be distinguished from an *ad hoc* combination of **hūs** with **belle** in the sense 'hill, knoll' or ***bel**[1], **bel**[2], **bēl**. Several Ess examples are known to derive from the transfer of a single family-name from Cambridgeshire: Ramsden Bellhouse 1261 Ess:168, Bellhouse 1393 Ess:399 and Belhus (*Belhousplace* 1389) Ess:122. Other instances include:
(*b*) Bell House 1307 YW:3·159, Bellhouses 1589 YW.

~ **belle, hūs.**
DOE *bell-hūs*; MED *bel(le-hŏus*; EDD —; OED *bellhouse*; DES *Bellhouse*.

bell-yetere ME 'bell-founder' is attested as a surname from the mid-13th century (MED, Fransson:138), and appears in Billiter Street (st.n. London; *Belȝeterslane* 1298).

~ **belle,** OE *gēotan* 'to pour, cast'.
MED *bel(le-yẹtere*; EDD —; OED —.

bēmere OE, *m.* 'trumpeter' could perhaps also refer to a bird (see Hough forthcoming). It appears in an OE charter boundary (in West Saxon form) in the phrase *to bymera cumbe* S:540 W.
(*a*) *Bemare(s)forlong* (f.n.) 1263–84 Gl:2·146 (**furlang**), *Bemerehill* 1574 W:225, *Bemerhills* 1570 W (**hyll**), *Bemersley* 1252 St (**lēah**), *Bemerton* 1086 W (**tūn**).

~ OE (Anglian) *bēme*, (West Saxon) *bīeme/bȳme* 'trumpet', from **bēam**.
DOE *bȳmere*; MED *bẹmere*; EDD —; OED *bemer*; DES *Beemer*.

bēn OE, *f.* 'prayer, request, favour' was applied in ME to gratuitous services, in kind or in labour, paid to landlord by his tenant or to a farmer by his neighbours (MED *bēne, bēne-rip, bēne-erthe*; EDD *boon*). Its use in this sense has been suggested for several Berkshire f.ns. The element could not be distinguished from **bēan** in ME spellings, but is more likely than that as a simplex. The term was also used for 'gift' in the ME period, a sense which could be relevant to p.ns. \
(*b*) The Bins (f.n.; *Great Been* 1698) Brk:67, The Been (f.n.) 1399 Brk:419.

~ **bón.**
DOE *bēn*; MED *bēne*. Cf. EDD *boon*; OED *boon*.

benc OE, *f.* 'bench' seems to have a topographical sense in many p.ns, where it refers to a ledge, terrace or bank (MELS:8–9). This use of the OE word may be due to the influence of ODan **banke**. (See **banke** also for a possible ON **benkr*: either this or Scandinavianised pronunciation of *benc* lies behind the variant *benk, bink*.)

The element clearly has the sense 'river-bank' in *Colnebenche* (f.n.)
1385 Ess:5 (r.n.), while in the Gloucestershire f.n. *le Lodebench'* 1497,
the site of a medieval fishery, it refers to a shelf of rock in the channel
(**ge-lād**) of the Severn (Gl:3·11).

(*a*) *Benchacre* (f.n.) 1235 W:423 (**æcer**), *Benchefurlong* (f.n.) 1570
W:423 (**furlang**), Bensham 1241–9 Du [NbDu:17] (**helm**), *Benechehurst*
(f.n.) 1509 W:423 (**hyrst**), *Benche lane* 1592 W:423 (**lane**), Bench Moors
(f.n.) 1573 Ch:2·149 (**mōr**).
(*b*) *le Bench* (f.n.) 13th Db:91, *the Bench* (f.n.) 1681 Gl:2·38.
(*c*) *Hokebench* (surn.) 1333 So [MELS:141], *Hokebenche* (f.n.) 1439
W:423 (**?āc**), Kate's Bench (*Cattenbenche* 1385) W (**catt**), Coxbench 1395
Db (**cocc²**), *Gretebenche* (f.n.) 1232 W:423 (**grēat**), *Myddle benche* (f.n.)
1592 W:423 (**middel**), Ninebanks 1228 Nb (**nigon**), *la Stanbench* (f.n.)
1255–90 Gl:1·126, *le Stanbench* (f.n.) 13th Db:716, Stone Bench 1654 Gl
(**stān**).

~ **banke**.

DOE *benc*; MED *bench(e*; EDD *bench*; OED *bench* sb.; DES *Bench*.

bend OE, *m*. 'band, fetter' may have an extended sense of 'something that
bends or twists' (cf. OE *wudu-bend* 'woodbine' and **binde**) in Bengrove
(*Bendegrave* 1271) Gl:2·152 (**grāf**), and—more dubiously—in the R.
Bowmont (*Bolbenda* c.1050 [12th]) Nb [ERN:45–6] (?OE *bōl* 'eel'). Bend
Gate 1571 YW, *bend gate* (f.n.) c.1650 L:4·180 and Bent Gates 1625 YW
probably contain ME *bende* (which is influenced by both the OE term and
OFr *bende*, 'band, ribbon'), referring to fastenings or strengthening bands.

DOE *bend*; cf. MED *běnd(e* n.¹; OED *bend* sb.¹

beneoðan OE, *prep*. 'beneath, under, below' often survives without the
unstressed initial syllable in compound p.ns. It is common in D (cf.
begeondan).
(*a*) *Benettebrugge* (f.n.) 1535 Gl:1·194 (**brycg**), *Benethedowne* (f.n.) 1338
Brk:533 (cf. nearby *Abovedoune* (f.n.) 1338), Neadon (*Beneadona* 1086,
Bynythedon 1333) D:482, (*Bynethedoune* 1294) D:424 (**dūn**), *Benethegate*
(f.n.) 1305 Ru:96 (**gata**), *Nethenhow* 1323 Hrt:207 (**hōh**), *Neath Towne
Close* (f.n.) 1649 [18th] Ru:146 (**tūn, clos**), Nethway 1384 D (**weg**),
Beneathwood 1337 Co [Svensson:80], Naithwood (*Bynethewode* 1361) D,
Neathwood 1509–47 Gl (**wudu**).

~ **bī**.

DOE *be-neoþan*; MED *binēthe(n*; EDD –; OED *beneath*.

*benti *adj*. ME, 'growing with rushes or coarse grass' appears to alternate
with the noun **beonet** in Bentley (*Bentiley* 13th, *Bentley* 1309) YW:3·85.

(a) ?Bennety Coppice (f.n.; *Bennett Coppice* 1590, *Bennettie* 1618) Do:2·204 (**copeis**), *the Benty Croft* (f.n.) 1611 Ch:1·158 (**croft**), Benty Doles (f.n.) c.1700 St:1·78 (**dāl**), *the Bentiefield* (f.n.) 1611 Ch:1·171 (**feld**), Benty Leys (f.n.; *le Bentileye Heye* 1399) Ch:2·288 (**lēah, gehæg**), *Bentylee launde* (f.n.) 1585 St:1·111 (**lēah, launde**), *Bentimore* (f.n.) 1608 YW:1·190 (**mōr**).

~ **beonet.**

MED −; EDD −; OED *benty.*

běo OE, *f.* 'bee' appears in OE charter bounds such as *ofer beocumb* S:1542 Brk:671 and *on beodune* S:501 K, but may sometimes be confused in p.ns with **bī**: thus Beeford 1086 YE (**ford**) has been analysed as both 'beside the ford' (YE:76) and 'bee ford' (DEPN, Mills 1991). The modern forms of Beestones c.1300 YW and Beestonely 13th YW more probably represent distortion of the common name Beeston, from ***běos** and **tūn**, than the *bee-stone* 'stone on which beehives were placed' or 'rock where bees were found' which is suggested at YW:3·49. A similar popular misunderstanding is evidenced in Beeston (*Buistane* 1086) Ch:3·302, which probably derives from **byge**[2] 'commerce' and **stān** 'stone', yet is translated into 15th-century Welsh as *y Fêl Allt* 'the honey rock'.

The compound *bee-stall* 'bee-hive' (OED 1572) appears in Beeston Brow (*Beestall-bancke* 1611) Ch:1·188 (**banke**); cf. **stall.**

(a) Bybrook (*æt beo broce* 940 S:464) K:415 (**brōc**), Beeby 1086 Lei (**bȳ**), Beckett 1086 Brk:376 (**cot**), Beacom 1292 Ch:1·302 (**cumb**), *the Beegarden* (f.n.) 1607 Gl:1·233 (**gardin**), the Bee-Garth (f.n.) 1704 We:2·116 (**garðr**), Bee Low 1285 Db:160 (**hlāw**), Beal 1208–10 Nb, Bee Hill 1349 Ru (**hyll**), Beaulieu 1258 (*Beleye* 1288) Do:3·241, Beoley (*into beo leahe* 972 S:786) Wo, Billow 1221 Gl (**lēah**), Bewick 1167 Nb, 1086 YE (**wīc**), Beauworth (*Beowyrð* 938 [?11th] S:444) Ha (**worð**).

~ **bīcere.**

DOE *běo*; MED *bę̄*; EDD *bee* sb.[1]; OED *bee*[1]; DOE *Bee.*

beofor OE, *m.* 'beaver' appears with words for streams, as in OE forms of Barbourne Wo (*Beferburnan*) and Beverley Brook Sr (*into beferiþi*). Beverley YE (*Beferlic*) may also belong with this group (see Ekwall 1931:58), though its second element is disputed (YE:193). The recorded, derived ME byname has been proposed for Beverston 12th ASC E s.a.1048 Gl:2·213, where there is no water. In Bevercotes Nt (**cot**) reference may be to the beaver's dam or dwelling (cf. Beevor Hall YW with **hol**[1]).

For further examples which possibly involve OE *bera* 'bear' instead, see **ber-ward**. See also Aybes & Yalden 1995.

The headword used here is the regular Anglian form with back mutation: unmutated *befor* and *befer* are also attested (OEG:§210).

(*a*) Beversbrook 1086 W (**brōc**), Barbourne 904 [11th] S:1280 Wo (**burna**), *Beverbuske* (f.n.) 1577 L:4·158 (***buskr**), Bevercotes 1192 Nt (**cot**), Bevere Island c.1150 Wo (**ēg**), Beevor Hall (*Beverhole* 1609) YW (**hol**[1]), Bewerley 1086 YW (**lēah**), Beverley c.1025 [11th] YE (?***licc**), *Beuernes* (f.n.) 13th Ch:2·36 (**nes**), Beverley Brook ?693 [11th] S:1248 Sr (**rīðig**), *Beuerwelle* (f.n.) 1306 Gl:3·61 (**welle**).

DOE *befer*; MED *bēver* n.[1]; EDD –; OED *beaver* sb.[1]; DES *Beaver*.

beolone OE, *f.* 'henbane' has been suggested as the origin of the r.n. *Bell* 1300 Wo, which gave its name to the settlement of Bell first recorded in an OE charter as *Beolne* 817 [11th] S:181; this village was joined with nearby *Broctun* in the 13th century to give the modern parish name Belbroughton (Wo:274–5). Both the plant-name and the derived r.n. have been proposed as the root of Bilton (*Bentone* 1086, *Beltone* c.1155) Wa (**tūn**), which lies on an unnamed stream. The word may also appear in combination with **æcer** in a derived ME surname *Belnacre* 1370 (Sundby 1959:110). However, none of these names is straightforward: first, the r.n. *Bell* may have a different Celtic origin; second, the simplex formation is curious and is only meaningful if ellipsis is inferred, giving 'river/settlement upon whose banks henbane grew'; and third, the early loss of the medial vowel may be problematic (ERN:32–3).

DOE *belene*; MED *belene*; EDD –; OED –.

beonet OE, 'coarse wild grass, bent-grass' is not found independently in OE, but is evidenced in the OE spellings of several instances of the common name Bentley, e.g. *æt Beonetleh* 963–75 [12th] S:823 Ha, *Benetleye* 1035–44 [14th] Ess:328 [ASWills:29] (**lēah**) and *beonot setena gemære* 851 [11th] S:201 Wo:141. In p.ns the element is widespread except in the east midlands, where the synonym ***bēos** is found. In ME the element was often used metonymically of 'place overgrown with wild grass' and more generally, of any tract of uncultivated land (MED *bent* n.[1] sense 2). This usage may well have been very common: it can presumably be inferred when the term is used as a simplex name or second element of a compound. The word survives in ModE *bent* and *bennet* which are applied to a range of stiff grasses, from reeds and rushes to sedge, the latter being particularly common in southern dialects.

The element is difficult to distinguish from **bēan** in Benton c.1190 Nb
(**tūn**). It seems to alternate with the adjective ***benti** in Bentley (*Bentiley*
13th, *Bentley* 1309) YW:3·85.

(*a*) Bentfield 1086 Ess, Binfield (*Benetfeld'* c.1160) Brk (**feld**), Benthall
1086 Sa:1·37, 1120 Sa:1·37 (**halh**), Bentham 1220 Gl, Bentham 1086 YW
(**hām/hamm**), Bent Head 1575 YW:3·192 (**hēofod**), *Bentle* (f.n.) 1346
Ru:36, Bentley (*Benedlege* 1086) Db:344, 1086 Db:530, 1086 YW:1·24,
1226 YW:2·218, c.1315 YW:4·138, (f.n.) 1347 Ch:3·308 (**lēah**),
Benteleg'yate (f.n.) c.1300 Ch:2·94 (**lēah**, **geat**), Bentley Royd 1275–1324
YW:3·145 (**lēah**, ***rod**[1]), Bensted 1086 K (**stede**).

(*b*) *le Benet* (f.n.) 1320 YW:4·30, Bent (f.n.) 1348 Ch:3·225, *le Bent*
1299 Db:303, Bents 1597 Cu, *le Bentes* (f.n.) 13th YW:1·161, *the Bents*
1647 YW:1·341, 1650 Db:199, *the Bentte* 1589 YW:6·101, Totley Bents
(*Bents* 1603) Db:316.

(*c*) *Ashenbenthe* (f.n.) 1544 YW:7·157 (**æscen**), Monubent 1205–11 YW
(**manig**), Merry Bent 1546 YW:3·68 (**myrig**), Chowbent c.1350 La
(pers.n.), *Tymeley Bent* 1624 YW (p.n.).

~ OHG *binuz*, OSax *binut*; ***benti**.

DOE –; MED *bent* n.[1]; EDD *bennet* sb.[1], *bent* sb.; OED *bennet* sb.[2], *bent* sb.[1];
DML *benta*; DES *Bent*.

beorn OE, *m.* 'man, warrior' cannot be formally distinguished from the
recorded pers.ns *Beorn* and *Beorna*, but has been preferred by some
scholars (C:39, Nth:179), particularly where OE forms show the element
without a genitive inflection, as *Byornham* 975–1016 S:1487, probably to
be identified as Barnham Sf (**hām**) and Barn Hill (*Beornhyll* 959 [12th]
S:681) YE (**hyll**). Others, however, have simply taken this to indicate that
in OE the inflection could have been omitted or already have fallen out
(DEPN, YE:252). In ME spellings the element cannot be distinguished
from **bere-ærn**. OE *beorn*, ME *bern* is almost entirely limited to poetic
texts.

DOE *beorn*; MED *bĕrn* n.[1]; EDD –; OED *berne*.

***bēos** OE, 'coarse grass, bent-grass' was proposed by Ekwall (1931:54–8)
on the basis of cognates in the Low German languages, to explain a
significant group of names beginning *Bees-* or *Bes-* for which no
satisfactory derivation had been given. The element seems to occur
predominantly in East Anglia and the east midlands, and may stand in
dialectal opposition to the synonym **beonet**, which is common outside this
area. Note that the attested ON pers.n. *Besi* could sometimes be involved.
(*a*) Bessacarr a.1166 YW (**æcer**), Beeston 1086 Bd, 1086 (×3) Nf, 1086

Nt, 1086 YW, 1254 Nf (tūn), Beasthorpe 13th [17th] L:3·163, Besthorpe 1086 Nt:183, 1147 Nt:201 (þorp).

~ MLG *bēse*, Du *bies*; *bēosuc.

DOE −; MED −; EDD −; OED −.

*bēosuc OE, 'tuft of bent-grass' was proposed by Ekwall for Bestwood Nt (1931:57–8), and would be a formation with *bēos parallel to riscuc 'tuft of rushes' (with risc) and hassuc 'tuft of coarse grass' (with *hæsse). (a) Bescar 1207 Nt (halh), *Beskroyde* (f.n.) 1328 YW:7·157 (*rod[1]), Bestwood (*Beskewuda* 1177) Nt (wudu).

~ *bēos.

DOE −, MED −, EDD −, OED −.

berc OE, *f.* 'birch-tree' existed alongside the weak form birce from which it might be distinguished by the retention of *-e-* or *-a-* and the unassibilated final consonant. A derived *bercet* 'clump of birch-trees' is possible in Bargate Hill (f.n.; *Barkett hill* 1682) Ru:75 (but see the discussion under *bircet). ·

The headform used here is Anglian, with smoothing. The West Saxon equivalent is *beorc* (DOE's *byrc* is a West Saxon *i*-mutated variant, perhaps produced by crossing with birce).

(a) Little Barford 1086 (*Berkeford* 1202) Bd (ford), Barkham 952 [13th] S:559 Brk (hamm), Berkhamsted 1086 Hrt:217 (hām-stede), Bartlow (*Berkelawe* 1232) C (hlāw), *Berklond* (f.n.) 1497 Gl:3·18 (land), Bartley 1086 Ha, Berkeley 824 [11th] S:1433 Gl:2·211, Berkley 1086 So, *Berkele* (f.n.) 1248 Brk:34 (lēah), *Berkeleymor'* (f.n.) 1376 Ch:4·113 (lēah, mōr), *Berkemore* (f.n.) 1231 Brk:210 (mōr), Barkway 1086 Hrt (weg).

~ birce, *bircen, *bircet, birki.

DOE *byrc*; MED *berk-* n.[2]; EDD −; OED −.

bere OE, *n.* 'barley' is found in Anglo-Saxon charters in *to bercrofte* S:1373, S:1593 Wo (croft) and *on berlandes heafda* S:1388 Wa (land). In compounds such as bærlic the word had a by-form *bær* (which would be indistinguishable in ME spellings from the cognate ON *barr*). The element is difficult to separate also from bār, bær, bǣr or a pers.n. *Bera* (equivalent to OE *bera* 'bear'). Most of the following examples denote places where barley was grown; those with ford are fords through which it was transported. Barcote Brk may be identical in meaning with bere-tūn, bere-wīc.

(a) Baracre 1253–4 K (æcer), Barcote 1216 Brk (cot), Bar Croft Bottom 13th YW, *Berecrofta* (f.n.) 1171–83 Gl:1·162 (croft), Barden c.1140 YW (denu), Bush 1147–82 K (ersc), Barford 1086 O, 1086 W, Barforth c.1130 YN (**ford**), Bearl 1242 Nb, *le Berehil* 1250 Lei:119 (**hyll**), *Berlond* 1450 Sx:209, *Berlondere* (surn.) 1332 Sr [Fransson:194] (**land**), Barlow 1086 Sa:1·30 (**lēah**), Baretilt 1285 K (**tilð**).

~ **bærlic, bere-ærn, bere-tūn, bere-wīc.**
DOE *bere*; MED *bēr(e* n.[2]; EDD *bear* sb.[2]; OED *bear* sb.[2]

bere-ærn OE, *n.* 'barn, storehouse for barley and other grain' already has the reduced forms *beren, bern* in OE as, for example, *to þæs bernes ende* S:179 Gl:2·19. As a first element it can hardly be distinguished from OE *beren* 'of barley, growing with barley', or, particularly where there is a medial -*e*-, from the pers.ns OE *Beorna*, ON *Bjarni*. ME forms in *barn* either evidence the change of *er* > *ar* (Jordan:§67), or involve the OE by-form *bær* (see **bere, bere-tūn**).

(*a*) Barnacre 1517 La (**æcer**), *barnecroftes* (f.n.) 13th Ch:2·191 (**croft**), Barden 1086 YN (**denu**), Barnage Wood 1448 Gl, Barnedge Hill 1282 Gl (**ecg**), *le Berneyorde* (f.n) 1466 Ch:5·xxviii (**geard**), *Le Bernhawe* (f.n.) 1319 Brk:34 (**haga**[1]), Barnacle 1086 Wa (**hangra**), *Bernhull* (f.n.) 1353 Ch:3·189 (**hyll**), *le bernelond* (f.n.) 1325 Ch:3·129 (**land**), Barlow (*Bernlege* c.1030) YW, *Berneslegh* 1360 Ch:1·52 (**lēah**), Barnwood 1086 Gl (**wudu**).

(*b*) Barnes 1269 Db:244, 1086 Sr, Barnes Hall (*Bernes* c.1267) YW, Barneshall (*La Neweberne* 1327, *Bernes* 1376) Wo, Barns 1325 Nb [NbDu:17], *Berne* (f.n.) 1316 Ch:2·94. Numerous instances in surnames are given by MELS:11–12.

(*c*) Abbey Barns 1465 Db (**abbaie**), *Aldeberne* (f.n.) 1148–79 Gl:1·159, *le Oldeberne* (f.n.) 1335 Db:182 (**ald**), *Catbarne Crofte* (f.n.) 1341 YW:4·114 (**catt**), *Le Heybern* (f.n.) 1309 Brk:95, *le Hayberne* (f.n.) 1339 Ch:2·250 (**hēg**), *Heldeberne* (f.n.) 13th YW:1·110 (**helde**), *le Wheteberne* (f.n.) 14th Db:716 (**hwǣte**), *Munkesberne* (f.n.) 1395 Ch:3·170 (**munuc**), Rowbarns (*la Ruebern* 1214) Sr:140 (**rūh**), *Tithe Barn* (bdg.n. Chester) 1713 Ch:5·34 (**tēoða**), *Godewynesberne* (f.n.) 1374 Gl:2·253 (pers.n.).

~ **bere, ærn.**
DOE *bere-ern*; MED *běrn* n.[2]; EDD *barn* sb.; OED *barn* sb.

bere-tūn OE, *m.* 'barley enclosure, barley farm' is also used once in OE of a 'threshing floor'. The usual sense, however, became 'outlying grange, demesne farm (especially one retained for the lord's use and not let to tenants)'. In origin and development it appears to be practically synonymous with **bere-wīc**, and the distribution of the two compounds is to some extent complementary (see Sa:1·42).

In the south, especially the south-west, *barton* survived in the senses 'farmyard' and 'large farm, demesne farm'. In the south-west, especially Devon, it is frequently added as a modern affix to settlement names. A citation in the EDD, from west Somerset, explains that 'very often it is the manor farm, or the principal holding in the parish, whether occupied by the owner or not—generally not—[which] takes the name of the parish preceding the barton'. Commonly, however, the farm-name is not that of a parish—e.g. Hayes Barton, Tidwell Barton (both in East Budleigh parish, D:583), Middlewick Barton, Stourton Barton (both in Thelbridge parish, D:396)—and the usual sense is perhaps simply 'large farm'. The EPNS publications unfortunately do not indicate the dates at which these affixes came into use. See the discussions in DCNQ 23 (1947–9):273–7, 326–8, though the early examples of the term adduced there are not clearly used as affixes.

A by-form *bær-tūn* (cf. **bere**) is evidenced in OE (if the 13th-century document is an accurate copy) only in the earliest record of Westcot Barton S:1425 O, but it seems to lie also behind the numerous early ME spellings in *Bar-* in the midlands and north, as in the DB forms of Barton La (×2), YN (×3), Db, Nt, Lei and Earls Barton Nth. Compare the following from the midlands and south, which have DB spellings in *Ber-* (from OE *bere-tūn* or the reduced *bertūn*): Barton Bd, Bk, Brk, C, Gl (×2), Ha, He, L, Nf (×2), O, Sf (×2), So, St, Wa and Barton Seagrave Nth. It appears that the choice of *Bær-* or *Ber-* is dialectal, though since *-e-* spellings may occasionally be written for OE *-æ-* in post-Conquest documents the line of the isogloss is not easy to fix precisely. Note that later in the ME period the change of *er* > *ar* removed any contrast (Jordan:§67, §270).

(*b*) It is usually uncompounded in p.ns, as Barton *passim*, and is frequently distinguished by affixes, as Abbot's Barton, King's Barton Gl, Barton Blount Db, Earls Barton Nth, Middle Barton, Steeple Barton O, Barton le Street YN, etc.

(*c*) Occasionally a distinguishing first element was added early: Down Barton 1397 (**dūne**), Mulbarton 1086 Nf (**meoluc**), Norbiton 1205 Sr (**norð**), Soberton 1086 Ha, Surbiton 1179 Sr (**sūð**).

   ~ **bere, tūn.**

DOE *bere-tūn*; MED *běrton*; EDD *barton*; OED *barton*[1]; DML *bertona*; DOE *Barton*.

bere-wīc OE, 'barley farm' seems to have developed the sense 'grange, outlying or demesne farm' already in the Anglo-Saxon period, as in *Medeshamstede & [þ]a berewican þa þar to heren, & Anlafestun & þam* *berewican þar to* S:1448 Nth. Cf. **bere-tūn**.

The compound element, like the simplex **wīc**, is recorded with a variety of grammatical forms: DOE notes that *bere-wīc(e)* can be both masculine or neuter and feminine; it is generally strong, but can apparently also be weak (cf. Ekwall 1964:10–11).

(*b*) Barwick 1219 So, 1086 YW, 1086 YN, Berwick 1086 (×2) Sa:1·41–2, 1120–47 YW, 1168 W:254, e.13th Gl, 1220 Ess:75, 1248 Ess:78, Borwick 1086 La.

~ **bere, wīc.**

DOE *bere-wīc*; MED *bĕr(e-wĭk*; EDD –; OED *berewick*; DML *berewica*; DOE *Berwick*.

berfroi OFr, *m.* 'shelter, tower, belfry'. 'Shelter' seems to have been the basic meaning: the word is used in L, Nt and So for a rough-built shed (EDD), and this sense is likely in the two L f.ns given below. In the ME period the term was applied to the various protective structures erected by soldiers besieging fortifications, from a simple hut or lean-to to a movable wooden tower (OED). Subsequently, the word seems to have been used for other kinds of tower—the Norwich building known as *le Berefry* in 1301 was described three years earlier as *campan[ile]* 'bell-tower'. However, the restriction of the term to this particular kind of tower may be due to the influence of a MLat reflex, *belefridum* (OED). This seems to be ultimately responsible for the ME form *belfrei*, and popular association with **belle** is likely to have given rise to the semantic range of ModE 'belfry'.

(*a*) *belfra garth* (f.n.) 1601 L:3·68, *Belfreygarth* (f.n.) 1558–79 L:3·176 (**garðr**).

(*b*) *Belffrey* (bdg.n. Tewkesbury) 1540 Gl:2·63, *Belfry* (bdg.n. Norwich; *le Berefry* 1301) Nf:1·28.

~ Gmc **bergfrid* (cf. OHG *bercfrit*, MDu *bergfert*) via Latin (OED). AND –; AFW *berfroi*; DML *berefredum*; MED *berfrei, belfrei*; EDD *belfry*; OED *belfry*.

berg OE, *m.* 'hill, mound' is common in p.ns. The basic meaning 'hill' survives in northern dialect *bargh, barf* (EDD). Topographically this sense is likely in many names, like Farnborough Wa and Grandborough Bk, and in West Yorkshire the element seems often to be used of drumlins, the hillocks formed when a glacier sheds its load of earth (Gelling 1988:133). The word is also used in OE literary texts of man-made hillocks such as Beowulf's burial mound, and Gelling (1988:132–4) argues that this specialised sense is common in p.ns south of Birmingham. There are tumuli at Barrow Ru, Barrowden Ru, Broughton Ha, Modbury Do,

Loosebarrow Do, Burgh Sr and Wigber Low Db, and it may be significant that in the last and most northerly of these names, the addition of a tautological **hlāw** became necessary. In other cases, it is the element with which *berg* is combined which suggests that the sense is 'barrow' rather than 'hill'. Idel Barrow Gl is 'empty' (**īdel**) and Brokenborough W could be 'broken into' (though **brocen** has other possible senses), while the boundary mark denoted in the phrase *be suðan þam longam beorge* S:1026 Gl has been identified as a Neolithic long barrow (Hooke 1980–1:14).

The nominative form of the element (whether Anglian *berg* or West Saxon *beorg*) should regularly give names in ME *bergh*, later *-bargh* or *-barf* (as in Barugh YN and Barpham Sx). The dative form *berge* should become early ME *berwe*, identical to some ME forms of **bearu** (see the full discussion there); both elements are represented in modern names as *-berrow* or *-barrow*. A large number of names that originally involved *berg* later became identified with the common **burh**, and thus the list of examples below includes a large number of p.ns that now end in *-borough*.

In the Danelaw and the north, OE *berg* could not be distinguished from ON *berg* and ON *bjarg* 'hill, mountain, rock, cliff'. (The two ON words cannot be distinguished formally from one another, and it must be doubtful whether any difference in their sense could be detected in England, for they have had varying precise applications in different parts of Scandinavia.)

The examples given below are mostly drawn from major names and could be supplemented by many minor ones.

(*a*) Berrier 1166 Cu (***ǽrgi**), Barrowby 1086 YW:5·40, Borrowby 1086 YN (×2) (**bȳ**), Barrowden 1086 Ru (**dūn**), Barway 1155 C (**ēg**), Burghfield 1086 Brk (**feld**), Barham 1086 C:109, 1086 [12th] Hu, Barpham 1121 Sx (**hām/hamm**), Bergholt 1086 Ess (**holt**), Broughton 1173 Ha, 1086 L (**tūn**).

(*b*) Barrow 1197 Ru, Barugh 1086 YN, 1086 YW, Berrow 973 [14th] S:793 So, 1275 Wo:63, 1190 [18th] Wo:96, 1221 Wo:318, Burf 1212 Wo, Burgh 1086 Sr.

(*c*) With an adjective: Blackberry Hill 12th [15th] Lei:139 (**blæc**), Brokenborough 956 [13th] S:629 W (**brocen**), Emborough 1086 So (**emn**), Grandborough 1042–9 [13th] S:1228 Bk (**grēne**[1]), Idel Barrow 1121 Gl (**īdel**), *Langeberge* c.1086 Do:2·87, Longborough 1086 Gl (**lang**[1]), Rowberrow 1177 So, Rowborough 1086 Wt:60, 1272–9 Wt:107 [& Mills 1996:88] (**rūh**).

With a noun descriptive of shape or soil quality: Backbarrow 1537 La (**bæc**), Chiselborough 1086 So (**cisel**), Flawborough 1086 Nt (**flōh**),

Limbery 1225–42 Db (**līm**), Samber 1235 Wt (**sand**), Stoberry 13th So, Stoborough 1086 Do:1·73 (**stān**).

With the names of wild creatures, or derived pers.ns: Caber c.1240 Cu, Kaber 12th We (***cā**), Crowborough 1292 Sx (**crāwe**), Durborough 1086 So (**dēor**), Ernsborough 1175 D (**earn**), Finborough 1086 Sf (**fīna**), Roxborough 1334 Mx (**hrōc**), Capple Barrow 1170–84 We:1·179 (**kapall**), Larborough 1225 W, Larkborough ?709 [12th] S:80 Wo (**lāwerce**), Loosebarrow 1130 Do:2·54 (**lūs**), Todber 1189–99 YW:6·179 (***todd**), Oldberrow ?709 [12th] S:79 Wa [Wo:267], *Oldborough* 1397 K (**ūle**), Wigber Low c.1230 Db (**wicga, hlāw**), Wolborough 1086 D (**wulf**).

With the names of domestic creatures: Ellesborough 1086 Bk (**eosol**), Hensborough c.1150 Wa (**hengest**), Harborough 1199–1216 Wo (**heord**).

With words for crops or vegetation: Brackenber 1303 YW (***brakni**), Aikber 1279–81 YN (& D:2·ix), Aigburth c.1200 La (**eik**), Farnborough 862 [?11th] S:331 K, 916 [13th] S:225 Brk, 990–1006 [12th] S:937 Wa (**fearn**), Risborough (*æt þæm easteran Hrisan byrge* 903 S:367) Bk, Riseborough c.1200 YN (**hrīs**), Whatborough 1086 Lei (**hwǣte**), Limber 1066–8 [12th] L:2·219 [ASWills:39] (**lind**), Riber e.13th Db (**ryge**), Wadborough 972 S:786 Wo (**wād**).

With numerals: ?Lymborough (*Endleuaberga* c.1090) K:561 (**endleofan**), *Fowerbereghes* 1260 C:312 (**fēower**), Seaborough 1086 Do (**seofon**), Thrybergh 1086 YW (**þrēo**).

With pers.ns: *Alvredesberge* c.1086 Do:2·194, Attleborough c.1150 Wa, Baltonsborough 744 [14th] S:1410 So, Edlesborough 1086 Bk, Handborough 1086 O, *Hunesberge* c.1086 Do:2·86, Inkberrow 789 [11th] S:1430 Wo, Rainborough 1145 YW, Symondsbury 1086 Do.

With other elements: *Bedeman's Berg* 1177 Ess (**ge-bed-mann**), Modbury 1086 D:279 (**mōt**), Scaliber 1276 YW (**skáli**), Sulber 1190 YW:6·220 (**sól**), Woodnesborough 1086 K (**Wōden**).

DOE *beorg*; MED *bergh*; EDD *bargh, barrow* sb.³; OED *bargh, barrow* sb.¹; DES *Barrow, Bergh*.

berht OE, *adj.* 'bright, clear' is not common in p.ns, the more usual OE term being **scīr**². Its sense is expressed in an Anglo-Saxon charter as Lat *declaratam fontem* S:523 for Brightwell Brk. The metathesised form *breht* appears only in the north in OE, but spreads southward during the ME period (Jordan:§165). The head-form is Anglian, with smoothing; the southern equivalent is *beorht*. The element would often be difficult to distinguish formally from the OE pers.n. *Be(o)rht(a)*. It is probable in: (*a*) *Bertie Grove* 1199 Sr (**grāf**), Brightholmlee a.1209 YW (**holmr, lēah**), Birtley 1183 Du, 1229 Nb, *Birtley* 1324 Gl (**lēah**), Breightmet 1246 La (mēd), Breighton 1086 YE (tūn), Brightwell 854 [12th] S:307 Brk, 887 [11th] S:217 O:120, 1086 Sf (welle).

DOE *beorht* adj.; MED *bright*; EDD *bright* adj.; OED *bright* a.; DES *Bright, Burt*.

berige OE, *f.* 'berry' probably appears in OE charter bounds in the phrase *ofer berigancumb* S:229 W, and is also possible in several p.ns in combination with **stall** and **stōw**, giving 'place where berries grow'. *Berige* and **beger** alternate with both *stall* and *stōw* in spellings of Berristall Ch:1·131: *Bistale* c.1270 [17th], *Berestowe* 1347, *Berystowe* 1357 and *Berystall* 1567.

(*a*) Berristal 1499 YW (**stall**), Berrister (*Beristowe* 1503) Ch:1·142 (**stōw**).

(*c*) Brownborrioo 1671 YW (**brūn**[1]).

~ ***beg, beger, *blæc-berige**.

DOE *berie*; MED *berie*; EDD *berry* sb.[1]; OED *berry* sb.[1]

*berkarie ME, 'sheep-fold'; alternatively perhaps a sheep-walk or a lambing shed (DML). The word was sometimes associated with **bark** and the meaning 'tan-house' (OED). The confusion was largely occasioned by the change of *-er-* > *-ar-* which probably began in the north before the 14th century (Jordan:§67); the OED's earliest instance of the word, in either sense, is 1594, but Lat *bercaria* appears with the meaning 'tan-house' in the 15th century (DML *bercaria*[1]). The spelling *Bark-* in the single example here, as early as the 12th century, suggests that some confusion of form—if not of sense—may already have taken place.

(*b*) Barkers Field (*Barkarie* 12th) YE.

~ MLat *bercaria*, OFr *bergerie*.

DML *bercaria*[2]; AND *bercherie*; MED –; OED *barkary*.

*berse ME, appears to denote a forest-enclosure, but the etymology and precise sense are uncertain. It has been connected with a MLat *bersa* 'hedge made with stakes' and MLG *bersa, brisa* 'pleached hedge' (EPNE), or with OFr *berser* 'to shoot', especially 'to shoot game' (DML). A Latin *bersella* is also recorded (DML), and may be relevant to the f.n. *Berselhok* below. It is perhaps a diminutive of *bersa*—of whatever origin—as DML tentatively suggests, offering '(?) enclosure'. But MED records ME *bersel* (OFr *bersal*) 'archery butt'; alternatively there is OFr *bercil* 'sheepfold' (AFW *bercil*, AND *berzil*).

(*a*) Bracebridge 1100–35 [14th] Nt (**brycg**), ?Brizlincote (*Bersicot* c.1100) Db (**cot**), *Berselehok* (f.n.) 1398 Ch:4·175 (?**lēah, hōc**), *Bersewell* (f.n.) 12th Gl:2·162 (**welle**).

(*b*) Bearse 1270 Gl, *Berse* 1230 Wo:389.

DOE –; MED –; EDD –; OED –; DML *bersa*.

ber-ward ME, 'bear-keeper'. Bears provided popular medieval entertainment, used in the sport of bear-baiting and trained to perform tricks (Nth:7). Bearbinder Lane (st.n London) 1338–9 and *Barebinder Lane* (st.n. Poplar) 1617 Mx:135, may perhaps refer to bear-tamers, though 'bearbinder' is not on record, and there may instead be a connection with *bearbind* 'convolvulus' (OED *bearbine*).

Ekwall (DEPN) doubts whether Bearwardcote 1086 Db is a genuine instance of OE **bera-weard*, ME *ber-ward*, because the OED first records *bearward* in 1399. (He suggests instead an OE pers.n. **Beornweard* for Bearwardcote.) The st.ns given below, and instances of the element as a ME surname which take it back to 1179 (Thuresson:190–1), make the identification more acceptable, however.

Note that p.ns have sometimes been taken to offer further evidence for bears in early England in Barbon We and *Atteberburne* (surn.) 1309 Sx [MELS:10] (**brunnr/burna**). However, ON **bjórr** 'beaver' would be an alternative in the former name (see there), while the example of Barbourne Wo—*Beferburnan* 904 [11th] S:1280, *Bereburn* 13th—suggests that the Sx example might similarly involve OE **beofor** 'beaver'.

(*a*) *berwardbryg* (f.n.) 1464 L:4·127 (**brycg**), Bearwardcote (*Beruerdescote* 1086) Db (**cot**), *le Bereworde Gate* (st.n Nottingham) c.1240 Nt:19 (**gata**), *Berewerdishill* (f.n.) 1552 Brk:181 (**hyll**), Berewards Lane (st.n London ×2) 1279 Ldn:112, 1285 Ldn:112, *Bereward Lone* (st.n Chester) c.1240 Ch:5·9 (**lane**), Bearward St (st.n. Northampton) 1281 Nth:7 (**strēt**).

DOE –; MED *bēr(e-wărd(e*; OED *bearward*; DML *berewardus*; DES *Bearward*.

besma OE, *m.* 'broom, brush' appears in *Bessome-lane* (st.n. Chester) 1656 Ch:5·67, where they were perhaps for sale, and in Beesoms Hill (f.n.; *Besemehull* 1339) Ch:2·62, where the twigs of broom, heather or birch were perhaps collected. (The word is also recorded simply denoting the broom-plant itself, but EDD *besom* sb.[2] notes this only in the south-west.) Beesom Stail (f.n.) 1844 Ch may be, as Ch:3·220 suggests, for 'besom's tail' (**tægl**), an expression applied to long, bushy tails. Alternatively 'besom-stail' is a term for 'broom-handle' (EDD; cf. OED *stale* sb.[2]). In either case there would presumably be some topographical application here.

DOE *besma*; MED *bĕsm(e*; EDD *besom* sb.[1]; OED *besom* sb.[1]; cf. DES *Bessemer*.

beste OFr, *f.* 'beast' was first used of any living creature. Its sense was gradually narrowed to animals alone (as opposed to humans, fish, birds and reptiles), and by the 16th century was generally restricted to livestock, especially cattle.

(a) Beastgate (f.n.) 1767 Db:165 (**gata/geat**), *the beast howse* (bdg.n. Lincoln) 1581 L:1·137 (**hūs**), Beastmarket Hill (st.n Nottingham, *Beast Hill* 1744) Nt:15 (**hyll**), The Beast Market (st.n Chester) 1533 Ch:5·9, *Beast Market* 1610 L:1·19 (**market**), *le Bestmor* (f.n.) 1369 YW:2·17 (**mōr**).

~ Lat *bestia*.

AND *beste*[1]; AFW *beste*; MED *bēst(e*; EDD *beast*; OED *beast* sb.; DML *bestia*; DES *Best*.

*bete ME, lying behind ModE *beat* 'turf cut away and burned in preparing land for cultivation', is likely in Beatland Corner *(la Beate Beathlonde* 14th) D. The element is found again in *Beate* (f.n.) 1652 YW:1·33 and perhaps in some of the modern f.ns given by Field:16 under *Beaten Flat*. The sense is close to that of **beak**, ***burn-bake** and some link seems evident since *beat* is similarly partnered by *burn-beat* (EDD, OED). The details of the connection are obscure, however. As first element in a compound, ME **bete* could not be distinguished from OE *bēte* 'beetroot', which is possible in Bedhampton 1086 Ha (**-hǣma-tūn**), but has otherwise not been suggested for p.ns.

~ of uncertain origin. It might very tentatively be related to MED *bēte* n.[3] '(?) an implement for beating flax'; cf. the apparent origin of **beak** as the name of an implement.

EDD *beat* sb.[1]; OED *beat* sb.[3]

betwēonan OE, *prep.* 'between, amongst' usually occurs in compound p.ns with elliptical sense 'the place between'. Both the unstressed initial syllable and the sense of the element were lost early in the charter form *at Twynham* 934 [17th] S:391, the Anglo-Saxon name of Christchurch Ha. As here, the preposition frequently combines with elements denoting streams or rivers. Another example is *Bituinæum* 814 [11th] S:172, an early form of Twyning Gl. Both names contain the dative plural of **ēa**—they are situated between the rivers Avon and the Stour and the rivers Severn and Avon respectively.

Christchurch Ha also has an alternative OE form *æt Tweoxneam* 10th ASC A s.a.900, with the synonymous preposition *betwēoxn* (OED *betwixen*). Further evidence for this in p.ns is scarce: only Twixen Dykes (f.n.) 1844 Ru:170 (**dík**) has been noted.

(a) Twambrook 1.12th Ch:2·195, Twambrooks (f.n.; *Twenebrok* 1331) Ch:3·157, *Twembroke* 1260 Ch:2·141, *Twenebrokes* (f.n.) 1337 Ch:3·130, *Twene brooke* (f.n.) 1605 Gl:2·108 (**brōc**), *Bitwenedik* (f.n.) 1309 Gl:3·165, *Twenedich* (f.n.) c.1225–50 Brk:442 (**dīc**), Tinhay 1194 D,

Twineham 1087–1100 Sx, Twinney 1166–7 K, Twinyeo 1086 D, Twyning c.740 [12th] Gl (ēa), Between Gates (f.n.; *Tweene gates* 1633) Ru:26, Twin-gates (f.n.) 1634 Ru:226, *Betwenyegates* (f.n.) 1355 YW:1·97 (**gata/geat**), *La Tweneheghe* (f.n.) 1222–3 Brk:381 (**hege**), Tween Mills (f.n.) 1624 Ch:3·226 (**myln**, i.e. Frodsham Mills), *Bytwenestret'* (f.n.) 1337 Brk:50 (**strēt**), *Bytweene Townes* (f.n.) 1519 Brk:349, *Tweentown Pieces* (f.n.) 1688 Brk:416 (**tūn**), *Tweene Walls* (f.n.) 1653 Gl:1·60 (**wall**), *Bytwynewayes* (f.n.) 1519 Brk:349, Tweenaways 1567 D (**weg**), Tanwood 1290 Wo (**wudu**).

~ **bī.**

DOE *be-twēonan*; MED *bitwę̄ne* prep.; EDD *between*; OED *between*.

betws MW, 'prayer-house, chapel' is a loan from OE **bed-hūs**. It appears in Bettws-y-Crwyn 1256 Sa, which refers to a medieval chapel (*capelle de Betteus* 1256). The affix, Welsh *crwyn* 'skin, animal hide' (or possibly Welsh *crowyn* 'pigsty'), does not appear until the 19th century. *Betws* is common in p.ns in Wales.

GPC *betws*[1].

*beð ON, *n.* 'embankment, river-bank' may perhaps appear in English p.ns. The singular is unattested, and reconstructed from the plural *bjǫð*, which is recorded only in poetry (Moberg 1951). The sense probably better suits the topography of the two (related) We instances than does that of the apparent alternative, ON *bjóð* 'table, plateau' (see We:1·67–8 and xiv).

(*a*) Beela 1190–9 We (**á**), *Bethesclogh* (f.n.) e.13th YW:3·209 (***clōh**).
(*b*) Beetham 1086 We (dat.pl.).

OGNS (R&T) *bjǫð*.

bī OE, *prep.* with dative, 'by, near' tends to be used elliptically in p.ns; so Bywood would mean 'place near the wood', Bythorn 'place near the thorn-tree', etc. It was fully incorporated into the name at an early date, so that another preposition could precede it; thus *æt Biggrafan* e.11th for Bygrave Hrt, *æt Bifleote* ?1062 [13th] S:1035 for Byfleet Sr.

Ritter 1927–8 argues, citing Germanic parallels, that *bī* could be a prefix with the sense 'surrounding': Bythorn might therefore be 'encircling thorn-hedge', etc. This could perhaps be so for some names in England, but it will hardly suit the topography of many examples. See YN:xliii. A greater problem sometimes lies in distinguishing *bī* (which had also short and less stressed forms *bi* and *be*) from other elements. DEPN, for instance, derives Byfield Nth and Bywell Nb from **byge**[1] 'bend', and Beeford YE from **bēo** 'bee', while Bybeck We could be from ON **bȳ** 'village'. For Bicker L and Byker Nb, see **kjarr.**

Cox 1989–90 explores the Ch dialect term *byflete* 'piece of land cut off by the change of a river's course, which used to belong to the other side'. He argues that this developed sense of *bī* and OE **flēot** 'stream' may well be found in a number of Ch f.ns, including Bye Flatt (*Byflet* 1423) Ch:2·299, *the byflett* 15th Ch:3·105 and *pastura que dicitur Biflet* (f.n.) 1241 Ch:4·186. Cox suggests that the sense might be taken earlier still, and extended beyond Ch and neighbouring St, to include an Anglo-Saxon boundary from Ess (*oð bifleot* 963 S:717) and perhaps also the settlement of Byfleet 933 [13th] S:420 Sr, usually interpreted as '(the place) by the stream'.

Bī is combined with **ēastan, sūðan, norðan, westan,** to denote 'place on the east, south, north, west side of', see DOE sense I.A.2, MED sense 1a (d), OED *be-east, benorth* etc. Examples include *bi Northanuude* 727 [13th] S:26 K and Eastwood (*Byestewode* 1351) D:150 (**wudu**). With the latter may be compared a series of Devon surnames, *John Byestewode* 1339 D:98, *William Bynorthewey* 1330 D:529, *Walter Bysoutheweye* 1333 D:529 which refer to men from places that survived as Eastwood, Northway and Southway. Occasionally, however, *bī* survives in the modern name, as Bestwall 1086 Do:1·157 (**wall**), the place east of the town-walls of Wareham. It is clear that such names should be analysed as *bī ēastan* + *wall* 'on the east side of the wall', and not *bī* + *ēast-wall* 'by the east wall', not only because the *-an* of the OE adverb tends to survive in ME spellings as medial *-e-*, but also because any instances of *bī* prefixed to a compound p.n. are very hard to find. The f.ns *Biþenorthestanlond* 1290 St:1·53 (**norð(an), stān, land**) and *Biþerevelonde* 13th Gl:1·32 (**ge-rēfa, land**) are perhaps the nearest examples, and their status as names is questionable. Note, incidentally, that *bi* tends to appear without the definite article; contrast **æt** and **atte.**

For a discussion of the frequent use of prepositional prefixes in Devon names, see D:1·xxxvii.

(*a*) Bybeck c.1270 We (**bekkr**), Biddick c.1190 Du (**dīc**), Byfords (*Byfar'* 1248) Gl (**fær**), Byfield 1086 Nth (**feld**), Beeford 1086 YE (**ford**), Bygrave e.11th Hrt [ASWills:20] (**grafa; Hrt:155 says that 'there are ancient entrenchments here'), Beaute (*Byholte* 1327) K (**holt**), Bure 1154–89 Ha (**ōra**[1]), Bythorn 1086 Hu (**þyrne**), Bywell 1104–8 Nb (**welle**), Bywood 1086 D (**wudu**).

(*d*) The element is commonly used from the medieval period onwards in forming affixes, as Stanton by Dale Db, Aston by Sutton Ch, etc. It usually first appears as Latin *iuxta*; cf. Allerton Bywater YW, which is

juxta aquam 1258, *by ye water* 1430.
~ **begeondan, behindan, beneoðan, betwēonan, bufan.**
DOE *be*; MED *bī* prep.; EDD *by* prep.; OED *by* prep.

*bica OE, '(?) beak, point' is an element of frequent occurrence but uncertain meaning. It is discussed by Dietz 1985, where the instances in OE charter bounds and later-recorded p.ns are detailed exhaustively. The OE material points overwhelmingly to a weak noun compounded in the genitive, as *on bican bricge* S:522 W, *on bican hyrste* S:360 Ha—the nominative might be either **bica* or **bice*. Although formally it could not be distinguished from the attested pers.n. *Bica*, there are too many instances for this to be the general explanation. The word is compounded with a variety of elements, most of them topographical; it is predominantly found in the west midlands and the south. Connection with ME *bike* 'nest of bees' is unlikely in the great majority of instances—Dietz argues convincingly that *bike* is a relatively late northern word, a ME back-formation from OE **bīcere** 'bee-keeper'. Instead, Dietz follows the majority of scholars in associating the element with a group represented by Ger *Bicke(l)*, OE *becca* 'pick-axe' (cf. **beak**), suggesting a general sense 'something pointed'. Since the only name in which **bica* seems to act as generic is Purbeck Do, with **pūr** 'bittern, snipe', there is some strength in the suggestion, first made by Ekwall, that the precise sense is 'beak, bill'. Purbeck could then be a name like Cockbill (see **bile**), the name referring to a prominent chalk ridge (Do:1·1). The other instances would similarly involve the sense transferred to topography.
(*a*) Bicknoller 1291 So (**alor**), Bicknacre 1186 Ess:275 (**æcer**), Bigbury c.1222 Wt [& Mills 1996:28] (**berg**), Bigbrook 1230 D (**brōc**), Bickham (*Bichecoma* 1086) D:387 (**cumb**), Bicton 1086 Sa:1·47 (**dūn**), Bickford 1086 D (**ford**), Bickleigh 1086 D:224, 1086 D:554, Bickley 1185 YN, 1240 Wo, 1279 K [KPN:230] (**lēah**), Bicknor (*Bicanofre* 1086) Gl (**ofer**[2]), Bicknor 1185–6 K [KPN:231], 1311 D (**ōra**[1]), Bickton 1086 Ha (**tūn**).
(*c*) Purbeck 948 [15th] S:534 Do:1·1 (**pūr**).
DOE –; MED –; EDD –; OED –.

bicce OE, *f.* 'bitch, female dog' seems to appear in a number of names in **haugr** and **hyll**, where it would perhaps mean 'hill/mound frequented by bitches' or 'where dogs were bred' (cf. instances of H(o)undhill; see **hund**[1]). The element is difficult to distinguish from the pers.n. *Bicca* (Redin:85) unless it appears in the gen.pl. *biccena*, as Beechen Cliff (*Biccheneclyve* 1259) So [& W:319] (**clif**), Beechingstoke (1086 *Bichenestoch*) W (**stoc**).

(a) *Bychow* (f.n.) 1278 We:2·220, *Bytchehowe* (f.n.) 1577 We:1·165 (**haugr**), Beech Hill (*Bychill* 1231) YW:5·111, *Bitch Hill* 1314 YW:2·166, Beech Hill (*Bitchell* 1692) We:1·162 (**hyll**).

~ **cur-bich**.

DOE *bicce*; MED *bicche*; EDD *bitch* sb.[1]; OED *bitch* sb.[1]

bīcere OE, *m.* 'bee-keeper'. The word is found as *bikere* only in a gloss of c.1200 (DOE), but nearly all of the p.n. evidence demands Anglian OE *bīcere*, rather than the better attested West Saxon *bēocere*. The Anglian form is probably attested in the Anglo-Saxon forms *Biceratuna* for *Bickerton* YW, and perhaps in *bycera fald* S:786 He. As Dietz argues (1985:8), the *ī* represents smoothing of the diphthong in original *bīocora. Outside the Anglian area, Bickerton D, despite its modern form, is *Bekerton* in the only medieval spelling noted (D:333). This is what would be expected from West Saxon *bēocere*, which is also apparently attested in *beocera gente* [probably for *geate*] S:857 Ha. All of the OE forms could be gen.pl. 'of the bee-keepers' (and cf. the DB spelling *Bicretone* for Bickerton Ch, He and YW), while Bickerston Nf apparently contains the gen.sg. The word is also attested as a ME surname, *Biker*, the distribution again favouring the Anglian north and east (Thuresson:115).

The etymology of *bīcere* is of interest: it seems to represent **bēo** (earlier *bīo*) 'bee' combined with the reflex of Germanic **kaza-* 'container' and turned into a *nomen agentis* (Dietz 1985:8; cf. the cognates listed below). Its root-meaning, in other words, would be 'bee-hiver'. It is possible that this 'bee-hive' itself also survived into OE, as Anglian *bīcær, or more probably *bīcer with reduced stress on the second element. If so, then 'bee-hive' would be an alternative meaning in p.ns, and it seems to offer better sense in some cases. The *Bycera fald* mentioned above, for instance, contains **fald** 'animal enclosure', and an 'enclosure of bee-hives' is perhaps the most satisfactory sense that can be suggested. A similar name may be *Le Bikersegh'* (f.n.) 1371 Ch:1·158 (**ge-hæg**).

Bickerthwaite (f.n.; *Bekerystwayt* 1428) YW:5·106 (**þveit**) and *le Bykereslegh* (f.n.) 1384 Ch:1·147 (**lēah**) may also belong to *bīcere* or *bīcer, though instances involving woods may be better explained by **biker** 'dispute'. Bickerstaffe a.1190 La is another possibility, though its second element is uncertain: it may be ON **staðr**, 'place, site', ON **stǫð** 'landing-place' or OE **stæð** 'river-bank', though the only waterways in the parish are small brooks. For further very uncertain instances see **biker** and **kjarr**, and cf. Ekwall 1933:73–4.

(a) Bickerston 1086 Nf, *Bickerton* c.1030 YW:5·56, Bickerton 1086

Ch:4·4, 1086 He, 1086 YW:4·247, 1236 Nb, 1509–47 D (**tūn**).

~ **bēo**. Cf. OHG *char*, ON *ker* 'container' and OS, MHG *bīkar*, MLG *bî(en)kar*, MDu *biencaer* 'bee-hive'. Ger *Imker* and Du *Ijmker* 'bee-keeper' are comparable, while Frankish **bîkari* (> OFr *bigre* 'bee-keeper') would be identical with OE *bīcere*.

DOE *bēocere*; MED –; EDD –; OED –; DES *Bicker*; cf. DML *bicarius*.

bield ModE, 'shelter' is a northern word. It usually describes a small mountain hut (We:1·205), as in Beldoo Hill (*Beldhow hill* 1687) We:2·74 (**haugr, hyll**). Later occurrences with animal names indicate local use for a den or 'a natural shelter of rocks, under which an animal could get' (We:1·200): see for example Cat Bield 1847 We:1·200 (**catt**) and the modern name Fox Bield Cu:344.

(*b*) Beeld (f.n.) 1595 YW:7·156, Beilds (f.n.) 1642 YW:6·95.

(*c*) Howes Bield 1859 We (pers.n.), Nan Bield 1823 We (?pers.n.).

~ probably OE *beldo* 'boldness', ME *belde* 'boldness, security'. For a different view, relating it to *bold* (see **boðl**), cf. EPNE:73.

EDD *bield*; OED *bield* sb.

*big ME, 'building'. This term, apparently a derivative of ME *biggen* (< ON *byggja*) and parallel to **bigging**, has not previously been noted. It occurs in *Canonbig* 1372 L:5 (Great Grimsby) and *Newbig* m.13th L:6 (Haxey), the runs of forms (*Canonbyg* 1372, *Canonbigge* 1514; *Neubug* m.13th, *Le Neubygfeld* 1328) clearly excluding **bȳ**.

~ **bigging**.

bigging ME, 'building' is common in the north of England, but early examples are also found surprisingly far south. MED indicates that besides 'building', the senses 'dwelling, habitation' and even 'town' are attested. OED suggests that it came also to have the specific meaning 'an outbuilding as distinguished from a house' in northern dialect.

(*b*) Biggin c.1260 C:142, 1490 Nb [NbDu:21], 1301 Sr:52, *Biggin* 1280 Bk, 1379 YW:5·209, Biggins (*Bygging* 1257) Nt:90, Biggins 1200–26 We:1·43, *Biggyng* (f.n.) 1453 C:313, *Biggyngge* (f.n.) 1361 Ess:575.

(*c*) Combination with **nīwe** is so common as to suggest that the compound functioned as an appellative: *Neubigging* (f.n.) 1329 Bd:292, Newbegin 1310 YN, Newbiggin c.1200 Cu:188, 1202 Cu:184, 1292 Cu:149, 1208–10 Du, 1316 Du, 1187 Nb, 1208–10 Nb, 1242 Nb, 1378 Nb, 1179 We:2·126, 1154–89 [17th] We:2·32, 1190 We:1·37, 1187 YN:104, 1228 YN:262, New Biggin 1274 YW:2·108, *Newbigging* (f.n.) 1185 YW:4·120, 1215 La:155, (f.n.) 1457 C:313. In several examples the novelty wears off: Biggin (*Newbigging* 1223–39) Db:531, Biggin

(*Neubigging* 1240) Db:314, Biggin (*Newbigging* 1244) Db:368, Biggin
(*Neuebiggynge, le Biggyng* 13th) YW:4·63, Bramham Biggin (*Neubiging*
12th) YW. (Bishop 1935–6:17–18 states that *Newbigging* was used of
newly cleared or reclaimed land in Yorkshire in the 12th and 13th
centuries, but this sense is not recorded by the dictionaries and requires
confirmation.)
   Combination with other elements is not common, but the following
have been noted: *Aldbyggyng Strete* (st.n. Richmond) 1536 YN:287 (**ald**),
Dowbiggin 1321 YW (**dūfe**), *Ravenesbiggyng* (f.n.) 13th We:2·163
(**hræfn**/pers.n.), Sunbiggin 1310 We (**sunne**), Arnold's Biggin 1226 YW
(pers.n.), Biggin (*Percybigginge* 1262) YN (pers.n.).
   ~ ON *byggja* 'to settle, dwell, build'. borrowed into ME with all of its
senses as *biggen*. **Bigging** may well be a ME formation from this verb;
ON *bygging/bygning* 'building' appears to be late. Cf. ***big**.
   MED *bigginge*; EDD *biggin(g*; OED *bigging*; cf. OGNS *bygging*.

biker ME, 'dispute, fight'. Terms with similar meaning, like þrēap,
chalenge and *ge*-**flit**, are applied to contested territory. Ownership of
woods forming boundaries seems sometimes to have been disputed, cf.
Threapwood Ch, Threepwood Nb, and *biker* may well appear in the
following instances. Note, however, that the word would be formally
indistinguishable from **bīcere**, and might also be confused with *bȳ-kjarr*
etc. (see **kjarr**).
   (*a*) Bickershaw c.1200 La (**sceaga**), *Bikerwode* (f.n.) 1371 Ru:7, Vicar
Wood (*Bikerwode* c.1220) Db (**wudu**).
   ~ of uncertain origin.
   MED *biker* n.²; EDD *bicker* v. & sb.¹; OED *bicker* sb.²

bilberry ModE, 'bilberry' is recorded relatively early in *Billberry ditch*
(f.n.) 1675 Db:76 (**dīc**). Cf. **blá-ber**.
   ~ possibly of ON origin (OED), **berige**.
   EDD *bilberry*; OED *bilberry*.

bile OE, *m*. 'bill, beak' is used of a pointed projection, either with
reference to topography (a promontory or pointed hill) or to the shape of
a boundary. Note the recurring compound *Cockbill* in Wa (see below), and
the analagous modern f.n. Sparrow Bill Piece Brk:321. Selsey Bill Sx is
considered 'not particularly "beak-like" in shape' (Sx:84), but may have
been altered by coastal erosion. For further discussion, and an instance in
a Wo surname, see MELS:13. *Bile* 'beak' is probably related to OE *bill*
'sword', which may have a similar topographical application—'(?) ridge,
hill'—and from which it could hardly be distinguished. The latter is

preferred by DEPN and Mills 1991 for Bilston ?994 [17th] S:1380 St, which is OE *Bilsǣtnatūn*, **tūn** of the dwellers at *Bill/Bile*. Both *bile* and *bill* may be relevant to the hill-term *****billing**.

(*a*) *Bilefeld* (f.n.) 1348 Brk:307 (**feld**), Bilham 1272–1307 K (**hamm**).

(*b*) Bill Gut (*la bylle* 1527) Sx, *Bilheath* (*the byll heathe* 1562, *the Byll* 1567) St:1·39.

(*c*) *Cockbill* (*to Coccebyle* 998 S:892) Wa:145, *Cockebile* (f.n.) 1199 Wa:145 (**cocc**[2]; and see two further modern instances, one of them in the form *Cockbillock, ibid.*), Portland Bill (*the Bill of Portland* 1649) Do:1·220, Selsey Bill 1740 Sx (both p.ns). Amble 1204 Nb perhaps combines a pers.n. *****Amma** with *bile*.

> DOE *bile*; MED *bile* n.[1]; EDD –; OED *bill* sb.[2]; DES *Biles, Bill*.

billere OE, *m.* and *n.* renders Latin terms for 'cress' in OE glossaries. In ME it denotes any of several water plants used medicinally, especially 'watercress' and 'water-parsnip', and the p.n. element commonly compounds with words denoting watery sites. The use of ModE *bilders, billers* for related water plants characterised by umbrella-shaped flower heads, such as water-dropwort (Wt, D and Co) and perhaps fool's watercress, may explain the subsequent extension of sense in Somerset and western Devon to any plant with this distinguishing feature, such as the dryland species chervil, cow parsley and hognut (EDD, OED). Note that *bilder* 'a horse' (OED) and *bilder* 'a mallet used for breaking clods', 'to level ground by breaking clods' (EDD) may occasionally be relevant alternatives; so too may *biller* 'maker of halberds', attested as a surname (MED *biller(e* n.[1], Fransson:152).

(*a*) Bilbrook (*Bilrebroch* 1086) St, (*Bilrebroc* 1227) So (**brōc**), Billacombe (*Billercombe* 1319) D (**cumb**), *Bilderflatt* (f.n.) 1539 YW:6·64 (**flat**), *Bylremor* 1355 Wa:68 (**mōr**), *Bylrewell* (f.n.) 1337 Brk:50, *Bilrewell* 1206 Wa:68 (**welle**).

> ~ apparently Celtic: cf. Middle Irish *birar, bilar*, Old Cornish *beler* (CPNE:19–20), Welsh *berwr*, Gaulish *berula* 'cress'. MLat *berula* probably comes from Celtic.
>
> DOE *billere*; MED *biller(e* n.[2]; EDD *bilder(s*; OED *bilders*; cf. DML *berula*.

*****billing** OE, *m.* is a hill-term derived from OE *bill* 'sword' (or, as *****biling*, from OE **bile** 'beak') with an *-ing* suffix. It is discussed in detail by Dodgson (1967:326–32 and Ch:1·138–9). He shows that individual names sometimes offer a variety of spellings, suggesting that a range of confusible terms and grammatical forms were in use from an early date. *****Bil(l)ing*, meaning 'hill-place', was accompanied by *****Bil(l)inge*, with assibilation of the final consonant group, representing a locative p.n. 'at *Bil(l)ing*'. Several p.ns indicate—either instead or as well—*Belling(e)*, which could be parallel formations from **belle** 'bell-shaped hill'. And some seem to suggest that folk-names *Bil(l)ingas*/*Bellingas* 'people living at the *Bil(l)*/*Bell*' could alternate with the topographical terms. While the frequent occurrence of the forms, together with topography that is often clearly suitable, indicates that hill-terms are usually to be reckoned with in Billing-/Belling- names, alternative derivations often cannot be ruled out—*Billing*, for instance, is an attested OE pers.n., *Billingas* could be 'followers of *Billa*' or 'people of the sword-blade' etc.

(*a*) Billingborough 1086 L (**burh**), Billington 1196 Bd, 1196 La:71 (**dūn**), Bellingham c.1170, Billingham c.1050 [12th] Du (**hām**), Billinghurst 1241 Sr, Billingshurst 1202 Sx (**hyrst**), Billington 1086 St:1·135 (**tūn**), Bellington Hill 1622 Db (**tūn, hyll**).

(*b*) Billing 1086 Nth, Billinge c.1200 La:104, 13th La:66, 1503 Ch:1·138, 1503 Ch:3·298, 1534–47 Ch:2·198.

binde OE, *f.* 'climbing plant'. In OE the simplex is attested only with the sense 'band, ribbon', but it is applied to a plant in the compound *wudu-binde* (cf. **bend**). In ME the simplex can have the sense 'vine'; ModE dialect *bind, bine* is used of various climbing plants. The element may appear in Binthwaite (*Byndetwayth* 1297) Cu (**þveit**), and perhaps also in Bineham 1296 Sx (**hamm**) and *Byne* 1261 Sx:185, though the form without -*d*- is not certainly recorded before 1548 (OED *woodbine*).
  DOE *binde*; MED *bĭnd(e*; EDD *bind* sb.[1] and sb.[2]; OED *bind* sb., *bine*.

***bing** OE, '(?) a hollow'. This is a difficult element. An OE *bing* seems to be found in *to binguuellan* in the bounds of Icklesham Sx (772 [13th] S:108), while there is a predominantly north-country dialect *bing* recorded with the senses 'heap' and 'bin, receptacle'. The source of the dialect term is likely to be ON *bingr*, which certainly provides the sense 'heap' and perhaps 'bin' as well, for *bingr* also meant 'boxed-off chamber, stall' (and cf. Danish *bing*, Swedish *binge* 'bin'). Presumably, however, ON *bingr* is not the source of the Sussex *binguuellan*, and for this MHG *binge* 'kettle-shaped hollow in the hills' and ModHG *binge* 'forest-ditch' have been compared—'spring in a hollow' seems to offer reasonable sense for the OE compound. Whether ***bing** 'hollow' occurs more widely is uncertain, however. The following names may be relevant:

(*a*) Bingfield 1181 Nb (**feld**), Bingham 1086 Nt (**hām**), *Bingelandes* (f.n.) c.1220 Nt:220 (**land**), Bingletts (*Byngelegh* 1327) Sx, Bingley 1086 YW (**lēah**).

On one hand, several of these could contain the Norse loan-word; on the other, it is striking that all of them have regular early medial -*e*- which would surprisingly suggest the consistent use of an inflected form. To account for the -*e*- it has been suggested that *Binge*- does not represent a common noun, but rather a reduction of an earlier genitival group-name such as *Bynninga* (DEPN); against this, however, is the persistence and completeness of the reduction in all these names (Nt:220–1).

Several Cheshire f.ns contain a common noun of the form *bing*, though it is not clear in which sense:

(*b*) Bing 1838 Ch:3·257, Bings Mdw (*The benges* 1345) Ch:1·185.

(*c*) Far & Near Bing (f.n.) 1838 Ch:2·261.

DOE –. Cf. for dialect 'heap, bin' OGNS *bingr*; MED *bing*; EDD *bing* sb.[1] & sb.[2]; OED *bing* sb.[1]; DES *Bing, Binne*.

binn OE, *f.* 'basket, manger, stall' is perhaps found in Binchester c.1050 [12th] Du (**cæster**). DEPN speculates that 'The old fort may have been used as a shelter for cattle', though since the site is to be identified with Romano-British *Vinovia/Vinovium* the first element may have arisen from some kind of word-play or 'folk-etymology' (PNRB:504). Smith (1980:31–2) has observed that in the Latin of the Hispanic *Vettones*, a tribe known to have provided garrison-troops for the fort, *b* for *v* was frequent, and argues that **Binovia* or **Binobia* may thus have been the form passed on to the Anglo-Saxons.

For Binbrook L Kristensson has suggested that *binn* may appear in a transferred topographical sense 'valley', which would be appropriate to the site (see L:3·2, L:4·xiii).

Note that the term may well have been confused in usage with ***bing**, and that it would often be difficult to distinguish from **binnan**. There was also an OE pers.n. *Bynna* (Redin:61–2).

OE *binne*, a weak variant, is also recorded.

(*a*) *Binboghe* 1426 YW:2·277 (**boga**), Binbrook 1086 L:3·2 (**brōc**), Binfield 1709 YW:2·289 (**feld**), Binn Royd 1536 YW, *Bynsrode* (f.n.) 1275 YW:3·103 (***rod**[1]).

(*b*) *Atte Binne* (surn./f.n.) 1327 L:3·129, Binns 1536 YW:3·90.

~ ?Celtic (cf. Welsh *ben* 'cart').

DOE *binn*; MED *binne* n.; EDD *bin* sb.[1]; OED *bin* sb.; DES *Binne*.

binnan OE, *prep.* 'within' is used elliptically in p.ns of 'a place within'. This is clearly the case with both St Mary's Benniwerk 1239 L [EPNS collection], a church located within the medieval castle (**ge-weorc**) at Stamford, and Bingley's Island K (**ēa**), first recorded in an Anglo-Saxon

Latin charter as *in loco qui dicitur Binnanea . . . inter duos rivos gremiales fluminis quod dicitur Stur* 814 [13th] S:176. The element is used of 'land within' or 'on this side of' in Bembridge 1316 (*infra pontem* 1324) Wt:34 (**brycg**); once known as the Isle of Bembridge, this town was until the 19th century separated from the rest of Wight by a tidal creek and marshes, which could only be crossed by a bridge, built c.1300, at Yarbridge (see Mills 1996:27). In Binbrook Lane (st.n. Cambridge) 1199–1216 C:44 (**brōc**) the sense 'land enclosed by the brook' is preserved, a meaning which may be relevant in other p.ns. Both of the examples of Norbin(s) given below seem to denote a place in the extreme north of a parish or town. Confusion with the OE pers.n. *Bynna* and the element **binn** 'manger, stall' would sometimes be possible.

(*a*) *Byndyche* (f.n.) 1440–1 Brk:419 (**dīc**; the dike is Mere Dyke), Bindon 1154–9 Do:1·189 (**dūn**), Binney 1291 K:122, Binny 1254 K:269 (**ēa**), *Binholme* (*Binham* 13th) Wo (**hamm**), Bin Marsh (f.n.) 1550 Brk:235 (**mersc**), Benwell (*Bynnewalle* c.1050 [12th]) Nb (**wall**; Hadrian's wall), The Binn Wall 1670 Gl:3·138 (**wall**; the sea-wall along the Severn).

(*c*) Norbins Wd (*boscus qui vocatur Northbynn* 1239–40) Brk:316 (**norð**).

(*d*) Barton Bendish (*Bertuna* 1086, *Berton Binnedich* 1249) Nf (**dīc**; Devil's Dyke).

DOE *binnan*; MED *binne* adv. & prep.; OED *bin* adv. & prep.

birce OE, *f.* 'birch-tree' can usually be distinguished in p.ns from the related **berc** by its assibilated final consonant. It sometimes alternates with the derived adjective *bircen and, in the north, spellings in -*k*- suggest the influence of ON **birki**: Birkenhead Ch:4·313 is *Bircheveth* 1190–1216, *Byrkeheveht* 1259, *Byrchenid* 1277 and *Birkenhed* 1278 (**hēafod**). In *Lithtebyrches*, the earliest spelling of Birch Db, the element appears with **lēoht** 'light': the compound may refer to the silver-birch.

The element is attested in OE boundary clauses, e.g. *ofer byrce leage* S:1338 Gl:3·186 (**lēah**). MELS:13–14 gives examples from ME surnames.

The form *Bircheles* recurs in Ch and Db names, e.g. Birchill 1086 Db:110, Birtles m.12th Ch:1·72 and *le Byrcheles* (f.n.) 1280 Ch:2·315. The names perhaps contain an OE diminutive *bircel.

(*a*) With generics denoting 'wood': Bircholt (*on norþweardan Biricholte* 996 [14th] S:877) K [KPN:344], *Bircholt* (f.n.) 1286 Ch:1·79 (**holt**), *Birchehurst* 1272–1307 Brk:62 (**hyrst**), *Bircheleg'* (f.n.) 1265–91 Ch:2·322, *Birchlega* (f.n.) 1139–48 Gl:3·162, *Byrchleyhey* (f.n.) 1423 Ch:2·155 (**lēah**, **ge-hæg**), Birchwood 1269 Db:591 (**wudu**).

With other topographical generics: *Bircheden* (f.n.) 1334 Ch:3·176 (**denu**), *Bircheage* (f.n.) 13th YW:7·158 (?**ēg**), *Birchfurlongesyate* (f.n.)

1347 Ch:3·244 (**furlang, gēat**), *Bircheham* (f.n.) 1448 Gl:1·43 (**hamm**), Birchitt (*Birceheved* c.1260) Db (**hēafod**), Birchills (*Byrchehull* 1275) St [DEPN], Birch Hill 1645 Gl (**hyll**), Bescar (*Birchecar* 1331) La (**kjarr**), Birchover (*Barcovere* 1086) Db, Bircher 1212 He, Birchall c.1300 Ch:3·62 (**ofer²**), *Bircherowe* (f.n.) 1327–77 Ch:2·191 (**rāw**), Ingbirchworth (*Berceuuorde* 1086) YW, Roughbirchworth (*Berceuuorde* 1086) YW (**worð**).

(*b*) Birch 1202 Brk:246, 1252 He, Birch Hall (*del Byrches* 1418) Db, *la Birche* (f.n.) c.1240 Gl:3·180, 1265–91 Ch:2·185, *le Byrches* (f.n.) 13th Ch:2·109.

(*c*) Birch (*Lithtebyrches* 1251) Db:60 (**lēoht**), Freebirch (*Threbirches* 1271) Db (**þrēo**), Heybridge (*Heyebirches* m.13th) Ch:1·194 (**hēah**).

~ **berc, *bircen, *bircet, birki**.

DOE *byrc*; MED *birch(e*; EDD –; OED *birch* sb.; DES *Birch*.

*bircen OE, *adj.* 'birchen, growing with birch-trees' seems to alternate with **birce** in Birkenhead Ch (see **birce**): the spelling in -*k*- may suggest the influence of ON **birki** here as in other northern names. In simplex names the adjective appears to be used elliptically of 'a place where birch-trees grow'.

In ME and later spellings the element would be hard to distinguish from inflected forms of **birce**.

(*a*) With words denoting or suggesting woodland: *le Birchenegrof* (f.n.) e.14th Ch:1·103, Birchen Grove 1282 Gl (**grāf**), *Bircheneleg'* (f.n.) 1320 Ch:4·19, Birchinlee 1285 Db (**lēah**), *Birkinroid* (f.n.) c.1190 YW:3·42 (***rod¹**), Birkenshaw 1274 YW, *le Byrchenschawe* (f.n.) 1357 Ch:3·244, *le Byrchineschagh* (f.n.) c.1325 Ch:1·192 (**sceaga**).

With other topographical terms: Birchencliff 1611 Ch:1·133, *Birchencliffe* (f.n.) 1306 Ch:4·6 (**clif**), Birch Clough (*Birkinclough* 1589) YW (***clōh**), *Le Birchyn Close* (f.n.) 1547 Brk:301 (**clos**), *Burchencrofte* (f.n.) 1551–2 Brk:182 (**croft**), *le Birchenfeld* (f.n.) 1334 Ch:2·70 (**feld**), *Le Bircheneflattes* (f.n.) 1315 Ch:1·217 (**flat**), *Byrchenehalflond* (f.n.) 1321 Ch:4·63 (**half, land**), Birchenough 1285 Db, (f.n.; *del Byrchenhalgh* 1354) Ch:1·156 (**halh**), *Burchyn haye* (f.n.) 1606 Gl:2·100 (**ge-hæg**), *Birchenhewed* (f.n.) 12th [17th] Ch:2·50 (**hēafod**), *le birchenehul* (f.n.) 1313 Ch:3·322 (**hyll**), *le Birchenlond* (f.n.) 13th Ch:2·221 (**land**), Birkenside 1262 Nb (**sīde**).

(*b*) Birkin c.1030 YW, Birkinheath (cf. *de Berkyn* 1348) Ch:2·58.

~ **birce**.

DOE –; MED *birchen*; EDD *birchen*; OED *birchen*.

*bircet OE, 'birch copse' occurs predominantly in p.ns of the south-east. The analogous formation *bercet* (with **berc** rather than **birce**) may perhaps be recorded late as far north as Ru (see **berc**), but cf. Birchitt Db:198, which is shown by medieval spellings to involve **birce** and **hēafod**.

MELS:14 presents many further examples from Sx and Sr surnames.
(*a*) *Burchat Coppis* (f.n.) 1650–1 Brk:99 (**copeis**), Birchetts (*Birchettfeld* 1239) K (**feld**).
(*b*) *la Berchitte* 1294 Sr:359, *Birchet* (f.n.) 1206 Ess:578, *Le Birchet* (f.n.) 1420 Brk:124, Birchett Copse (*le Byrchet* 1462) Sr, Birchett Wood (cf. *Byrchletts* 1562) K, Birchetts Green 1296 Sx, Birchetts Plantation c.1280 Sr, Birchett's Wood 1327 Sx, Burkitt's Lane (*Birchet* 1291) Ess.
~ **birce, -et.**
DOE –; MED –; EDD –; OED –; DES *Birchett.*

birki ON, *n.* 'place growing with birch-trees, birch wood' is generally to be distinguished from OE **birce** by final -*k* (though this might sometimes have arisen in **birce** from the influence of OE **berc**). *Birk-* may represent a Scandinavianisation of **birce**, and in Birklands Nt, recorded as *Birchwude* in 1188, there is an example of a complete substitution of ON for OE. This instance seems to indicate incidentally that, though **birki** was properly a collective noun 'a group of birch-trees', it came to be used in England identically with words for specific singular 'birch'. The ON specific term was *bjǫrk*, which has not been identified in English names (though it would be indistinguishable from **berc**).
(*a*) Birker 1279 Cu (***ǽrgi**), Birk Beck 1279 We (**bekkr**), Birk Fell 1279 We (**fjall**), Birka 1281 YW:5·187 (**haugr**), *Birkeheued* c.1150 We:2·186 (**hēafod**), Birklands 1251 Nt (**lundr**), *Birkshaw* 1278 We (**sceaga**), Briscoe 1230 YW:5·49, c.1250 YN:306 (**skógr**), *Birketon* (surn.) 1308 Y [METT:49] (**tūn**), Birthwaite 12th YW:1·319, Burthwaite 1323 We (**þveit**), Birkwith 1189–94 YW:6·218 (**viðr**).
(*b*) Birks 1292 YW:6·118, The Birks 1330 Db.
(*c*) Brown Birks 1331 YW (**brūn**[1]).
~ **berc, birce.**
OGNS – (cf. *birkiviðr, björk*).

biscop OE, *m.* 'bishop' occurs in OE charter forms of Stoke Bishop Gl, *æt Bisceopes stoce* 969 [11th] S:1317 and *æt Bysceopes stoce* 984 [11th] S:1346. It is usually applied in p.ns to the possessions and manors of a bishopric, though occasionally reference may be to a particular bishop— Bishopstrow 1086 W (**trēow**) owes its name to legendary association with St Aldhelm, an Anglo-Saxon Bishop of Sherborne. In names where the element appears as an affix, Lat *episcopus* is often recorded significantly earlier: thus Bishop's Caundle, a manor owned by the bishops of Salisbury, appears as *Kaundele Episcopi* from 1268 and with the English element in 1294 (Do:3·311), while Bishop Thornton YW, in the Archbishop of York's manor of Ripon, is *Thornton episcopi* as early as 1198, almost 200 years before *biscop* appears in the name. Where the identity of the bishop or bishopric is not known, such p.ns may sometimes contain the derived OE pers.n. *Biscop*, as perhaps in Bishopdale 1202 YN (**dæl**). Several names evidence the contracted form *bisp* (OED s.v.).

In the north and east it would not be possible to distinguish a Scandinavianised *biscop* from ON *biskup*: an example is Biscathorpe 1086 L (**þorp**).

(*a*) Bear Wd (*Bissopesbir'* 1256) Brk (**bǣr** or **bearu**), Bustabeck (*Biscopbek'* 1285) Cu:244 (**bekkr**), Bushbury (*Byscopesbyri* ?994 [17th] S:1380 St (**burh**), Biscot 1086 Bd (**cot**), Bushcomb (*Bisshopescumbe* 1299) Gl (**cumb**), Bispediche 1354 [14th] Ch:4·130 (**dīc**), Bisshopefeld (f.n.) 1352 We:1·94 (**feld**), Bischophalle 1310 L:1·32 (**hall**), Bispham 1190–1213 La:136 [& Kenyon:77], 1086 La:156 (**hām**), *Bisschopishaye* (f.n.) 1353 Ch:3·284 (*ge*-**hæg**), Biscopholm (f.n.) 1184–90 We:2·234 (**holmr**), Bishop's Moor 1481 YW (**mōr**), *Byshopesrudyng* (f.n.) 1302 Gl:2·170 (***ryding**), Bishopside 1459 YW (**sīde**), *Byschopeslade* (f.n.) 1276 Gl:3·213 (**slæd**), *Byshopstelles* (f.n.) 1362 YW:4·39 (**stell**), *Biscopsti* (f.n.) 13th YW:7·158 (**stīg**), *Biscopstrothes* (f.n.) 12th YW:5·179 (**storð**), Bishopstone 1227 Bk, 1166 He, Bishopton c.1030 YW, Bishton 1061–5 Gl, 1086 Sa:1·49, 1086 St, Bushton 1242 W (**tūn**), *Biscopethweyt* 1285 Cu:244 (**þveit**), Bishopsworth 1086 So (**worð**), Bishop's Wood 1270 Gl–He, Bishopwood 1655 YW, Bushwood 1197 Wa (**wudu**).

(*d*) Bishop Monkton 1402 YW, Bishop's Caundle 1268 Do:3·311, Bishop's Cleeve 1284 Gl, Bishop's Sutton 1167 Ha, Bishopstoke c.1270 Ha, Bishopthorpe 1275 YW, Cropwell Bishop 1280 Nt.

DOE *bisceop*; MED *bishop*; EDD *bishop* sb.; OED *bishop* sb.; DES *Bishop*.

bismer OE, *m.* or *n.* (and once *f.*) 'shame, disgrace'. In *Bismereforlong* (f.n.) 1248–52 Brk:321 (**furlang**), this perhaps alludes to the site of a medieval crime (Field:21); alternatively it may be a derogatory term for the land (Brk:540). In *Bysmarerowe* (f.n.) 1307 YW:2·111 (**rāw**), houses of ill-repute may be denoted.

DOE *bysmor*; MED *bĭ-smār(e*; EDD –; OED *bismer* sb.

bite ME, 'bit' is found in minor names where it is often taken to mean 'small piece of land'. This is possible, though the dictionaries do not offer independent examples of the usage. The senses 'food for animals' and 'pasturage' are better supported (cf. OED *bit* sb.[2] sense 1b, EDD *bite* sense 3, ON **beit**) and would perhaps better suit some of the compounds noted below.

ME *bite* is derived from two OE words: *bita* 'piece bitten off, morsel' and *bite* 'a bite'. The equivalent ON pair *bit, biti* could also be involved. 'Dog-bite' is evidently the meaning in *Hundebite* (f.n.) 13th YW:7·159 (**hund**[1]), but the significance is unknown.

(*a*) *Byteleyes* (f.n.) 1627 Ru:46 (**lēah**), *Bytenooke* (f.n.) 1627 Ru:46 (**noke**).

(*b*) *Bitts* in 16th-century and later Cu f.ns; see Cu:461.

(*c*) *Benbytes* (f.n.) 1316 YW:7·159 (**bēan**), *Dunnebitis* (f.n.) 1227 YW:7·159 (**dunn**), *Wytebite* (f.n.) 1267 YW:7·159 (**hwīt**), *Litelbyte* (f.n.) 13th YW:7·159 (**lȳtel**), Sweet Bits 1617 YW (**swēte**), *Gibbs Bitt* (f.n.) 1632 Ru:186 (pers.n.).

~ **beit**.

DOE *bita*[2], *bite*; MED *bite*; EDD *bit* sb.[1], *bite* sb.; OED *bit* sb.[1] & sb.[2], *bite* sb.

bitela OE, *m.* 'insect, grub, beetle' seems originally to have been applied in OE and ME to various kinds of biting parasite.

(*a*) *Bitelfelde* (f.n.) 1462 YW:2·245 (**feld**), *Bittewell* (f.n.) 1610 (*Bittlewell* 1684) Ru:100 (**welle**).

~ **bite**.

DOE *bitela*; MED *bitil*; EDD –; OED *beetle* sb.[2]

biter OE, *adj.* 'bitter' appears in f.ns, where it may be used of waterlogged land (cf. **sūr**)—the sense 'brackish' is attested (DOE, MED). It may also be used in a figurative sense as a derogatory name for unproductive fields. It would be hard to distinguish from ME *bitter* 'water-carrier', which has been suggested for *Biterham* Gl.

(*a*) *Biterham* (f.n.) 1250–75 Gl:1·55 (**hamm**), Bitterum (f.n.; *Bitterholm* c.1235) C:362 (**holmr**), *Bittermede* (f.n.) 1251 C:362 (**mēd**).

DOE *biter*; MED *bitter* n.; EDD *bitter*; OED *bitter* a. & sb.[1]

bjórr ON, *m.* 'beaver' is more likely than a pers.n. or OE *bera* 'bear' in:

(*a*) Barbon 1086 We (**brunnr**), Bardale 1280 YN (**dalr**; perhaps **á, dalr**).

~ **beofor**.

OGNS *bjórr*.

blá-ber ON, *n.* 'bilberry'. 'Blaeberry' survives in northern dialect. Note that some spellings preserve the ON form of the second element: OE **berige** came to be substituted, and appears in all the instances in MED,

EDD and OED.

(*a*) Blaberry Croft 1558 YW (**croft**), *Blabirland* (f.n.) 13th YW:1·297 (**land**), *Blaberimorgate* (f.n.) e.14th YN [Lindkvist 1912:177] (**mōr, gata**), *Blaburthwaite* (*Blaberithweyt* 1272, *Blayberthwayt* 1380) Cu:201 (**þveit**).

~ **blár, beger, berige**; cf. **bilberry**.

OGNS *bláber*; MED *blō-berī*; EDD *blaeberry*; OED *blaeberry*.

*blakno- Brit, 'point, summit'. The PrW and PrCu form of the element would have been **blain* (see LHEB:362 n.1, JEPNS:1·44). In Blennerhasset and Blencow ON elements seem to have been added to names beginning with *Blen-*: their original second elements cannot be recognised. Initial *P-* appears in all the forms of Plenmeller and, if the element is correctly identified, presumably represents an early English substitution.

(*a*) Blencow 1231 Cu (**haugr**), Blennerhasset 1188 Cu (**hēg, sǽtr**), Blencarn 1159 Cu (**karno-*), Blindcrake 1154–89 Cu (**krakjo-*), Blencogo c.1190 Cu (**kukā*), Plenmeller 1256 Nb (**mailo-, *brigā*).

GPC *blaen*; CPNE *blyn*.

*blak-ote ME, 'black oats', a cultivated species distinguished from the red oat, the pill oat and the rough oat (OED).

(*a*) *Blakeoteacre* (f.n.) 1450 Db:435 (**æcer**), *Blachateridding* (f.n.) c.1200 We:1·49 (**ryding*).

~ **blæc, āte**.

MED −; EDD −; cf. OED *oat* sense 2a.

blanche OFr, *adj.* (*f.*) 'white'. The masculine equivalent *blanc* has been thought to appear in Aston Blank 1685 Gl with an extended sense 'bare' (in 1194 the name has the affix Cold and in 1275 *frigida*). However, this sense is not attested in ME, and this form of the element would be difficult to distinguish from the derived French surname *Blanc*. The feminine *blanche* is perhaps easier to identify in p.ns (though this also appears as a surname). It often refers to the colour of the soil: Blanch 1153 YE was in its earliest spelling *Blanchemarl* (**marle**), named from the chalk pits in the area, and *the blanch field* (f.n.) 1611 Ch:1·192 (**feld**) is opposed to the field called *the black Earth* in the same parish. *Blauncheland* (f.n.) 1422 We:2·134 may also belong among the straightforward names, combined with OE **land**. The name of the abbey of Blanchland Nb (*Blanchelande* 1165, *Alba landa* 1203), however, may have been transferred from the well-known abbey of Blanchelande near Cherbourg, Normandy (DEPN, NbDu:25), which contains OFr **launde**

'glade, woodland pasture' as second element.

AND *blanc*; AFW *blanc*; MED *blaunk*; EDD –; OED *blanch* a., *blank* a.

blanda ON, *f.* 'a mixture of fluids (especially of milk and water)', from *blanda* 'to mix, blend', cannot be distinguished from an ON byname *Blanda* (probably with the force 'wishy-washy'). There are Scandinavian parallels for a r.n. of this form meaning 'muddy' or 'milky', and this may well appear in Blansby 1086 YN (**bȳ**) (SSNY:22, Janzén 1957:203–7) and in *the Blande* 14th We:2·60. *Bland* 1226 YW, however, refers to a hillside, and it has been suggested that it might denote something 'mixed up and disorderly' (We:2·61). Alternatively, Ekwall (DEPN) speculates that this name may contain the OE cognate *(ge)bland*, also 'mixture', but used in images for 'tumult, storm'—the site is high and exposed.

OGNS *blanda*.

blár ON, *adj.* 'lead-coloured, the colours of a bruise, dark'. ME *blo* probably had also the extended sense 'cheerless, cold, exposed' which is recorded in northern dialect *blae*. There may have been influence from OFr *blo*, *bloi* 'pale, blue, sad' and perhaps from OE *blāwan* 'to blow' (cf. *blāw, from which *blár* cannot always be securely distinguished).
(*a*) Blea Beck 12th We, 1280 We, 1325 We (**bekkr**), *blabargh* (f.n.) c.1414 L:4·70, *blabergh* (f.n.) e.13th L:3·66 (**berg**), *Blafen* (f.n.) e.13th L:3·73 (**fenn**), Bleagate 1279 Cu (**gata**), Blagill 1278 Cu, Blea Gill 1580 YW:6·118 (**gil**), *Blailand'* (f.n.) 1259 L:3·111 (**land**), Blayshaw 1346 YW (**sceaga**), *Blosike* 1276 YW:2·15 (**sík**), Blasterfield (*Blascher* c.1160 [13th]) We (**sker**), Bleatarn 1199 We:2·82 [& JEPNS:2·71], c.1240 Cu:92 (**tjǫrn**), Blow Gill (*Blawathgila* 1170–2) YN (**vað, gil**), Bleawick 1256 We, Blea Wyke 1108–14 YN (**vík**), Blawith 1276 La (**viðr**).
(*d*) Blo Norton 1291 Nf.
 ~ **blá-ber, *blāw, blǽingr.**

OGNS *blár*; MED *blō* adj.; EDD *blae, bloa*; OED *blae, blo*; DES *Blaw*.

*blather ME, 'liquid mud, slime, sludge' survives in L and Y dialect (EDD). It appears early in the YW f.n. *Blather*, described as a *stagnum* 'pool', and *Blether hill'* YW, described as 'a moss hill' (cf. **mos** 'bog').
(*a*) *Blether hill'* (f.n.) 1594 YW:3·209 (**hyll**).
(*b*) *Blather* (f.n.) 12th YW:5·152.

MED –; EDD *blather* sb.²; OED –.

*blāw OE, *adj.* 'blue'. The evidence relating to this word in OE is problematic. A noun *blāw* '(blue) pigment' is usually deduced from the Erfurt III gloss *blata: pigmentum, hauiblauum*, though the details of this gloss (and even the language of the sequence *hauiblauum*) do not appear straightforward. Nonetheless, an adjective *blǣ* (presumably for **blǣw*) is attested once, and forms the basis of *blǣhǣwen* and *blǣwen*. *Blǣ(w)* would be an *i*-mutated form of **blāw*, which would be expected to exist on the evidence of cognates, though its scarcity suggests that it died out early. *Hǣwen* was the more general word for the colour in OE; in ME this came to be replaced by OFr **bleu** and ON **blár**.

The extent to which **blāw* may appear in p.ns is then another question. It might be suggested that OE *blāwan* 'to blow' might be involved either directly (a noun *blou* 'blast of wind' is attested in ME and could enter into names) or indirectly (by influencing the sense of 'blue' towards 'windy, exposed'). There is also ON *blár*, from which **blāw* might formally be distinguished in ME by the retention of final *u̯*, though it would clearly be possible either for **blāw* to lose the semi-vowel in combination, or for *blár* to gain it by analogy, so that the distinction cannot be rigorously maintained.

Formally, moreover, any of the names except Blofield Nf, which has early forms in *Bla-*, *Blawe-*, might alternatively be related to OE *blōwan* 'to bloom'. OED notes, however, that the noun *blow* 'blossom' seems to be 'of recent origin'—its first citations come from the 18th century.
(*a*) Blowden 1270 D (**dūn**), Blofield 1086 Nf (**feld**), Blowhead 1438 C (**hēafod**), *Blouhulle* (f.n.) 12th Gl:2·38, *blowe hill* (f.n.) 1577–80 L:3·11 (**hyll**), *Blowelond* (f.n.) 1378 D:282, *Blowland* (f.n.) 1631 Ru:263, *Blowlande* (f.n.) 1601 L:4·187 (**land**).
(*b*) *the Blowes* (f.n.) 1688 Ru:217.
   ~ **blár**
   MED –; EDD –; OED –; DES *Blaw*; cf. DOE *blǣ*.

blāwere OE, *m*. 'blower' is attested in OE in the sense 'furnace' and in ME both as the term for a smelter (one who operates the bellows in a foundry; cf. ***ore-blowere**) and for the bellows themselves. ME also records the senses 'horn' and 'hornblower' (cf. **horn-blāwere**) and a figurative application to a braggard or gossip (cf. EDD *blow* v.² sense 13(1)). The term could reflect any of these senses, and may of course appear in the p.n. instance as the derived ME surname.
(*a*) *Blauoruland* (f.n.) 1380 YW:4·11 (**land**).
   ~ OE *blāwan* 'to blow'; **horn-blāwere**, ***ore-blowere**.
   DOE *blāwere*; MED *blouere*; EDD –; OED *blower*¹; DES *Blower*.

blæc OE, *adj*. 'black' is often formally indistinguishable from its antonym *blāc* 'pale, white'. Under normal circumstances, *blāc* would come into

ME as *blōk* (*blāk* remaining in the north), *blæc* as *blak*. But, partly as a result of regular sound-changes, such as the shortening of *blāc-* in compounds, and the lengthening of the open syllable in inflected *blacan*, the two words can hardly be kept apart; ME *blak* and *blok* can each mean either 'pale' or 'black' (MED).

In p.ns, therefore, the elements can normally only be distinguished by context. Blockmoor, Block Moors and Blockfen, the names of peat marshes in C, are likely to go back to *blæc*. Linguistic context, especially the interchange of *blac-* with other elements, can also be helpful. Black Burn Cu has early spellings from ON **bleikr** 'pale', which supports a derivation from *blāc* (cf. *Blaykeburn* c.1170 with a diphthong and *Blacheburne* 1189–99 without). Similarly, ModE *bleak*, recorded outside p.ns from the 16th century, sometimes appears to alternate with spellings which indicate *blæc/blāc* and *bleikr*: Bleak Bank YW:6·233 (**banke**) is recorded as *Blaikebank* 1608, *Blakebanke* and *Blekebanke* 1621. Two Westmorland streams called Black Beck have sporadic spellings in *Bla-*, from ON **blár** 'blue, dark', suggesting that the English element is *blæc*—one, in Middleton parish, is *Blabec* 1180–1206 and *Blakebec* 1260; the other, near Bowness, is *Blacbec* 1170–84 and *Blabec* 1200–14 (We:1·3–4, ERN:36).

In early ModE, *black* may also have the sense 'fertile' in contrast to *white* 'infertile' (Ru:286), and in the combinations *black acre* (OED; cf. *le Blakacres* (f.n.) 1432 Ch:4·195) and *black-crop* (OED *black* a. sense 19), can refer to the cultivation of peas and beans as opposed to that of corn.

In *Blackmooneday buske* (f.n.) 1608 YW:1·75 (***buskr**), 'Black Monday' is Easter Monday, considered unlucky.

Examples with *o*-spellings (where there could also be confusion with **blok** 'stump, log'):

(*a*) Block Fen (*le Blokfen* 1340) C:250 (**fenn**), Blockmoor (*Blokmoor* 1397) C:198, Block Moors (*Blockemor* 1326) C:230, (*Blokemor* 1459) C:241 (**mōr**).

Examples with *a*-spellings:

(*a*) *Blakebroc* (f.n.) 1147–54 YW:6·37 (**brōc**), Blackborough 1086 D, c.1150 Nf (**burh**), Blackburn 1086 La, 1313 Du [NbDu:24] (**burna**), Blakedon (*Blakedene* 1280) Db (**denu**), Blagdon 1086 So, 1234 Do:2·207, 1238 D:77, 1242 D:518, 1244 D:123 etc. (**dūn**), Blakeney 1185 Gl:3·251, 1242 Nf (**ēg**), *Blakefenne* (surn.) 1297 Sr [MELS:15] (**fenn**), *Blackamore* (*mora de Blachou* c.1160) YN (**haugr, mōr**), Blakeley (*Blakelowefurlang* 13th) Db (**hlāw**), Blacup 1226 YW (**hop**), *Blakehurst* (surn.) 1262 Sx

[MELS:15] (**hyrst**), Blacklache c.1250 La (***læcc**), Blackmoor 1212 Do:3·274, Blackmore 1213 Ess (**mōr**), *Blacmyld* (f.n.) 1275 [16th] Ru:302 (***mylde**), Blackrod c.1188–9 La:45 [& Kenyon:37] (***rod**[1]), *Blakroodes* (f.n.) 1619 Ru:72 (**rōd**[1]), Blaxton 1213 YW (**stān**), *Blakestrod* (sum.) 1296 Sx [MELS:16] (**strōd**), Blackwell 1086 Db:46, 978 [11th] S:1337 Wo:172, 1100–35 [14th] Db:212 (**welle**). (*d*) Black Notley 1252 Ess.

~ ***blak-ote, *blæc-berige, *blæcen, *blæc-þorn, bleikr.**
Pale: DOE *blāc*; MED *blǎk* a. sense 6, *blōk* a.; EDD *blake* adj.[1-2]; OED *blake* a., *blok(e* a.
Dark: DOE *blæc*; MED *blǎk* a., *blōk* a.; EDD *black*; OED *black* a., *blok(e* a.

*blæc-berige OE, *f.* 'blackberry, bramble' is not recorded in OE as a 'true' compound, though the combination appears several times in glosses to Latin plant-names with the adjective inflected, as *blæcu berie* (DOE s.v. *blæc*).

(*a*) Bleaberry Gill (*Blakberygyll* 1307–27 [16th]) Cu:5 (**gil**), *blakberegreves* (f.n.) 1466 Ch:3·256 [& Ch:5·xxxvii] (**grǽfe**), *Blakeberilond* (f.n.) 12th Gl:2·50 (**land**), Blackpennywall (*Blakbery Wall* 1633) Gl (**welle**).

~ **blæc, berige.**
DOE s.v. *blæc*; MED *blǎk-berie* s.v. *blǎk* adj. sense 4d; EDD *blackberry*; OED *blackberry*.

*blǽcen OE, 'bleaching' has been suggested for Blashenwell Do, site of a calcareous spring (Do:1·9). It is also possible in *Blechefeld* We, perhaps with reference to the bleaching of cloth there. Either the present participle of the verb 'to bleach' (OED *bleaching* ppl.a) or the verbal noun with the sense 'bleachery' (OED *bleaching* vbl.sb.[1] sense 2) appears in later f.ns.
Blexterehole (f.n.) 1292 Nf:1·91 **hol**[1] is first recorded as *Blekestereshole*, and may contain the ME *nomina agentis bleikstere* (MED) or the derived surname (Fransson:109).
(*a*) Bleaching Croft (f.n.) 1840 Ch:2·303 (**croft**), *Blechefeld* (f.n.) 1425 We:2·8 (**feld**), *Bleachinge garthes* (f.n.) 1600 L:1·179, *bleaching garth* (f.n.) 1671 L:2·306 (**garðr**), Blashenwell 955 [14th] S:573 Do:1·8–9 (**welle**).

~ OE *blǽcan* 'to bleach'; *blāc* (see **blæc**).
DOE –; MED *blēchinge*; EDD –; OED *bleaching* ppl.a. & vbl.sb.[1].

*blæc-þorn OE, *m.* 'blackthorn, sloe-tree' occurs in phrases of the type *of þane blake þornen* S:485 Do in OE boundary clauses, though a true compound form with uninflected adjective is not attested in OE.

(*a*) *Blackthornemedowe* (f.n.) 1436 Gl:3·235 (**mēd**).
(*b*) Blackthorn 1190 O, Blackthorns 1626 Gl, *Blakethorn* (f.n.) 13th Db:498, *les Blakethornes* (f.n.) 1333 Db:625, Blaythorn 1255 Wo.
The variant **blæc-þyrne*, a feminine form with *i*-mutation in the final element, may preserve some distinction in meaning (see **þorn**). It is also attested, with inflected adjective, in OE boundaries (e.g. *on ða blacan þyrne* S:1599 Wo).
(*b*) *Blakethurne* (f.n.) 1250–60 Gl:1·139, *Blakeyern* (f.n.) e.13th Brk:341, *Le Blakeyurne* (f.n.) 13th Brk:327.

~ **blæc, þorn.**

> DOE –; MED *blak-thorn* s.v. *blăk* a. 4; EDD *blackthorn*; OED *black-thorn*; DES *Blackthorn*.

blæd OE, *n.* 'blade, leaf' may have a topographical sense such as 'ledge, terrace' in Chesterblade 1065 So (**cæster**) and the surname *del Blad* 1332 Y [METT:21]. In *Gibbon˙Blades* 1630 L:3·137 (surn.) and *the Blades* (f.n.) 1630 L:3·140, the sense is perhaps 'grassland', extended from 'blade of grass'.

~ ***bur-blade.**

> DOE *blæd*; MED *blăd(e*; EDD *blade* sb.[1]; OED *blade* sb.

blædre OE, *f.* 'bladder' appears in the London st.n. Bladder Street. This is one of the city's chief butchers' quarters, said to have been named from the sale there of bladders, which were used to make various products from fishing floats to medicines (Ldn:77). However, the word seems also to have been used as a plant-name—it apparently glosses *berula* 'cardamine' in a 15th-century herbal (OED *bladder* sense 8), and occurs in the modern names of plants like *bladderwort* and *bladderwrack*. In this sense it has been suggested for Blatherwycke 1086 Nth (**wīc**), though the identification is far from secure (Wa:xlvi, JEPNS:1·12, Ekwall 1957:138).
(*a*) Bladder Street (st.n. London) 1603 (**strēt**).

> DOE *blǣdre*; MED *bladdre*; EDD *bladder*; OED *bladder* sb.

blǣge OE, *f.* 'blay, gudgeon; a small freshwater fish'. The gen.pl. *blǣgna* may combine with **ford** in Blandford (*Blaneford* 1086) Do:2·87 and *Blaneford* (f.n.) 1276 Gl:3·55. For Blannicombe (*Blanecumbe* 1238) D, the combination *blǣgna*, **ēa**, **cumb** 'valley of the blay river' has been suggested (Ekwall 1931:62), though there are other possibilities (D:639–40).

> DOE *blǣge*; MED –; EDD –; OED *blay* sb.

blǽingr ON, *m.* 'the dark one' is recorded as a poetical term for a raven (LexPoet *blæingr*), but in p.ns is applied to rivers and, in the case of Blean, transferred to a settlement (ERN:37). The word also occurs as a pers.n. and it is probably as a pers.n. that it seems to appear as the first element in Blingsby 1086 Db (SSNEM:37–8).

(*a*) Blean (*Blayngbek* 1153) YN (**bekkr**).
(*b*) Bleng 1391 Cu.

~ **blár.**

OGNS –.

blēat OE, *adj.* 'wretched, miserable' is the etymon of ME *blete* 'bare' and southern dialect *bleat* 'cold, bleak' (EDD). It seems to appear in Bleatham c.1121 Sx:101 (**hām**) and *La Blete More* (f.n.) 1240 Brk:213 (**mōr**).

DOE *blēat*; MED *blēt* adj. & n. (cf. *blǣð*); EDD *bleat*; OED *blete*.

bleikr ON, *adj.* 'pale' would generally be identical to the ON pers.n. *Bleiki*. It can be distinguished from the cognate OE *blāc* by its diphthong, which—as examples given under **blæc** illustrate—sometimes alternates in p.ns with the -*a*- and -*e*- forms proper to *blāc* and ModE *bleak*. This latter word is of uncertain origin; one suggestion is that it originates in 16th-century spellings of ME *bleik* (OED).

(*a*) Blaika 1793 We (**haugr**), Blaithwaite 1278 Cu (**þveit**).

~ **blāc.**

OGNS *bleikr*; MED *bleik*; OED *blayk(e* (cf. EDD *blake* adj.[1–2]; OED *blake* a.).

blēo OE, *n.* 'appearance, colour' is apparently used with adjectival force to mean 'coloured, variegated'. Comparable recorded OE compounds include *blēo-bord* 'gaming board', where *blēo* presumably means 'coloured' or 'checked', and *blēo-stǣning* 'coloured stonework', which glosses a lemma (wrongly) interpreted as 'mosaic' (see DOE). Of the p.ns, the hillside of Bleadon So is said to have 'green parts interchanging with white, where the limestone comes to the surface' (DEPN), while the soil at Blewbury is 'creamy-white chalk', which would give a variegated appearance when under cultivation (Brk:153).

(*a*) Blewbury ?942 [13th] S:496 Brk (**burh**), Bleadon 956 [12th] S:606 So (**dūn**), ?Blea Moor (*Blemor* 1293) YW (**mōr**).

DOE *blēo*; MED *blę̄*; EDD *blee* sb.[1], *bly*; OED *blee, bly.*

blesi ON, *m.* 'bare spot on a hillside', transferred from 'white spot (on a horse's forehead), blaze'. Formally it cannot be distinguished from a byname *Blesi*, though this name is not common (SSNEM:37). See Ekwall 1920.

(*a*) Bleasby 956 [14th] S:659 Nt, Bleasby 1086 L (**bȳ**), Bleasdale 1228 La (**dalr**).

(*b*) Blaes 1588 We, Blease 1420 We:1·127, Bleaze a.1219 La.

OGNS (R&T) *blesi* (cf. OGNS *blesóttr*).

ge-bletsod OE, *past part. adj.* 'blessed, happy' appears in *le Blesedrode* (f.n.) 1377 Db:59, where it might be combined with **rod*[1] 'clearing' or rōd[2] 'cross'. The former combination might designate a field owned by the church or denote productive land; the latter would appear to refer to a (?the) holy cross. Perhaps the ambiguity is deliberate.

~ OE *ge-bletsian* 'to bless'.

DOE *ge bletsod*; MED *blessod*; EDD *blessed*; OED *blessed*; DES *Blessed*.

bleu OFr, *adj.* 'blue'. The compound 'bluestone' in *Blueston feild* (f.n.) 1630 L:4·154 may refer to copper sulphate (OED *blue* a. sense 12c).

(*a*) *the blew acre* (f.n.) 1662 L:1·179 (**æcer**), Blue Burnings 1540 YW (**brún**[2], **eng**), *Blewlands* (f.n.) 1566 Db:273 (**land**), Bloomer Hill 1579 YW (**mýrr**), Blue Scar 1579 YW:6·114 (**sker**), *the Blewe Stone* 1620 Ch:5·84 (**stān**).

~ cf. **blár**, ***blāw**.

AND *blef*; AFW *blo*; MED *bleu* adj.; EDD –; OED *blue* a.

blind OE, *adj.* 'blind', indistinguishable from ON *blindr*, appears in p.ns meaning 'concealed', 'dark' or 'closed at one end' (cf. DOE senses 4–6, MED senses 3–4). With reference to streams—a usage attested in OE boundary clauses like *to þere blinde wylle* S:115 Gl and *on þone blindan will* S:1003 D—the sense is probably 'overgrown' or 'underground'. Blind Hardwick (*Herdwic* 12th, *Blynd Hardwicke* 1584) YW:2·79 is so called because there is no thoroughfare through the hamlet.

(*a*) *Blind Beck* 1190–1210 We:1·4, Blind Beck 1549 YW:6·221 (**bekkr**), *Blindeburn* 1228 Nb [ERN:37] (**burna**), Blind Gate (st.n. Bristol) 1285 (*portam cecam* 1492) Gl:3·86, *Blind Gate* (st.n Gloucester) 1455 Gl:2·127 (**geat**), *Blyndkelde* (f.n.) a.1300 We:2·186, Blind Keld 1323 Cu (**kelda**), Blind Lane 1709 YW:3·116, 1735 YW:3·163, *le Blynde Lane* (f.n.) 1549 Ru:185 (**lane**), Blind Meend 1609 Gl:3·227 (**munede**), Blindtarn Gill 1717 We (**tjǫrn**, **gil**), *Blindwell* c.1270 O:13, *Blindewelle* (f.n.) 12th YW:1·273, *Blyndwell* (f.n.) 1205–11 YW:6·164 (**welle**).

DOE *blind*; MED *blĭnd* a.; EDD *blind* adj.; OED *blind* a.; DES *Blind*.

blīðe OE, *adj.* 'blithe' ranges in meaning from 'cheerful, merry' to 'quiet, gentle'. In r.ns, where the element is most common, either of these extremes may be applicable, or the sense may be no more specific than 'pleasant'. In compound p.ns the adjective could not be distinguished from an OE pers.n. *Blīđa*, a short form of attested compound names in *Blīđ-*. (*a*) Bethnal (*Blithehale* 13th) Mx:83 (**halh**), ?*Bleytherudyng* (f.n.) 1325 Ch:3·157 (***ryding**), Blidworth 1086 Nt (**worđ**).

(*b*) All of the following instances are r.ns (see ERN:38–9): *Blithe* 944 S:495 Nth:11, Blyth 958 [14th] S:679 Nt, 1133–40 Nb [ERN:39], Blythe 1154–89 Wa:2, 996 S:878 (ASCh:2·27) St:1·5. In addition, Blyford c.1050 [13th] S:1516 (**ford**) and Blythburgh 1086 (**burh**) contain the name of the R. Blyth Sf, itself first independently noted in 1586.

    DOE *blīþe*; MED *blīthe* adj.; EDD *blithe*; OED *blithe* a.; DES *Bly*.

blōd OE, *n.* 'blood' appears in connection with trees, woods and water, and may refer to colour. An adjectival sense of *blōd*, meaning 'bloody' or possibly 'blood-coloured' is noted by MED from c.1300. Reference to the physical presence of blood on some occasion cannot be ruled out (cf. *Blodyforlong*, under **blōdig**).
(*a*) Bladbean 1226 K:431 (**bēam**), *le Blodgreueland* (f.n.) 1278–81 Ch:4·334 (**grǣfe**, **land**), Llanyblodwel (*Blodwelle* c.1200) Sa:1·178 (**welle**).

    ~ **blōdig, blōd-lēas.**

    DOE *blōd*; MED *blǫd* n.¹, *blǫd* adj.; EDD *blood* sb.; OED *blood* sb.; DES *Blood*.

blōdig OE, *adj.* 'bloody'. In Bloody Beck (*Bludebec* 1268, *Blodybek* 13th) YN:113 it appears to alternate with the noun **blōd**. The name may refer to a stream with a bed of reddish soil; *blōdig* is used for 'blood-coloured' in OE (DOE sense 1b) and later (OED sense A7). *Blodyforlong* 1498 Gl:2·67 (**furlang**), on the other hand, is near to the site of the Battle of Tewkesbury, fought in 1471.

    ~ **blōd, blōd-lēas.**

    OED *blōdig*; MED *blǫdī* adj.; EDD *bloody*; OED *bloody* a. & adv.

blōd-lēas OE, *adj.* 'bloodless' seems to occur in *Bloudlesacre* (f.n.) 1346 Ch:3·227 (**æcer**), where it may refer to a field with pale soil, or one that is barren (MED). Alternatively, the root of the name may be OE *blōd-lǣs* 'blood-letting': in this case, the name could refer to an unproductive field that 'bleeds its owners dry'.

    ~ **blōd, blōdig.**

    DOE *blōd-lēas*; MED *blǫdlēs*; EDD –; OED *bloodless*.

blok ME, 'block, stump, log'. From the 16th century OED records various senses under the heading 'a bulky piece of any substance', and EDD has one instance meaning 'clod of earth' in Hrt. Such applications may be relevant to p.ns.

(*b*) *Bloc* (f.n.) 13th YE:319, *la Blok* (f.n.) 1485–1509 Sr:367.

(*c*) *Boweres Blocke* (f.n.) 1575 Gl:2·186 (pers.n.), *Uuermare Blockes* (f.n.) 13th YE:319 (pers.n.).

~ OHG *bloh*, MDu *bloc*, probably entering ME via OFr *bloc*.

AFW *bloc*; MED *blok(ke*; EDD *block*; OED *block* sb.; DES *Block*.

blōma OE, *m.* 'lump or ingot of metal' probably appears in Bloom Ho. (*Blomehouse Grene* 1584) YW:1·318 (**hūs**), where it would denote a building used for smelting—the place is situated in an area where the industry was practised from an early date (YW:7·11). A certain instance io *Blomoomithy* (f.n.) 1585 St:1·111 (**omiðjo**).

~ **blōmere*.

DOE *blōma*; MED *blǫme*; EDD *bloom* sb.[2]; OED *bloom* sb.[2]

*blōmere OE, *m.* 'smelter' is recorded in ME surnames from the 13th century. As a common noun or derived surname it appears in:

(*a*) *Blomerfeld* (f.n.) 1341 YW:3·253, *le Blomeresfeld* (f.n) 1371 Ch:3·50 (**feld**), *Blomer rydding* (f.n.) 1570 St:1·64 (***ryding**).

~ *blōma*.

DOE –; MED *blǫmere*; EDD –; OED – (cf. *bloomery*[1]); DES *Bloomer*.

*blōr OE, of uncertain meaning, has been suggested for a group of St names. The sense of ME *blure* proposed by Stratman, 'swelling, blister', was once accepted as a solution, and taken to refer in these p.ns to a hill or mound (EPNE **blōr*, DEPN, Mills 1991 *Blore*). However, MED assigns Stratman's evidence to *blǫre* 'crying, wailing'. Duignan 1912:18 links the St names with ModE *blore* 'gust' (cf. **blāw*), noting that several are in exposed sites. DEPN also suggests a connection with OE *blere* 'bald'. However, neither of these possibilities seems entirely satisfactory for the simplex examples.

(*a*) Blurton (*Blorton* 1195) St (**tūn**), *Blore Wood* (f.n.) 1337 St:1·64 (**wudu**).

(*b*) Blore (nr Ashbourne) 1086 St, Blore (nr Market Drayton) 1293 St.

blōstm OE, *m.* 'blossom, flower'. A feminine form is occasionally recorded, and the word is attested weak as well as strong in both genders (DOE).

(*a*) *Blossomtore* (f.n.) 1415 Db:348 (**torr**).

DOE *blōstm*; MED *blosme*; EDD *blossom* sb.[1]; OED *blossom*.

bluber ME, 'bubble' and the associated verb *bloberen*, are applied to seething or bubbling water. This is presumably the case in *Blubberwell* (f.n.) 1579 Gl:3·248 (**welle**) and the Sx local surname *Blobermere* 1296 (**mere**[1]) cited by MED. Blubberhouses 1172 YW:5·120 (**hūs**) is more problematic—*Bluber* was used as a ME byname (*Walter Bluber* 1229), and that could be the solution in this instance. Alternatively, if the element does here refer to water, it might denote a feature of the R. Washburn, though this would leave unexplained the nearby *Blubber Lane* (st.n. Fewston) 1771 and *Blubber Fell* 1771 YW:5·120. If these are neither repeated instances of the byname, nor back-formations from Blubberhouses, it may be—as YW:5·120 suggests—that ME *bluber* was used in an extended sense of 'that which bubbles out, spring'. There are several springs in the vicinity.

~ probably onomatopoeic.

MED *blober*; EDD *blobber* sb. & v.[1]; OED *blubber* sb.[1]

*****blukko-** Brit, *adj.* 'bald, bare' is shown by Quentel (1955) to occur in Lamplugh c.1150 Cu (*****nanto-**). Padel 1980–2:524 (cf. CPNE:23) gives further supporting evidence for the element, which would be PrCu *****bluch**. Nanplough Co is an exact parallel to the Cumbric name.

~ MCo *blogh*, MW *blwch*, Breton *blouc'h*.

GPC –; CPNE *blogh*.

bobbe ME, 'clump, spray' is used of plants, as in *holyn bobbe* 'spray of holly', *Sir Gawain* 206—cf. Hollin Bob Close (f.n.) 1841 YW:2·138. (*c*) *the Rise bobb* (f.n.) 1600 YW:2·135 (**hrīs**), Ling Bob 1769 YW:3·206 (**lyng**).

~ uncertain origin.

MED *bobbe*; EDD *bob* sb.[1]; OED *bob* sb.[1]

bōc[1] OE, 'beech-tree' is hardly recorded in independent use after the OE period (MED has only compounds). There is rarely interchange with the side-form **bēce** in p.ns, but it does occur in Bookham Sr (*Bocheham* 1086, *Becheham* 1165, 1174, *Bocham* 1225 etc.). It is possible that some habitative names, such as Boughton, do not belong here; see **bōc**[2]. (*a*) *Boke Greues* (f.n.) 1454 Ch:4·286 (**grǣfe**), Bookham 1086 Sr (**hām**), Bockhampton 1086 Brk, 1295 Ha [DEPN] (**hām-tūn**), Bockhanger a.1212 K (**hangra**), Buckhold 1109–20 [13th] Brk, Buckholt 724 [13th] S:1180 K [KPN:34], 1086 Ha, 1121 Gl:1·158, 1121 Sx:491 (**holt**), Buckhurst 1226 K:319, 1178 Brk:143, 1135 Ess, 1199 Sx:370 (**hyrst**), Buckover 1167 Gl (**ofer**[2]), *Bochestede* (f.n.) 1294 We:2·102 (**stede**), Baughton 1038 [18th] S:1392 Wo, Boughton 1086 Ch:4·123, 1086 K (×4) (**tūn**).

(*b*) *atte Buk* (surn.) 1327 Sf [Carlsson:31], *atte Boke* (surn.) 1332 Nf [Carlsson:31].
(*c*) *Setebuck* (f.n.) 1284 Ch:3·317 (*ge*-**set**).
~ **bēce, *bōcen.**
DOE *bōc*²; MED *bǫk*- n.²; EDD –; OED –.

bōc² OE, *f.* 'book' occurs in the compound **bōc-land** and may be found in a similar sense when combined with other terms for areas of land. A probable case is *Burhuuare boc aceras*, 'the "book-acres" of the townspeople' S:1629 K; Bucks (*Bochewys* 1086) D (**hīwisc**) is another possibility. It has also been cogently argued that some instances of Doughton, given here under **bōc¹**, might instead belong here, giving 'settlement held by charter' (K:300–1).
~ **bōc-land.**
DOE *bōc¹*, *boc-æcer*; MED *bǫk* n.¹; OED *book* sb.

*bōcen OE, *adj.* 'growing with beech-trees'.
(*a*) Bockenfield 1206 Nb [NbDu:26] (**feld**), Bokenhale (f.n.) 1356 Ch:2·41 (**halh**), Buckenhill 1328 He, Bucknall (f.n.) 1357 Ch:4·260 (**hyll**).
~ **bōc¹, bēcen.**
DOE –; MED –; EDD –; OED –.

bocher OFr, *m.* 'butcher'.
(*a*) *the Butchers Field* (f.n.) 1650 Ch:4·120 (**feld**), *the Botchers Hey* (f.n.) 1549 Ch:4·152 (*ge*-**hæg**), *Butcher Row* (st.n. Cirencester) 1460 Gl:1·62, Butcher Row (st.n. Beverley) 1633 (cf. *rangea carnificium* 1456) YE, Butcher's Row (st.n. Bristol) 1540 Gl:3·87 (**rāw**), Butcher Royds (f.n.) 1529 YW:4·95 (***rod¹**).
~ **bocherie.**
AND *bocher*; AFW *bochier*; MED *bǒchěr*; EDD *butcher*; OED *butcher* sb.; DML *bucherius*; DES *Butcher*.

bocherie OFr, *f.* 'slaughter-house, butcher's shop, butchers' quarter'. An early form which has been linked with The Butchery, Ely, is *Bocherisrowe* 1382; this may belong here or under **bocher**.
(*b*) *the Buchery* (Hull) 1443 YE:211, *The Butchery* (Gloucester) 1413 (cf. *Vico Macerrariorum* c.1250) Gl:2·128, The Butchery (st.n. Ely) 1418 C:215, *Butchery St.* (Lincoln; *Bucheriam* 1201) L:1·56.
~ **bocher.**
AND *bocherie*; AFW *bocherie*; MED *bǒcherīe*; EDD –; OED *butchery*; DML *bucheria*.

bōc-land OE, *n.* 'land held by royal charter', a technical term in Anglo-Saxon land-tenure. By the early 10th century all land in England was held either as **folc-land** or as *bōc-land*. The holder of an estate of *folcland* owed dues and services to the king, and was subject to custom in matters of succession and disputed title. The holder of *bōcland* had greater freedom over its disposal, and was exempt from most of the royal dues and services. (Wormald 1984:20–3 discusses various solutions to the problem of the exact nature of *bōcland*.)

Rumble has noted (1987:219–29) that a tiny minority of the Anglo-Saxon estates held as *bōcland* took the term as their name, and suggests that only when a new estate was specifically created by the royal charter was *bōcland* used as an appellative.

Rumble details the 29 instances of Buckland (the modern form wherever it has survived) recorded up to 1086. They occur in Brk, Bk, D (×13), Do (×2), Gl, Ha, Hrt, K (×4), Mx, So (×3), Sr. The earliest recorded is the Mx example, an unidentified *æt Boclonde* 825 S:1436.

A number of instances of Buckland are first recorded after 1086. Some of these may be Anglo-Saxon estates omitted by the Domesday Survey, others may be transferred instances of the element, being named from an owner who took his byname or surname from one of the Anglo-Saxon estates. Rumble suggests that, amongst others, Bucklands 1294 Brk and Buckland 1288 He may be instances of the first category, and that *Boclond* 1260 Ch:4·2 and Buckland Grange (cf. *Nigel de Boclonde* 13th) Wt may represent the second. Sometimes, especially when the name survives only as a f.n. (as *Bokelond* 1326 C:313, *Bocland* 1220 Ess:575), it is possible that **bōc**[1] is involved instead.

~ **bōc**[2], **land**; cf. *bōc-æcer* under **bōc**[2].

DOE *bōc-land*; MED *bok-lond* s.v. *bọ̄k* n.[1] sense 7; EDD –; OED *bookland*; DML *bochelanda*; DES *Buckland*.

bog ME, 'bog, marsh' is common in later minor names. Cheshire dialect *bog* evidences a specific sense 'tuft of grass or reeds' (EDD *bog* sb.[3]) which may perhaps be relevant elsewhere.

(*a*) Bogthorn 1670 YW:6·8 (þorn).

(*b*) Black Bog (*le Bog* 1382) Nb [NbDu:24], The Bog 1578 Cu:316, *Boggs* 1691 Cu:278.

(*c*) Lolly Bog 1769 YW:5·136 (pers.n.).

~ Irish *bog* 'soft', *bogach* 'marsh'.

MED *bog*; EDD *bog* sb.[1]; OED *bog* sb.[1]; DES *Bogg*.

boga OE, *m*. 'bow, arch, bend' would be indistinguishable from ON *bogi* of similar meaning.

(1) Meaning 'arch' or 'arched bridge'.

(*a*) *le Boghbrugge* 1349 Ch:2·233, *Boubrig* (f.n.) 1407 YW:4·288, Bow Bridge 1370 YE:222 (**brycg**).

(*b*) *Bow Lane* (st.n. London: *le Bowe* 1307, alternating with OFr *arche*) Ldn:149.

(*c*) *Mynstirbowe* (st.n. Beverley) 1449 YE:197 (**mynster**), *Stanbowe* 1282 Wo:168, Stonebow 1147 [13th] L:1·41, 1574 Wo (**stān**), Bow Bridge (*Ste[n]enebogh* 1315) D:315 (**stænen**), Stonebow (st.n. York; *Staynbowe* 1275) YE:298 (**steinn**).

(*d*) Stratford at Bow 1279 Mx.

(2) Otherwise in most cases with the transferred meaning 'something curved or bent', as 'curved valley' or 'river-bend'. Some p.ns denoting woods may indicate the source of material for making bows. Other names listed here may of course refer to unidentified arches or bridges.

(*a*) *boweacer* (f.n.) 1566 L:3·75 (**æcer**), Buckleigh 1333 D (**clif**), Bow Croft (f.n.) 1550 Brk:278 (**croft**), Bowden 1216–72 Db:61, 1257 W:338, 1270 D:28, 1333 D:37, 1262 D:48, 12th D:485, Bowdon 1086 Ch:2·15 (**dūn**), *Bo[u]hfeld* (f.n.) 1309 Db:441 (**feld**), *Bougham* 1327 Gl:3·204 (**hamm**), Bowhill 1249 D:438 (**hyll**), Bowland 1102–14 YW:6·112 (**land**; the 'bow' is probably the curving course of the Hodder valley), *Bowlonds* (f.n.) 1519 Brk:349 (**land**), Bowley 1086 D (**lēah**), Bowness c.1225 Cu:123 (**nes**), Bowscale 1361 Cu:181 (**skáli**), *Bowestedewong* (f.n.) 1349 Ru:279 (**stede, wang**), Bowerthy 1249 D (**worð**), Boode (*Boghewode* 1330) D, Bowda (*Boghewode* 1330) D, Bowood 1333 D:625, Buda (*Bowode* 1287) D:96, Bude (*Boghewode* 1330) D:83 (**wudu**).

(*b*) Bowes 1172 YN (perhaps bends in the R. Greta), Bow c.1224 YW:6·185 (probably a bend in the R. Ribble).

(*c*) Holbeton 1229 D (**hol¹, tūn**), Windbow 1242 D (**wōh**), *Wodebowe* (f.n.) 1425 Gl:2·205 (**wudu**).

The element is disproportionately common in Devon—see D:37–8, which notes 17 compounds with **dūn** and 13 with **wudu**, together with a number of less frequent combinations. An OE diminutive *bogel has been suggested for Bolas 1198 Sa (***wæsse**): see Sa:1·51 and cf. OED *boul* 'anything bent into a curve'.

~ OE *būgan* 'to bend'; **bow-bearer, bowe-man, bowyer, byge¹, *bycge, byht.**

DOE *boga*; MED *boue* n.¹; EDD *bow* sb.¹; OED *bow* sb.¹; DES *Bow*.

boggard ModE, 'ghost, goblin' is well attested outside p.ns in the forms *boggard* and *boggart* in the north of England (EDD, OED). *Boggard* would be indistinguishable from ModE *boggard* 'a privy' (OED sb.²).
(*a*) Boggart Close (f.n.) 1824 Db:603 (**clos**), ?*Bogger Furlong* (f.n.) 1649 L:2·93 (**furlang**), *Boggard Ho* 1623 YW:3·133, Boggard Ho 1797 YW:3·108 (**hūs**).
~ uncertain origin.

MED –; EDD *boggart* sb.¹; OED *boggard*¹.

*boia OE, 'boy, servant, knave'. This element may appear in a number of p.ns from Domesday Book, and possibly earlier in *boiwic* 785 [12th] S:124 Hrt, though it is not independently recorded until c.1300. Its etymology and language of origin are disputed, and have been discussed at length by Dobson 1940 and Dietz 1981. The sense in p.ns is also problematic; Insley has recently suggested that the names *Boydale* and *Boydole*, found in Nf and L, might denote a share of land appropriate to a boy, but not to a man (L:4·137).

The attested OE pers.n. *Boia* (Feilitzen:205), perhaps the same word, cannot be distinguished in p.ns; nor can the ODan pers.n. *Boie*, which may be particularly likely in Boythorpe 1086 Db, 1086 YE (**þorp**). Confusion with OFr **bois** is also possible in some names.
(*a*) Boycott 1086 Bk, c.1189 Wo, 1291–2 Sa:2·31, Boy Court 1240 K, Bycott c.1200 D:549 (**cot**), Boycombe 1278 D (**cumb**), *Bondesboydole* (f.n.) 1214–29 Nf [Insley 1994:98] (**dāl**), *Boydale* (f.n.) c.1216–44 L:4·136 (?**deill**), *Boyfield* 1248 Gl (**feld**), Bayford 1243 So, Byford (f.n.) 1286 Ess:614 (**ford**), Boynal 1278–9 O (**halh**), Boyland 1086 Nf, 1204 D:435 [& C:liv] (**land**), Bystock 1242 D (**stoc**), Boyton 1086 Co, 1086 W, 1086 Sf, 1086 Ess:426, 1202–3 K, 1348 Ess:498 (**tūn**), Bayford (*Boywurthe* 1442) K:272 (**worð**).

DOE –; MED *boie* n.¹; EDD *boy*; OED *boy* sb.¹

bois OFr, *m.* 'wood'. Some instances, such as *le grauntboys de Hoton* (f.n.) 1402 Ch:4·191 (**grant**), probably simply translate English elements in French documents, but in others the nature of the compound suggests that the term had been adopted locally.
(*c*) *Northboys* (f.n.) 1255 YW:4·18 (**norð**), *le Southboys* (f.n.) 1339 C:313 (**sūð**), Woodboice (f.n.; *Hood Boyse* 1777) YW:1·305 (pers.n.).
~ originally Germanic, related to **busc**.

AND *bois*; AFW *bois*; MED *bois*; EDD –; OED –.

bol OE, *m.* 'tree-trunk, stump'. ME *bole* has often been derived from ON *bolr*, but OE *bol* is attested once in the *Lacnunga* recipes, apparently (but not certainly) referring to the stem of ivy. This occurrence in a manuscript of c.1000 might be classed as an early appearance of the ON loan, but in the light of the early Gl instances, below, it is likely that the OE cognate did exist. The combinations with **cot** and **hūs** suggest that the range of meanings may have included 'log'.

The element is very hard to distinguish both from *bole and from a possible *bol 'rounded hill', which has been suggested on the strength of German cognates (Mawer 1913:59–60), and would suit the topography of Boldon c.1170 Du (**dūn**).

(a) Balburrow 13th Gl (**bearu**), Bow Beck (*Bollebec* c.1125) YW (**bekkr**), Bowcote c.1250 Gl:2·241, 13th Gl:2·254 (**cot**), *Bolgrave* (f.n.) 1374 Gl:2·252 (**grāf**), Bullar (f.n.) 1328 Ch:2·40 & 5·xxiv (**halh**), *Bolehustede* (f.n.) 1346 Ch:4·43 (**hūs**, **stede**), Bellmarsh (*Bolemos* 1307) Ch:2·227 (**mos**), Bow Shaw 1203 YW, Bowshaws l.12th YW (**sceaga**).

(b) Bole 1086 Nt (dat.pl.), Bolham 1258 [14th] Nt (dat.pl.).

~ *bolled, *bolling.

DOE *bol*; OGNS *bolr*; MED *bōle* n.[2]; EDD –; OED *bole*[1].

bolas-tre ME, 'bullace-tree, wild plum-tree'. The regional *bully*, recorded in YW and the east midlands (EDD), is found in Bully Trees 1773 YW:3·269 and *Bully-tree feild* (f.n.) 1684 YW:1·301 (**feld**). Bullace Trees YW:3·28 shows variation between *Bulitrees* 1783 and *Bullas Trees* 1817. Another variant is presumably represented in *Bullonstree Croft* (f.n.) 1639 Ch:2·94; cf. the spelling *bullin(s)* noted in Sa (EDD).

(a) Bullace Tree Close (f.n.) 1845 YW:2·24 (**clos**), Bullace Tree Croft (f.n.) 1843 Ch:3·89 (**croft**), *the Bullistree flatt* 1716 YW:5·127 (**flat**).

(b) Bolsters (f.n.; *del Bolastre* 1365) Ch:1·129, Bullacetree (f.n.) 1847 Db:391, Bullace Trees 1778 YW:3·150.

~ OFr *beloce* 'sloe', MLat *bolluca* 'small wild fruit' (du Cange).

MED *bolās*; EDD *bullace, bullister*; OED *bullace, bullester*, cf. *bully* sb.[4]

*****bole** ME, 'place where ore was smelted' refers to smelting lead, and perhaps iron, before the invention of furnaces (Db:1·xlv). The hearth was 'often made on a hill-top so as to utilize the prevailing winds' (Kirkham 1949:3), and according to the EDD (*bole* sb.[3]) was usually in a round cavity on that hill-top. Although formally the element could be confused with **bol** the distribution in Db is conclusive for the names in this county, where the use of the term is frequent and goes back to the 13th century (see below and cf. also Ralph le Bolere 1300 Db:92). Outside Db it is possible that *bole* appears in some names generally thought to contain *bol*; this would be especially likely in the other counties where EDD records the term: Nb, We, YN and YW. In particular, instances of Bole Hill in neighbouring YW, and perhaps also Ch, probably relate to the Db group. *Bole howe* (f.n.) 1519 Ru:54 (**haugr**) is perhaps a less certain instance. (*a*) *Boleacre* 13th Db:230 (**æcer**), *Bolehul* (f.n.) 1308 Ch:2·314, Bole Hill 1364 Db:265, *Bolehull* (f.n.) c.1386 Db:42, *Bolhill* (f.n.) 1425 YW:2·143, Bole Hill 1562 Db:35 [& Db:3·vi], Bolehill 1570 Db:285, Bole Hill 1587 YW:1·197 (**hyll**). (*b*) *le Boles* (f.n.) 14th Db:716, *the Boole* 1561 Db:315. (*d*) Burton Bole 1319 [16th] Db.

~ obscure; it has been equated with **bolla** (EDD, Db:673), *bol* 'rounded hill' (Mawer 1913:60), **bál** (Björkman:88) and **bōli** (Ch:5·108).
MED –; EDD *bole* sb.³; OED *bole*⁴.

bōli ODan, *n.* 'dwelling, homestead' appears in only one major name, Newball c.1110 L (**nīwe**). The earliest source for this name, 1086 Domesday Book, has *-berie* (from **burh**), perhaps substituting a familiar element for an ON one that was clearly rare in England (SSNEM:214).

~ **boðl**.
Cf. OGNS *ból*.

bolla OE, *m.* 'bowl' may appear with a topographical sense in some p.ns. Bowling 1086 YW (**-ing**²) is a likely case, since a plausible bowl-shaped hollow can be identified (YW:3·244). The early spellings of this name, moreover, preserve consistent *-ll-*. Otherwise, the element is hard to distinguish from several others, including **bol** and ***bula**.
Bollewell (f.n.) 1327 Gl:1·67 and *Bollewellethorne* (f.n.) 1292–3 Brk:395, may belong to a group of names in which **welle** is combined with a word for a receptacle for water, as Brk:395 notes (cf. **byden**). A single *-oll-* spelling, however, is not certain evidence, and these names could contain ***bula**.
DOE *bolla*; MED *bolle*; EDD *bowl* sb.¹; OED *boll* sb.¹, *bowl* sb.¹

***bolled** ME, *adj.* 'pollarded', an adjective formed (in the OE or ME period) from **bol**. Spellings with and without *-d-* alternate in Boldshay. (*a*) Boldshay 1292 St/YW:3·243, *Bolledesaghe* (f.n.) c.1190 YW:4·122 (**sceaga**); cf. *Bollershaw* 1459 YW:7·160.

~ **bol**.
MED –; EDD –; OED –.

***bolling** ME, 'pollard tree' is found in Bolding Hatch (*Bollinggehach'* 1297) Ess (**hæcc**) and perhaps also in *Bollenshawehefed* 1291 Ch:1·244 (**sceaga**, **hēafod**), though the latter is *Bolshagh'* 1380 etc., apparently with

bol. Like ***bolled**, the formation could formally date back to OE.
~ bol.
MED –; EDD *bolling*; OED *bolling* sb.

bolt OE, *m*. 'bolt, arrow'. This element seems to be used in a topographical sense to denote a straight stretch of high coastland west of Salcombe D. It gave its name to Bolberry 1086 (**burh**), Bolt Head (*Bult poynt* 1577), Bolt Tail 1765 and probably *Boltbay* 1451 (**baie**). See D:307.
In ModE dialects, *bolt* has several uses: a bundle of cloth, hay or reeds, a narrow passage between houses, a stone drain or dam, and wood cut into straight lengths for lath-making (EDD). These senses may be relevant to later names, like Bolt Platt (f n) 1840 Brk;94 (**plat**) or Boltshaw (f.n.) 1848 Ch:1·163 (**sceaga**).
DOE *bolt*; MED *bolt*; EDD *bolt* sb.¹; OED *bolt* sb.¹

bón ON, *f*. 'prayer, request' developed in ME to mean also both 'favour, gift' and 'demand, requirement'. Boon work was a service required by a feudal lord of his tenants (MED), and where the element appears in p.ns it may relate to this. Identifying the term is problematic, however, since in ME spellings it would often be indistinguishable from **bān**. Of the two medieval examples given here, *Bonacres* We is a particularly likely instance because *bān* should retain *ā* north of the Humber–Ribble line. *Boneweir's Marsh* Gl, however, is very uncertain: Gl:3·202 speculates that it refers to a fishery granted as a favour.
(*a*) *Bonacres* (f.n.) e.14th We:2·xiii (**æcer**), Boon Dikes (f.n.) 1844 YW:6·121 (**dīc**), *Boneweir's Marsh* 1402 Gl (**wer, mersc**), Boon Wood (f.n.) 1801 Db:113 (**wudu**).
   ~ bēn. MED suggests that there may also have been an OE *bōn, which would be partly the source of the ME term.
OGNS *bón*; MED *bōn* n.2; EDD *boon* sb.²; OED *boon* sb.¹

bóndi ON, *m*. 'peasant landowner' was borrowed into OE as *bōnda*, where it retained the application to freemen (DOE). In ME it came to be used of unfree feudal tenants, sometimes specifically of a villager ranking between a freeman and a cottar (MED). In the f.n. *les bondgardins* 1413 L:3·161 (**gardin**) the related ME *bond*, denoting the feudal obligation, may appear, giving 'gardens held by tenure of bond service or rent'.
P.ns might also contain the derived ON pers.n. *Bóndi* or ME surname *Bonde* (Thuresson:50).
(*a*) Bonbusk 1227 Nt (***buskr**), Bonby 1086 L:2·56, Bomby 1292 We (**bȳ**), Bond Ings 1329 YW:4·81, 1548 YW:4·62 (**eng**), Bond Gate (st.n. Pontefract) c.1220 YW:2·76, Bongate (probably *vetus Appilby ubi villani*

manent 1199–1216, *Bondegate* 1279) We:2·93 (**gata**), Bone's Gote 1438 C (***gota**), *Bondeholm* (f.n.) 1170–1240 YW:4·52 (**holmr**).

(*d*) *Bond Burstwick* 1260 YE (certain *bondi* held land here of the king in 1297 according to YE:33).

~ ON *búa* 'to dwell' (cf. **bȳ**), **bond-man**. In ME the originally free *bóndi* became associated with *bond* 'fetter'.

OGNS *bóndi*; DOE *bōnda*; MED *bŏnd(e* n.¹; OED *bond* sb.² & a.; DES *Bond*.

bond-man ME, 'husbandman, unfree villager, serf', recorded as a ME surname (DES).

(*a*) *Bondmanscroft* (f.n.) 1334 L:4·88 (**croft**), *le Bondmanwode* (f.n.) c.1200 [15th] L:3·61 (**wudu**).

~ **bóndi, mann**.

MED *bŏnd(e-man*; EDD –; OED *bondman*; DML *bondemannus*; DES *Bondman*.

bon-fir ME, 'bonfire, fire on which bones were burned' is found in Bonfire Hall (*Baynfierhowe* 1641) We (**haugr**). The earliest spelling retains the northern form of OE *bān* 'bone' and/or is influenced by ON *bein*.

~ OE **bān, fȳr**.

MED *bŏn-fīr*; EDD *bonefire*; OED *bonfire* sb.

booty ModE, *adj*. 'sticky (of soil)' is recorded in Cheshire dialect by EDD and, despite Ch:5·111, is presumably to be preferred to 'booty, common spoils' in the following:

(*a*) *the Bootiefeild* (f.n.) 1654 Ch:1·105, the *Booty Sandy Fd* (f.n.) 1696 Ch:2·142 (**feld**), The Hoole (*Bootie Hoo* 1665, *Bootee Hoole* 1712) Ch:4·128 (**hol¹**).

MED –; EDD *booty* adj.¹; OED –.

*bor OE, 'elevation, hill' has been discussed at length by Ekwall (1936:131–3). He suggests that it lies behind a group of names in *Bor-* which are traditionally derived from OE **bār** 'boar' but have consistent spellings in *o* from an early date and tend to be situated on raised land. On the other hand, the sound-change *ā* > *ō* seems to have begun early in the 12th century, and even in the late OE period sporadic writings of *o* for *ā* are attested (Jordan:§44), so that derivation from *bār* can rarely be ruled out, apart from in the simplex instances.

(*a*) Boreham 1035–44 [14th] Ess [ASWills:29], 1188 Hrt, 12th Sx:483, 1249 W:305 (**hām**), Borret 1608 YW:6·266 (**hēafod**).

(*b*) Bore Place (*atte Bore* 1313) K, *la Bore* (surn.) 1279 O [METT:21].

~ MLG *bor* 'high', Swedish dialect *bor* 'ridge, hill', OE *beran* 'to lift, carry', OE *borlice* 'excellently'.

DOE –; MED –; OED –.

bord OE, *n.* 'board, plank', probably also 'border'. The sense 'border' belongs to a homonym attested in OE *utan-bordes* 'abroad' and *innan-bordes* 'at home', and supported by cognates (see below, and cf. DOE *borda*² 'ornamental border, embroidery'). Some contexts suggest that it is probably also found in English p.ns. In OE boundary clauses, *ofer bord dene* S:619 Ha and *on norðan bord dæne* S:1620 K (**denu**) could be 'valleys on the border', *on bord riðig* S:786 Wo (**rīðig**) a 'boundary stream'. In each case there are alternatives, such as 'valleys where boards are obtained' and, perhaps, 'stream crossed by a plank bridge'—while these seem less likely explanations, they cannot be excluded. Some ambiguity is always present with this element, and is neatly encapsulated in Borthwood Wt, which could be said to combine both features: the forest was situated on a parish boundary and provided timber for the construction of a castle in Henry VIII's reign (Mills 1996:31).

The element would also be difficult to distinguish from a dissimilated form of the OE pers.n. Brorda (Feilitzen:208, Redin:45); the early forms of Bordley YW, which often have a medial *-e-*, make the pers.n. a particular possibility in that name (though there was also a weak noun *borda*, as noted above). There may also have been a related OE pers.n. *Bord, which has been proposed for a large number of p.ns, including Balsall Heath (*Bordeshale* 1275) Wo (**halh**) and the neighbouring Bordesley 1175 Wa (**lēah**). Alternatively such names could involve genitival composition with *bord* in one of its senses. Finally OFr *bord* 'cottage' is not independently recorded in English, but could conceivably appear in p.ns (cf. **bordel** and, less probably, **bord-land**).

Bord sometimes denotes a table upon which goods were displayed for sale (see MED *bŏrd* sense 3(c)): *The King's Board* (bdg.n. Gloucester) 1455 Gl:2·134 (**cyning**) was 'a small ornamental market-stall, erected or repaired by Richard II, assigned for the sale of butter and cheese', while *The Fish Board* (bdg.n. Chester) 1356 Ch:5·31 (**fisc**) was a fishmonger's stall in the medieval market.

(*a*) Bordhaw Lane (st.n. London) 1305 (**haga**¹), *le Bordholyns* (f.n.) 14th Db:197 (**holegn**), Bord Hill 1648 YW:1·341 (**hyll**), Bordley 1086 YW (**lēah**), Borthwood (*Bordovrde* 1086, *Bordwode* c.1222) Wt (**wudu**).

~ OHG *bort*, ON *borð*, MDu *bort* 'plank, board'; OHG *bort*, ON *borð*, MDu *boort* 'edge, border, side of a ship'; **borden, bord-land, bred, breden.**

DOE *bord*; MED *bŏrd*; EDD *board* sb.¹ & *bord*; OED *board* sb.

bordel OFr, *m.* 'bordello, brothel', earlier 'cottage'. The word is a diminutive of OFr *bord* 'cottage', and originally meant 'small cottage, hut'. This sense is not attested for ME *bordel*—which is commonly attested from c.1300 as 'brothel' (MED)—but it is found in Anglo-Norman and in 12th- and 13th-century instances of the Latinised *bordellum* from Britain (DML). A *hermitagü voc' le Bordell* 1384 (f.n.) YW:2·81 suggests that the meaning may at one time also have been represented in the vernacular.

The term may appear also, with either sense, in *Bordelcroft* (f.n.) 1208–37 YW:4·252, *le Bordelcroft* (f.n.) 1317 Db:385 (**croft**) and *Bordelleʒ* (f.n.) 1535 YW:4·35 (?**lēah**). As a first element, however, it can be difficult to identify, since there may have been an OE pers.n. *Bordel and there was an OFr pers.n. *Burdel*; see the discussion of *Bordelby* 1086 YN in SSNY:22.

~ OFr *bord* 'cottage'; **bord-land**.

AND *bordel*; AFW *bordel*; MED *bordĕl*; EDD *bordel*; OED *bordel*; DML *bordellum*.

borden ME, 'made of boards or planks' is often combined with **brycg** (cf. *boarding-bridge* 'a plank laid across a running stream, as a substitute for a bridge' EDD *boarden* sense 2(1)).

(*b*) Boarden Bridge (f.n.) 1662 L:2·186, *Borden Bridge* (f.n.) 1607 Brk:50, *borden Bridge* (f.n.) 1715 L:4·191, *the borden bridge* (f.n.) 1629 L:2·85 (**brycg**).

~ **bord, breden**.

MED *bŏrden* adj.; EDD *boarden*; OED *boarden* a.

bord-land ME, 'demesne land, land which supplied food for the lord's table'. Winchester 1986 shows that this sense, from **bord** 'board, table', is preferable to 'land held by a bordar (cottager)', from OFr *bord* 'cottage'. Winchester 1986:136–9 gives further examples, including many from Scotland, where the term is frequent.

(*b*) Birtlands 1494 Gl, *Bordeland* (f.n.) 1409 L:4·88, (f.n.) 1480 Db:716, (f.n.) 1462 YW:2·288, (f.n.) 1465 YW:3·19, *Bordelandes* (f.n.) 1551 Brk:485, (f.n.) 1547–53 Brk:401, *le Bordland* (f.n.) 1315 YW:2·171, *Bordelond* (f.n.) 1466 Do:1·172, *prat' voc' Bourdelandes* (f.n.) 1559 Do:1·264, *Bourdlond* (f.n.) 1508 Brk:124.

~ **bord, land**.

MED *bŏrd-lŏnd*; EDD –; OED *bord-land*.

borg[1] ON, *f.* 'fortified place' is found in Borrow Beck (*Borra watter*, *torrentis de Borra* 1170–84) We. It is combined with ON **á** 'river', probably as gen.sg. *borgar* (cf. the spellings *Bargera* 1279 and *Borgherey* 1558). The fort referred to is Roman (We:1·138). Borrowdale (*Borgheredal* 1175–84) We (**dalr**) is named from the same fort, either directly as **borgar-dalr* or from the river as **borgar-á-dalr*. There is a closely similar pair in Cu: *Borghra* 1211 [15th] is a name used for part of the Derwent (ERN:40) and Borrowdale c.1170 is its valley (see Cu:349). It is uncertain which fortified place is referred to here, as it is in the case of *le Borgh* (f.n.) 1256 YW:6·107. A Lincolnshire f.n. shows alternation with the cognate OE **burh**: *Borg, Retro Borg* 1231–40, but *Bure, Bihindeburc* c.1216–44 L:3·28.

It is worth noting that ON *borg* is also used of small, round hills, though that sense has not been proposed in English names.

Medieval Scandinavian legend suggests that Scarborough 1155–63 YN was founded as *Skarðaborg* by a 10th-century Viking nicknamed Skarði, and Gordon 1926–7 argues that Flamborough YE may similarly owe its origins to one Fleinn. The early spellings of both names, however, suggest OE **burh** as the second element, and they may be hybrids, or earlier English p.ns Scandinavianised. See also **fleinn** and **skarð**.

  ~ **burh**.

OGNS *borg*.

borg[2] OE, *m.* 'pledge, surety, guarantor', used since at least the laws of Cnut in the technical sense 'association of householders jointly answerable before the law' (DOE sense 3a, MED sense 4). As with the similar *tithing*, the term came to be applied to administrative regions; hence the vills *Northborgh, Middelborgh* and *Southborgh*, the three divisions of Barcombe Hundred Sx, first recorded in 1327 (Sx:312). Such divisions can be traced back to at least the first half of the 13th century (Stevenson 1913:299). Used in this way, the term may be limited to Sx and K.

  ~ **borg-stall**.

DOE *borg*; MED *borgh* n.; EDD *borrow* sb.; OED *borrow* sb.; DML *borga*.

borg-stall OE, *m.* 'pathway up a steep hill'. This sense is noted for *borstal* in the dialects of Sf, K, Sr, Sx and W (EDD, OED). It is perhaps implied also by an instance of OE *burhsteal* which is linked with **helde** 'slope' to gloss Latin *clivus* 'slope' and *descensus* 'descent', though formally *burhsteal* must here have been confused with **burh-stall**. How 'pathway up a steep hill' is derived from the compound is not clear: *borg-stall* appears to contain **borg**[2] and **stall**, and might once have meant 'place of refuge'. It may be relevant to note that **borg**[2] 'surety, guarantee of security' and **berg** 'hill' are cognate. Outside p.n. instances in Anglo-

Saxon charters, *borg-stall* is not securely attested in OE. It is difficult to be sure what meaning enters into p.ns, though the gloss already mentioned and the lost *Gealtborgsteal* ?791 [14th] S:1178 Sx (probably with ***galt** 'boar') support the supposition that 'steep path' was in use early.

There is a tantalising connection between this compound and the evidence for **ānstīg** 'path, steep path', which is once linked with *faestin* (i.e. **fæsten** 'stronghold') in an obscure gloss on *termofilas*, apparently Thermopylae (Pheifer 1974:1042).

(*b*) Borstal 10th S:165 (a charter of 811, the name recorded in a 10th-century endorsement; see ASCh:1·17) K [KPN:124], Borstal 1240 K:256, Borstalhill (*atte Borstal* 1323) K:494, ?Boshill (*atte Bostall* 1330) D:636, Bostal 1296 Sx:287, 1327 Sx:415, Bostall 1254 K:31.

~ **borg**^{2}, **stall**.

DOE – (cf. *borg* and *burh-steall*); MED –; EDD *borstal*; OED *borstall*.

*bors OE, 'a spiky plant' would be related to OE *byrst*, ***byrstel** 'bristle' and ME *burre*, *borre* used of various wild plants with bristly seed-cases, such as burdock, dock, goosegrass, etc. (MED *burre*, OED *bur*; cf. ***bur-blade**). The element seems to appear in the OE form of Boasley D, and might therefore be suspected in other combinations with **lēah**, though **bār** (ME *bor*) 'boar' can rarely be excluded from names first attested in the ME period; ***bor** 'hill' might also be thought of. See also ***bōs**.

The OE charter boundary *to borsenan beorge* S:448 Brk:660 may contain an adjective *borsen* 'growing with ***bors**' (cf. **æcen**, **æscen**, ***bircen** etc.).

(*a*) Boasley (*æt borslea* c.970 BCS:1247) D:174, *Borsle* 1362 W:361, Boseleys (*Borseley* 1570) W, ?Boseley (f.n.) 1575 Gl:2·221 (**lēah**).

DOE –; MED –; EDD –; OED –.

*bōs OE, 'stall for animals, cow-stall', surviving as dialect *boose*. The element can be difficult to distinguish from an OE pers.n. *Bōsa* (Redin:86) and from ***bors** (cf. Boseley Gl:3·202, where late spellings in *Bors-* raise the possibility that *-r-* is obscured in the earlier run of *Bos(e)-* forms).

(*a*) Boosbeck 1375 YN (**bekkr**), *the Boose Crofts* (f.n.) 1683 Ch:3·129, Cow Boose Croft 1845 Ch:2·122 (**croft**), Boarsden 1579 YW (**denu**), *Bosewalle* (f.n.) 1397 Ch:2·171 (**welle**).

~ Goth *bansts*, Ger *banse* 'barn', **báss**, **bōsig**.

DOE –; MED *bōs* n.^{1}; EDD *boose* sb.^{1}; OED *boose* sb.

bōsig OE, 'stall for animals, cow-stall', a derivative of ***bōs** recorded in the OE Lindisfarne and Rushworth gospel glosses. As well as the single medieval example noted below, *boosy* and variants *boosing*, *bowsing*,

bowsen have been noted in modern minor and f.ns in Ch, Gl and Sa. When combined with *field, pasture* etc. they have a technical sense of land on which an outgoing tenant was allowed to pasture animals for an additional period (Sa:2·37, EDD).
(*a*) Buisey Pool (f.n.) 1378 Ch:3·225 (**pull*).
~ **bōs*.
DOE *bōsig*; MED −; EDD *boosy*; OED *boosy*.

bot ME, 'parasitical insect, grub' is recorded from the 15th century but might be much older since it seems to have a Dutch cognate (WNT *bot*) The word has denoted various insects: 'horse-fly' or 'grub' may be relevant to *Bottefildes* (f.n.) 1556 Ch:2·123 (**feld**).
~ etymology uncertain.
DOE −; MED *bot* n.²; EDD *bot* sb.¹; OED *bot*.

bōt OE, *f.* 'repair, remedy' has been suggested for Botwell (*Botewælle* 831 S:188) Mx (**welle**), where it might plausibly mean 'healing spring'. Two late-recorded f.ns, *Botewell Wood* 1677 Ru:100 and Botwell leaze 1839 Gl:2·232, might be identical. But Bottle 933 [14th] S:424 W appears to be of different origin, since the early forms (*to botan wylle* etc.) are inflected as a weak noun. The OE pers.ns *Bot(t)a* and *Bote* (Redin:45, 113) may instead be thought of here.
Another group of names in which *bōt* is possible is represented by at least seven instances of Botley (1086 Ha, 1167 Bk, a.1170 [13th] Brk, 1199 Wa, 1272–1307 W:355, 1296 Sx, 1331 Sr:338), together with Leebotwood (*Botewde* 1086) Sa:1·172 and Boothouse (*Bothurste* 1416) Ch:3·292. The combination with woods (**lēah, wudu, hyrst**) seems too frequent to be explained by the coincidental appearance of uncommon pers.ns. The p.ns should probably be related to a technical sense developed by *bōt*, 'the right of a tenant to take timber, etc. for repairs, firing, and other necessary purposes, from off the landlord's estate' (OED). In the compound *fire-boot*, 'the right to gather firewood', this sense is implied at least as early as 1222 (MED s.v. *fīr* n. sense 3); the Botleys etc. may well have been woods in which tenants could exercise this right. The modern development of Boothouse Ch, suggesting an original long vowel, offers some support for derivation from *bōt*. Generally, however, the vowel would be shortened before consonant groups in a compound (Jordan:§23). If this derivation is correct, spellings in *Bott(e)-* suggest that the shortening had already taken place by the earliest record of several of the Botleys.
DOE *bōt*; MED *bǭte* n.¹; EDD *boot* sb.²; OED *boot* sb.¹; DML *bota*¹.

both-hall ME, 'market-hall, town-hall'. This is not a straightforward compound with regard to origin or meaning. It has been recorded in three Gl towns and in Shrewsbury, Sa (the MED, EDD and OED refer only to the instances noted below). These are not areas where ODan bōð is otherwise common or where Scandinavian influence is marked. It may then be that *both* here represents a native OE *bōð(e)* (for the possibility cf. MELS:18, citing a 14th-century Sx instance). Alternatively, it is noteworthy that *Bohalle*, Winchcombe, and all four pre-14th-century spellings of Boothall, Gloucester, lack medial -*th*-, which might throw some doubt on the original first element of the compound (though Gl:2·134 explains the absence as due to Anglo-Norman influence). Cf., however, the equation with **toll-both** noted below.

Clues to the original meaning are late. In Gloucester in 1504 The Boothall certainly functioned as a market-hall (Gl:2·134); in 1712 it was equated with the town-hall (OED); the EDD calls it 'the great hall . . . in which assizes were held'. The Tewkesbury instance seems to be the same building that is called *le Tollboth* 1540; the edition gives the broad gloss 'guild-hall, customs-house, court-house' (Gl:2·xi, Gl:2·63).
(*b*) *Bohalle* 1154–89 (bdg.n. Winchcomb) Gl:2·31, The Boothall (bdg.n. Gloucester; *Buhall* 1219, *Bohalle* c.1230, *þe Bothhall* 1347) Gl:2·134, *le Bothehalle* (bdg.n. Tewkesbury) 1487 Gl:2·63, *La Bothhall* (bdg.n. Shrewsbury) 1324 Sa [Löfvenberg 1946:91].
~ **bōð, hall**.
MED *bōth-hall* s.v. *bōth*; EDD *booth-hall* s.v. *booth*; OED *boothall*.

botiler OFr (AN), *m*. 'butler' or 'bottlemaker', in either case probably as a surname. Both senses derive from OFr *boteille* 'bottle' (Thuresson:120).
(*a*) *les Botilerisbuttis* (f.n.) 1306 Ch:4·250 (**butte**).
~ **botilerie**.
Butler: AND *butiller*; AFW *boteillier*; MED *botelĕr* n.¹; OED *butler*; DML *butellarius*.
Bottlemaker: MED *botelĕr* n.²; OED *bottler*; DML *botellarius*.

botilerie OFr, *f*. 'buttery, wine-cellar' was used early in the sense 'pantry', the association with food strengthened, perhaps, by association with *butter* (OED). The word was also applied in ME to the domestic staff who served food and drink (MED), and is well attested as a ME surname, as in *Willielmus Buteri* 1205 (MED). The term seems to appear in *Old Botry field* (f.n.) 1399 YW:1·242 (**ald, feld**).
~ OFr *boteille*; **botiler**.
AFW *boteillerie*; AND *butillerie, buterie*; DML *butellaria*; MED *boterĭe*; EDD *buttery* sb.; OED *buttery* sb.

botm OE, *m.* 'bottom', in p.ns especially 'the floor of a valley'. Cole 1987–8 has studied the topography of around thirty names containing this or related elements (see **botn, bytme**). She concludes that the feature is often a wide, flat stretch of valley floor enclosed by steep slopes and a narrowing of the flood-plain at either end. She argues that this is a precise application that developed over time; several names that do not fit the pattern may have the more general sense 'damp valley floor', a meaning that may have been earlier.

Botm derives from earlier **boðm*, a change of fricative to stop labelled 'West Saxon' in the grammars (OEG:§419, Hogg:§7.10). The p.n. evidence suggests, however, that the area in which *botm* had developed—at least by the 14th century—extended as far north as C and Ru. From Db and Nt northwards, on the other hand, medieval forms retain the *-th-* of **boðm* very consistently, often to be replaced by the *t* of standard English from the 16th century. The clear north/south division is quite unlike the irregular pattern produced by *boðl* and *botl* (see **boðl**).

Adjectival use of *bottom* 'lowest', is first recorded in OED from 1561, suggesting that early appearances as a first element in p.ns more probably represent the noun. Note that, especially in spellings like *bothom* and *bothum*, *boðm* is difficult to distinguish, except on topographical grounds, from the dative plural of **bōð** 'booth', or from **boðen** 'rosemary' (cf. the spellings *bothom, bothum* etc. cited for this term by MED).

(*a*) *Bothumfeld'* (f.n.) c.1250 Db:490 (**feld**), *le Bothumforde* (f.n.) 1216–72 Ch:3·5 (**ford**), Botham Hall 1464 YW (**hall**), Bothampstead 1199 Brk (**hām-stede**), Bothenhampton 1107 [14th] Do (**hām-tūn**), *Bothumlandes* (f.n.) c.1300 Ch:1·223 (**land**), Bottomley 1246 YW:3·58 (**lēah**), Bothamsall 1086 Nt (?**scelf**).

(*b*) *le Botham* (f.n.) c.1260 Db:717, *le Bothem* (f.n.) 1260 YE:320, *Bothemes* (f.n.) c.1270 L:1·179, *Botme* c.1210 Gl:2·171, *le Botme* (f.n.) 1302 Mx:195, *le Botme* (f.n.) 1334 C:313, *Botteme* (f.n.) 1349 Ru:246, Bottom Barn (*Botme* 1295) Wt, The Bottoms (f.n.) 1289 Ch:3·225, Bottom's Hall (*Bothums* 1381) Db, Earl's Eye (*le Bothim* c.1256–7) Ch:5·46, Hawsker Bottoms (*Bothem* c.1230–40) YN.

(*c*) Oakenbottom 1246 La (**æcen**), Broad Bottom c.1250 YW:3·159, Broadbottom 1286 Ch:1·314 (**brād**), Brithem Bottom 1238 D (**bridd**), Cromwell Bottom a.1246 YW (**crumb, welle**), *Hermytesbothum* (f.n.) 1384 Ch:1·276 (**ermite**), Keld Bottom 1153 YN (**kelda**), Longbottom 1308 YW, *Longebothem* (f.n.) 1300 Nt:276 (**lang**[1]), *Oxebothem* (f.n.) 1216–72 Db:175 (**oxa**), Ramsbottom 1324 La (**ramm**), Elsingbottom 1182–5 YW (pers.n.), Bottom Boat (*Stanleiebothum* 1202) YW (p.n.),

Ladyshaw Bottom 1306 Db (p.n.), Higginbotham (f.n.) 1522 Ch:1·266
[cf. Ch:5·xxi] (?1st el.).

~ **botn, bytme.**

DOE *botm*; MED *botme*; EDD *bottom* sb.; OED *bottom* sb.

botn ON, *m.* 'the "bottom" of a valley', perhaps specifically either 'the
head of a valley', which is generally preferred for the ON term outside
England, or 'a wide flat stretch of valley floor', as Cole has suggested for
OE **botm**. Cole notes that either specific sense suits the topography of the
names where the ON term is to be preferred. Formally *botn* might be
distinguished from the OE cognate both by the final *n* and by the fact that
the latter regularly appears with *-th-* from the variant *boðm in the north.
Botton Cross (*Bothine* c.1200) YN might reflect either's influence on the
other.

(*a*) Starbotton 1086 YW (**stæf**), Wythburn c.1280 Cu (**víðir**).
(*b*) Botton c.1230 La.

~ **botm.**

OGNS *botn.*

bōð ODan, *f.* 'booth, temporary shelter, covered market-stall'; cf.
northern dialect *booth* 'cow-house, herdsman's hut'. The ODan form was
commonly adopted as ME *both*, but there is also evidence in England of
the variant *búð*, which is principally OWN. The origin of the distinction
between these forms is uncertain, but the distribution in England does
appear to reflect a division along the lines of dialect and nationality
(SSNNW:318): *búð*, giving spellings in *b(o)uth*, is found invariably in the
early-recorded names of Cu, We and northern La; *bōð*, spelled *both*, is
the only form encountered not only in the east midlands, where it might
have been expected, but also in Ch and La south of the Ribble. This seems
to suggest a Danish-influenced dialect in parts of these two north-western
counties. Occasional names containing *búð* in Y may have to do with
Norwegian settlers there, but they may instead indicate North Jutlandic
Danes, who would have shared the Norwegian form.

The ODan form was taken into standard usage, and ME *both* replaces
búð in Bootham YE and Boothroyd YW (Dewsbury). It also appears in
later-recorded names in We and Cu. The *-o-* spellings begin to compete
with *-u-* from the late 12th century in Bewcastle and from the 13th century
in Brotherikeld Cu.

Bootham YE (*Buthum* c.1150–60) demonstrates that the element could
be used in the dative plural 'at the booths'; note, however, that in its
ODan form dat.pl. *bōðum* would be hard to distinguish in medieval

spellings from *boðm* 'valley bottom' (see **botm**).

There is also some possibility (though the p.n. evidence is in the main against it) of a native OE **bōð(e)*; see **both-hall**.

Names containing ODan *bōð*, ME *both*:

(*a*) Boothby 1086 (×3) L (**bȳ**), *Bothefeld* (f.n.) c.1300 Ch:1·66 (**feld**), Booth Hay 1330 Db (**ge-hæg**), Boothroyd 1274 YW:3·38 (***rod**¹), Beaufit 13th Nt (**þveit**).

(*b*) *Attebothe* (surn.) 1288 Nf [Carlsson:27] (with **atte**), Booth 1330 Db:371, Booth Lane (*in Bothis de Medio Wico* [Middlewich] 1240) Ch:2·244, Booth Town (*Bothes* 1274) YW, *Bothes* (f.n.) c.1220 Ch·1·213, ?*Bothum* (f.n.) c.1190–1214 YN:325 (dat.pl.), Knutsford Booths (*Bothes* 1230) Ch:2·76.

(*c*) Barkbooth 1535 We (**bark**), *Herlesbothe* c.1270 [17th] Ch:1·181 (**eorl**), Armboth 1530 Cu (?**ermite**, ?**pers.n.**), Haw Booth 1324 La (**haga**¹), *Laxbothes* (f.n.) 1254 [14th] L:1·183 (**læx**), *Monkebothe* (f.n.) 1216–72 Nt:276 (**munuc**), Thurlowbooth 1154–89 Db (pers.n.), *Ysebelesbathes* (f.n.) 1217–32 (*-bothis* c.1301) Ch:1·124 (pers.n.), Oozebooth 1258 La (pers.n.).

Names containing OWN *búð* (or N. Jutlandic *būð*):

(*a*) Bewcastle c.1177 Cu (**cæster**), Bowderdale 1224 We:2·31, 1322 Cu (gen.sg. *búðar* or nom.pl. *búðir*, **dalr**), Boothroyd 1296 YW:2·185 (***rod**¹), Swarther (*Buthswardhout* 1200–46) We (?**svartr**, **hǫfuð**), Burthwaite 1211 Cu:349 (*búðar/búðir*, **þveit**), Brotherikeld c.1210 Cu (inversion compound, *búðir*, pers.n.).

(*b*) Bootham c.1150–60 YE (dat.pl.), Bouth 1336 La.

(*c*) *Hallebutherig* (f.n.) 1207 We:1·53 (**hallr**, **hryggr**), Scorborough 1086 YE (**skógr**), Waberthwaite c.1210 Cu (**veiðr**, **þveit**), Rulbuth 1508 La (pers.n.).

~ **both-hall, toll-both**.

OGNS *búð*; DOE –; MED *bōth*; EDD *booth*; OED *booth* sb.; DML *botha*; AND *bothe*.

boðen OE, *m.* or *n.* 'rosemary', also applied to other plants such as thyme, corn marigold and feverfew. The word might appear as first element in some compounds included under **botm** and **boðl**.

(*a*) Bothenwood 1323 Do:2·150 (**wudu**).

MED *bothel* n., *bothen* n.; EDD *botham* sb.², *buddle* sb.¹; OED *bottle* sb.⁴, *buddle* sb.¹

boðl OE, *n.* 'dwelling, house', with its variants *botl* and *bold*, is used in OE texts of dwellings both ordinary and exceptional. In p.ns there is a hint of the latter in Wychbold (*in regale villo quæ nominatur Wicbold* S:188), while a much more mundane building is suggested by Oxenbold Sa (with **oxa**, 'ox'). For Buddleswick 1317 D:396, interpreted as a **wīc** attached to a lost *Bothel*, MELS:19 argues that a fairly large homestead was meant. Otherwise there is little indication in the p.n. evidence of the dwelling's status; by far the most frequent compound is with the neutral **nīwe** 'new'. It is noteworthy that the element is rarely combined with a pers.n.; the one probable instance that has been noted is Lorbottle Nb, and that is not a certain case.

The relationship between the variant forms is examined in detail by Ekwall 1917, though his arguments are open to question, cf. OEG:§420 n.5. Fairly clear is the status of *bold*, a regular metathesised form of earlier *boðl* (OEG:§425, Hogg:§7.13). More difficult is the relationship between *botl* and *boðl*. Deriving the former from the latter is problematic since it involves a sound-change proper to the south of England (OEG:§419, Hogg:§7.10), while examples of *botl* are common in the north. The parallel with *botm* and **boðm* that is usually cited is misleading since that pair divides along regular dialectal lines (see **botm**). The original vowel-length is also problematic. Ekwall is probably correct that OE had forms of *bŏðl/bŏtl* with both long and short vowels. The single head-form used here is for convenience only.

The geographical distribution of the forms shows a fairly clear pattern. *Bold* is found in the the midlands, east and west, and as a sporadic spelling further north (e.g. *Bolde* for Bootle La). *Botl* is found in the north and in the midland counties of Nt, Ru, Nth and Bk. *Boðl*, giving spellings in *bothel* and *bodel*, is practically universal in the northern compound ***boðl-tūn**, and is otherwise also largely restricted to the north, save for a remarkable group in the south-west.

This distribution suggests that *bold* is principally a midland form, and it is particularly characteristic of the western part of the midlands since *botl* competes with it towards the east. The element is absent, in any of its forms, from most of the south-east and East Anglia. The instances in the south-west (principally D and So, but also Ha and Wt, see D:484 and Wt:182) are intriguing. They share the 'early' form *boðl* with the north, and presumably represent a local survival of the original form, though none of the examples is recorded earlier than the 14th century.

As a first element *boðl* might be confused with ME *bothel*, a well-attested corruption of **boðen** 'rosemary' (see MED s.v.).
(*a*) *Bothelford* 1086 We, Buddleford 1407 D (**ford**), Buddelheyes 1330 D (**ge-hæg**).
(*b*) Beadlam 1086 YN (dat.pl.), Bold 1204 La:107, 13th Sa, Bootle 1086

Cu, 1086 La:116, Bothel c.1125 Cu, Bould 1216–72 O, Budle 1166 Nb, Budleigh 1330 D:484.

(*c*) With **nīwe**: Newbald 963 [14th] S:716 YE, Newbold 1086 Db, 1086 Lei:523, c.1130 Lei:245, 1212 Lei:422, 1077 Wa:115, 1086 Wa:120, 1086 Wa:176, 1086 Wa:257, 991 [11th] S:1366 Wo, c.1200 La, 1203 Nth, *Newbold* 1086 Ch:2·286, 1086 Lei:293, 1086 Nt, 1255–6 Sa:2·135, *Newbottle* 1199 Bk, 1297 Ru, Newbottle 1196 Du, 13th Nt:184, Newbound 1287 Nt, Nobold 1284 Nth, Nobottle 1086 Nth.

With other elements: *Fordbottle* 1086 La (**ford**), Harbottle c.1220 Nb (?**hȳra**), *Long Bottles* 1349 YW (**lang**[1]), Oxenbold 1086 Sa:1·232 (**oxa**), Parbold 1195 La (?**peru**), Wychbold 831 S:188 Wo (**wīc**), Rigbolt 1251 L (?**wyrhta**), Lorbottle 1178 Nb (?pers.n.), Blindbothel 1278 Cu (?1st el.), Shilbottle 1228 Nb (?1st el.).

(*d*) Botolph Claydon 1224 Bk.

~ **bōli**, ***boðl-tūn**.
DOE *botl*; MED *bōld* n., *botel* n.[3]; EDD *bottle* sb.[3]; OED *bold* sb., *bottle* sb.[1]

***boðl-tūn** OE, *m*. 'house-enclosure, house-farm' is frequent in the north. Its precise significance is unknown. Suggestions have included 'collection of buildings', 'enclosure with some sort of building', 'settlement with a special building'; Ekwall (La:8) proposes that it may have had the sense of the similar OSwed *bólbýr* 'the village proper' as distinct from its outlying land. Save for one 19th-century Cheshire f.n. (Ch:1·191), the compound is not recorded south of La and Y. Boughton (*Boltone* 1275) Wo would disrupt this pattern, but it is so isolated that another explanation might perhaps be sought here (?**bol** or ***bula**). The northern instances have all become modern Bolton, and in nearly all cases there are early spellings in *Bothel-*, *Bodel-* to indicate that the compound had the form *boðl-tūn (rather than *botl-* or *bold-*).
(*b*) Bolton c.1170 Cu:394, 1086 La:186, La:210, 1185 La:45, 1201 La:41, 1200 Nb, 1100–33 We, 1086 YE, 1086 YN (×2), 1086 YW (×5), Boltons 1200 Cu:268.

~ **boðl**, **tūn**.
DOE –; MED –; EDD –; OED –.

bought ME, 'bend' probably appears in Boot (*Bought* 1587) Cu:389 situated where the valley of Eskdale forms an acute angle. Cf. also *close called boughte de bekk* 1578 Cu:389. Generally, however, this element cannot be distinguished from ModE *bought* 'sheep-fold, cattle-pen', well-attested in northern dialect. *Ye Bought of Dowcrag* 1687 We, noted at We:2·76, seems to be an instance of this sense, and it may be the more likely in most of the names given below. It is not improbable, however, that the two words are identical in origin: *bought* 'bend' is used for 'loop', and may well have been applied to an enclosure.

(*a*) Bolt Edge (*Bought Edge* 1545) Db (**ecg**), Boltgate (*Bought yait* 1542) YW (**geat**), *Boughtwalle* (f.n.) 1576 Db:397 (?**welle**).

(*b*) Boot (*Bought* 1777) We.

(*c*) Croft Boat (f.n.) 1688 We:2·106 (**croft**).

> ~ *bought* 'bend' may be from an OE *buht, a side-form of **byht** and directly cognate with MLG *bucht*. But it does not appear before c.1400, and OED prefers a late derivation from **boga**. No rival origin for *bought* 'sheep-pen' is obvious.
>
> Bend: MED *bught*; EDD *bought* sb.[1]; OED *bought* sb.[1]
> Sheep-fold: MED –; EDD *bought* sb.[2]; OED *bought* sb.[2]

bouker ME, 'bleacher of cloth', a recorded ME surname (Fransson:109–10). *Bouker place* (f.n.) 1449 Ch:2·15 is named from John son of William le Bouker 1427.

(*a*) *Bowkerscroft* 1501 Ch:2·221 (**croft**).

> ~ ME *bowken* 'to soak for the purpose of cleaning and bleaching' (from MDu, MLG *būken*).
>
> MED *bŏuker* n.; EDD – (cf. *buck* sb.[2], vb.[2]); OED – (cf. *buck* sb.[3] and vb.[1]).

boverie OFr, *f.* 'cattle-shed'. DML *bovaria*[1] also records the senses 'measure of land' and 'cattle-pasture', though *bovaria*[2] 'cow-shed' is more common. The word has not been noted in English outside p.ns, but cf. MED *bŏv(i)er* 'peasant, herdsman', which may be represented in *Bovieresflat* (f.n.) 1216–72 Db:646 (**flat**).

(*b*) *Boveries* 1199 Ess, *Boverie* (f.n.) 1293 Nth:274, *Bowveree* (f.n.) 1393 YW:5·23.

> AND *boverie*; AFW *boverie*; MED –; EDD –; OED –; DML *bovaria*[2].

bow-bearer ModE, 'archer' was also applied to the forest official responsible for protecting deer and their habitat from trespassers (OED).

(*a*) *le Bowe bearers Peece* (f.n.) 1596 Db:556 (**pece**).

> ~ **boga**.
>
> EDD *bow-bearer* s.v. *bow* sb.[1] sense 3(2); OED *bow-bearer*.

bowe-man ME, 'bowman, archer' is recorded as a surname from 1279 (MED). The word is recorded in *Bowmangill* (f.n.) 1620 YW:6·260 (**gil**) and *Boumanmede* (f.n.) 1509 Gl:2·184 (**mēd**), where it may refer to the ownership of the land, or possibly to its use for the practice of archery.

> ~ **boga, mann.**
>
> MED *boue-man* s.v. *boue* n.(1) sense 4b; EDD –; OED *bowman*[1]; DES *Bowman*.

bowling-alley ModE, 'bowling-alley' is common in minor names. There are also variants, as *Bowling Green* (st.n. Chester) 1745 Ch:5·65, *Bowling Platt* 1720 YW:2·226.

(*a*) *The Bowling Alley Close* (f.n.) 1673 Ru:166, *Bouling Ally lane* (f.n.) 1663 YW:5·26, *Bowling Alley piece* (f.n.) 1622 Gl:1·205.

(*b*) *Bowley Alley* (f.n.) 1673 YW:4·152, Bowling Alley (f.n.) 1628 Brk:484, *the Bowling Alley* (f.n.) 1649 L:1·179, *the Bowling Ally* (f.n.) 1681 Ru:254, *Bowlinge Allie* (st.n. Chester) 1630 Ch:5·78.

~ ME *boule* 'ball', **alee**.

MED – (cf. *alei(e* n. sense 3 and *bŏuling* ger.); EDD –; OED *bowling-alley*.

bowyer ME, 'maker or seller of bows, archer' has been suggested for the London st.n. Bowyer Row, where the sense 'bowmaker' or 'bowseller' is probable, and *Bowyardmede* (f.n.) Gl, though this might rather involve a compound of **boga** and **geard**. The alternative form *bowere* is possible in *Bower Hill* L and the Db f.n. *Bowerflat*. Both forms are attested as occupational surnames from the 13th century (Fransson:154–5).

(*a*) *Bowerflat* (f.n.) 1400 Db:646 (**flat**), *Bower Hill* 1349 L:1·17 (**hyll**), *Bowyardmede* (f.n.) 15th Gl:3·232 (**mēd**), Bowyer Row (st.n. London) 1359 (**rāw**).

~ **boga**.

MED *bouer*; EDD *bower* sb.²; OED *bower* sb.², *bowyer*; DES *Bower, Bowyer*.

box OE, *m.* or *n.* 'box-tree'. The element is found in the OE boundary *to ðere wican æt þam boxe* S:412 Ha. On a possible connection between *box* and Roman sites, see Coates forthcoming.

(*a*) Boxford 12th Sf (**ford**), Boxgrove Sx 1086 (**grāf**), Boxley 1086 K (**lēah**), Boxford (*Boxoran* 960 S:687) Brk (**ōra¹**), Boxwell 1086 Gl (**welle**).

(*b*) Box 1144 W, 1234 Gl. MELS:21 gives further ME examples from So and Sr surnames.

~ ***byxe**.

DOE *box¹*; MED *box* n.¹; OED *box* sb.¹; DES *Box*.

Check-List of Cross-References

This list offers a simple gloss on elements cited in cross-references. Details may be emended in later fascicles.

brād OE 'broad'.
*brakni ON 'braken'.
brēc OE 'breach, land broken up'.
bred OE 'board, plank'.
breden OE 'made of planks'.
breiðr ON 'broad, spacious'.
brekka OWN 'slope'.
brend ME 'burnt'.
brēow-ærn OE 'brewhouse'.
Brettas OE 'Britons'.
bridd OE 'bird'.
*brigā Brit 'hill'.
brike ME 'brick'.
brōc OE 'brook'.
brocc OE 'badger'.
brocc-hol OE 'badger's sett'.
brocen OE 'broken'.
brūn[1] OE 'brown'.
brún[2] ON 'edge'.
brunnr ON 'well, spring'.
brycg OE 'causeway, bridge'.
bú ON 'homestead'.
bufan OE 'above'.
*bula OE 'bull'.
*bur-blade ME 'spiky plant'.
*burg OE 'burrow'.
burh OE 'fortified place'.
burh-stall OE 'site of a *burh*'.
burna OE 'stream'.
*burn-bake ME 'land cleared for ploughing'.
*busc OE 'bush'.
*buskr ON 'bush'.
butte ME 'strip of land abutting a boundary'.
bȳ ODan 'village'.
*bycge OE, 'river-bend'.
byden OE 'tub'.
byge[1] OE 'bend'.
byge[2] OE 'commerce, traffic'.
byht OE 'bend, bight'.

bȳre OE 'byre, cowshed'.
bytme OE 'head of a valley'.
*byxe OE 'box-tree, box thicket'.
*cā OE 'jackdaw'.
cald OE 'cold'.
canne OE 'can'.
castel OE 'castle etc.'.
catt OE 'cat'.
causee OFr 'causeway'.
cærse OE 'cress'.
cæster OE '(Roman) city'.
cert OE 'rough ground'.
celde OE 'spring'.
cetel OE 'kettle'.
chalenge OFr 'challenge'.
chef OFr 'head, headland'.
cirice OE 'church'.
*cis OE 'gravel'.
cisel OE 'gravel'.
clæfre OE 'clover'.
clif OE 'cliff, bank'.
*clōh OE 'ravine'.
clos ME 'enclosure'.
cnæpp OE 'hilltop'.
cniht OE 'boy, servant'.
cnoll OE 'hilltop'.
cocc[2] OE 'cock'.
cofa OE 'chamber, cave'.
col OE 'coal, charcoal'.
commun OFr 'common'.
conestable OFr 'constable'.
copeis OFr 'coppice'.
copped OE 'pollarded'.
cot OE 'cottage'.
cot-stōw OE 'group of cottages'.
crab-tre ME 'crab-apple tree'.
crāwe OE 'crow'.
Crist OE 'Christ'.
*crocc-ærn OE 'pottery'.
croft OE 'small enclosed plot'.
cros OE 'cross'.

crumb OE 'crooked'.
*cryc OE 'hill'.
cū OE 'cow'.
cumb OE 'valley'.
*Cumbre OE 'Welshman, Cumbrian'.
cur-bich ME 'bitch cur'.
cwēad OE 'dirt'.
cwic-bēam OE '(?) juniper'.
cyne- OE 'royal'.
cyning OE 'king'.
dāl OE 'share, portion (of common field)'.
dalr ON 'valley'.
dauðr ON 'dead'.
dæl OE 'valley'.
dēad OE 'dead'.
deill ON 'share of land'.
dell OE 'pit, valley'.
denn OE 'woodland pasture'.
denu OE 'valley'.
dēor OE 'animal'.
desert OFr 'deserted place'.
dīc OE 'ditch'.
dík ON 'ditch'.
dile OE 'dill'.
*dolā Brit 'river meadow'.
drȳge OE 'dry'.
dūce OE 'duck'.
dūfe OE 'dove'.
dūn OE 'hill'.
dūne OE 'down, low'.
dunn OE 'dun, dull brown'.
*dylf OE 'digging, quarry'.
ēa OE 'river'.
ealh OE 'sanctuary, shelter'.
ēa-mōt OE 'confluence'.
*eard-ærn OE 'dwelling house'.
earn OE 'eagle'.
ēast OE 'east'.
ēastan OE 'east of'.
*eburo- Brit 'yew-tree etc.'.
ecg OE 'edge'.
edisc OE 'enclosure'.

ēdre OE 'water-course'.
efen OE 'even, level'.
ēg OE 'island'.
ēgeð OE 'small island'.
eik ON 'oak-tree'.
einn ON 'one'.
ēl[1] OE 'eel'.
eel-ark ModE 'eel-trap'.
ellern OE 'elder-tree'.
elm OE 'elm-tree'.
elri OE 'alder wood'.
ende OE 'end'.
ende-lēas OE 'endless'.
endleofan OE 'eleven'.
eng ON 'meadow'.
eorl OE 'nobleman'.
eosol OE 'ass'.
epli ON 'apple'.
ermite OFr 'hermit'.
ersc OE 'ploughed field'.
eski ON 'ash wood'.
espi ON 'aspen wood'.
essart OFr 'clearing'.
-et OE p.n. forming suffix.
ey ON 'island'.
eyrr ON 'gravel- or sand-bank'.
fald OE 'fold, animal enclosure'.
*ge-fall OE 'clearing'.
fæger OE 'fair'.
fær OE 'road, ferry, ford'.
fæsten OE 'stronghold'.
fearn OE 'fern'.
feld OE 'open country'.
felging OE 'fallow land'.
fenn OE 'fen'.
fēower OE 'four'.
fīf OE 'five'.
fīna OE 'woodpecker'.
*fīnig OE 'wood-heap, clearing'.
fisc OE 'fish'.
fjall ON 'mountain'.
flat ON 'level ground'.
*fleg ON 'iris, rush'.
fleinn ON 'arrow'.

flēot OE 'stream'.
ge-flit OE 'dispute'.
flōh OE 'fragment (of stone).
folc-land OE 'land held in return for service to the king'.
ford OE 'river-crossing'.
forester OFr (AN) 'forester'.
front OFr 'front'.
fūl OE 'foul'.
funta OE 'spring'.
furh OE 'furrow'.
furlang OE 'furlong',
fȳr OE 'fire'.
fyrhð OE 'wood'.
***galt** OE 'boar'.
gang OE 'path, passage'.
gāra OE 'point of land'.
gardin OFr 'garden'.
garðr ON 'enclosure'.
gāt OE 'goat'.
gata ON 'road'.
geard OE 'enclosure, yard'.
geat OE 'gap, pass, gate'.
geil ON 'ravine, narrow lane'.
geirr ON 'spear'.
gil ON 'ravine'.
gorst OE 'gorse'.
***gorstig** OE 'gorsey'.
gōs OE 'goose'.
***gota** OE 'watercourse'.
grāf OE 'grove, wood'.
***grafa** OE 'trench'.
grange OFr 'granary, barn, farm'.
grant OFr 'large'.
grǣfe OE 'grove, copse'.
grēat OE 'thick, bulky'.
grēne[1] OE '(the colour) green'.
grēne[2] OE '(village) green'.
gríss ON 'piglet'.
grjót ON 'gravel, stones'.
gylden OE 'golden'.
hafoc OE 'hawk'.
haga[1] OE 'hedge, enclosure'.
half OE 'half'.

halh OE 'nook, corner'.
hālig OE 'holy'.
hall OE 'hall'.
hallr ON 'slope, hill; boulder'.
hām OE 'village'.
hamm OE 'meadow'.
hām-stede OE 'homestead'.
hām-tūn OE 'home farm'.
hangra OE 'wood on a hill-side'.
hār[2] OE 'grey, hoary'.
hara OE 'hare'.
hassuc OE 'tuft of coarse grass'.
haugr ON 'hill, mound'.
hæcc OE 'hatch, grating'.
ge-hæg OE 'fence, enclosure'.
-hǣma-tūn OE 'farmstead of the dwellers in a certain place'.
hæsel OE 'hazel'.
***hæsse** OE 'coarse grass'.
hēafod OE 'headland'.
hēah OE 'high, tall'.
heard OE 'hard'.
hēg OE 'hay'.
hege OE 'hedge'.
***hegn** ON 'enclosure'.
helde OE 'slope'.
hella ON 'flat stone'.
helm OE 'helmet, hilltop'.
hengest OE 'horse'.
heord OE 'herd'.
hesli ON 'hazel'.
hīd OE 'hide, measure of land'.
hīwisc OE 'household'.
hlāw OE 'mound, hill'.
hlǣne OE 'lean, meagre'.
hlið[1] OE 'slope'.
hlíð ON 'slope'.
hnut-bēam OE 'nut-tree'.
hnutu OE 'nut'.
hōc OE 'hook'.
hofuð ON 'headland'.
hōh OE 'heel'.
hol[1] OE 'hole, hollow'.
hol[2] OE 'hollow'.

holegn OE 'holly'.
holmr ON 'island, water-meadow'.
holt OE 'wood'.
hop OE 'enclosed land (esp. in marshes)'.
hord-ærn OE 'treasury'.
*horn-beme ME 'hornbeam-tree'.
hraca OE 'throat'.
hræfn OE 'raven'.
hreysi ON 'cairn'.
hrīs OE 'brushwood'.
hrōc OE 'rook'.
hrycg OE 'ridge'. .
hryggr ON 'ridge'.
hund¹ OE 'dog'.
hunig OE 'honey'.
hūs OE 'house'.
*hvin ON 'whin, gorse'.
hvítr ON 'white'.
hwǣte OE 'wheat'.
hwēol OE 'wheel'.
hwīt OE 'white'.
hyll OE 'hill'.
hȳra OE 'hireling'.
hyrst OE 'wood'.
hȳð OE 'landing-place'.
īdel OE 'empty'.
-ing² OE p.n. forming suffix.
*innām OE 'land newly taken into cultivation'.
inntak ON 'land newly taken into cultivation'.
juge OFr 'judge'.
*kaito- Brit 'wood'.
*kambo- Brit 'crooked'.
*karno- Brit 'cairn'.
kapall ON 'horse'.
kelda ON 'spring, marsh'.
kirkja ON 'church'.
kjarr ON 'brushwood; marsh'.
kjóss ON 'creek, valley'.
klettr OWN 'cliff, rock'.
*koilo- Brit 'narrow'.
*krakjo- Brit 'rock, cliff'.

krókr ON 'crook, bend'.
*krumbo- Brit 'crooked'.
*kukā Brit 'cuckoo'.
kýr ON 'cow'.
lacu OE 'stream'.
ge-lād OE 'water-course; river-crossing'.
lah-man ME 'law-man'.
lake ME 'lake'.
land OE 'land'.
lane OE 'lane'.
lang¹ OE 'long'.
lang² OE 'long strip'.
launde OFr 'glade'.
lāwerce OE 'lark'.
*læcc OE 'stream, bog'.
lǣs OE 'pasture'.
læx OE 'salmon'.
lēac OE 'herb, vegetable'.
lēah OE 'clearing; wood'.
lēfer OE 'reed, yellow iris'.
lēoht OE 'light'.
*licc OE 'stream'.
lieu OFr 'place'.
līm OE 'lime'.
lim-kilne ME 'lime-kiln'.
līn OE 'flax'.
lind OE 'lime-tree'.
ljóss ON 'bright, bare'.
*losko- Brit 'burning'.
lundr ON 'grove'.
lūs OE 'louse'.
lyng ON 'heather'.
lytel OE 'little'.
*mailo- Brit 'bald'.
māl OE 'bargain, law-suit, tax'.
manig OE 'many'.
manoir OFr 'manor'.
mann OE 'man, person'.
*mapul OE 'maple'.
market OE 'market'.
marle OFr 'marl'.
marr ON 'fen, marsh'.
ge-mǣre OE 'boundary'.

mæðel OE 'speech, assembly'.
mearc OE 'boundary'.
mearð OE 'marten'.
mēd OE 'meadow'.
melr ON 'sand-bank, dune'.
meoluc OE 'milk'.
mere[1] OE 'pool'.
mersc OE 'marsh'.
mes OFr 'house, farm'.
micel OE 'large'.
middel OE 'middle'.
mikill ON 'large'.
minte OE 'mint'.
mixen OE 'dung-hill'.
mjór ON 'narrow, small'.
mont OFr 'mount'.
mōr OE 'wasteland; marsh'.
mos OE 'bog'.
mōt OE 'meeting'.
mōtere OE 'public speaker'.
mudde ME 'mud'.
munede ME 'forest waste-land'.
munuc OE 'monk'.
mūða OE 'river-mouth, estuary'.
***mylde** OE 'soil'.
myln OE 'mill'.
mynster OE 'monastery, monastery church'.
myrig OE 'pleasant'.
mýrr ON 'swamp'.
***nanto-** Brit 'valley, stream'.
næss OE 'headland'.
neoðera OE 'lower'.
nēp OE 'turnip'.
nes ON 'headland'.
netel OE 'nettle'.
nigon OE 'nine'.
nīwe OE 'new'.
noke ME 'nook'.
norð OE 'north'.
norðan OE 'north of'.
ofer[2] OE 'slope, hill, ridge'.
ōra[1] OE 'bank, edge'.
orceard OE 'garden, orchard'.

***ore-blowere** ME 'smelter'.
oxa OE 'ox'.
parc OFr 'enclosed tract of land for deer etc.'
pæð OE 'path'.
pece OFr 'piece, plot'.
***penno-ardwo-** Brit 'headland'.
persone OFr 'parson'.
peru OE 'pear-tree'.
***pīced** EE 'pointed'.
***pil-āte** OE 'pill-oats'.
***pinca** OE 'finch'.
place OFr 'plot, open space'.
plat ME 'plot'.
***plocc** OE 'plot'.
point OFr 'point'.
pōl OE 'pool'.
port[2] OE 'town, market'.
post OE 'post, pillar'.
***pott** OE 'pot'.
***pull** OE 'pool'.
pūr OE 'bittern, snipe'.
pytt OE 'pit'.
racu OE 'stream, stream bed'.
rād OE 'riding'.
ramm OE 'ram'.
rauðr ON 'red'.
rāw OE 'row'.
rēad OE 'red'.
ge-**rēfa** OE 'reeve'.
repaire OFr 'retreat'.
ribbe OE 'ribwort'.
***ric** OE 'narrow strip'.
risc OE 'rush'.
***ritu-** Brit 'ford'.
rīðig OE 'stream'.
***rod**[1] OE 'clearing'.
rōd[1] OE 'rood, measure of land'.
rūh OE 'rough'.
rūm[1] OE 'open space'.
***ryding** OE 'clearing'.
ryge OE 'rye'.
salt[1] OE 'salt'.
salt-ærn OE 'salt-works'.

sand OE 'sand'.
sandig OE 'sandy'.
*sasjo- Brit 'barley'.
sǣ OE 'sea, lake'.
sǽtr ON 'mountain pasture, shieling'.
sceaft OE 'shaft, pole'.
sceaga OE 'copse'.
sceard OE 'shard; cleft'.
scēat OE 'projecting corner of land'.
scelf OE 'shelf'.
scīr¹ OE 'shire'.
scīr² OE 'bright, clear'.
scite OE 'shit'.
sef ON 'sedge, rush'.
seisine OFr 'possession'.
sēlig OE 'blessed, lucky'.
seofon OE 'seven'.
ge-set OE 'dwelling, den'.
setl OE 'seat, abode'.
sīc OE 'stream'.
sīde OE 'side'.
sík ON 'ditch'.
skál ON 'bowl, hollow'.
skáli ON 'hut, shed'.
skarpr ON 'dried up'.
skarð ON 'gap'.
sker ON 'rock'.
skírr ON 'clear, bright'.
skógr ON 'wood'.
slāh-þorn OE 'sloe-thorn, blackthorn'.
slakki OWN 'shallow valley'.
slæd OE 'valley'.
smið OE 'smith'.
smiðja ON 'smithy'.
smoca OE 'smoke'.
snād OE 'something cut off, detached'.
sól ON 'sun'.
spell OE 'speech'.
spōn OE 'wood chipping'.
stafn ON 'pole'.

stall OE 'place, stall'.
stān OE 'stone'.
stapol OE 'pillar, post'.
staðr ON 'place, site'.
stæf OE 'staff, pole'.
stǣnen OE 'made of stone, stony'.
stæð OE 'river-bank, shore'.
stede OE 'place'.
steinn ON 'stone'.
stell OE 'enclosure'.
stīg OE 'path'.
stoc OE 'place, secondary settlement'.
stofn ON 'stem, trunk'.
storð ON 'plantation'.
stǫð ON 'landing-place'.
stōw OE 'place'.
strēt OE 'paved (esp. Roman) road'.
strōd OE 'brushy marshland'.
stubb OE 'tree-stump'.
sunne OE 'sun'.
sūr OE 'sour'.
sūð OE 'south'.
sūðan OE 'south of'.
sweart OE 'black'.
swēte OE 'sweet'.
*swelo- Brit 'turn'.
swīn OE 'pig'.
*tacca OE 'young sheep'.
tādige OE 'toad'.
*tagga OE 'young sheep'.
tægl OE 'tail'.
templ OE 'temple'.
tēn OE 'ten'.
tēoða OE 'tenth, tithe'.
tigel OE 'tile'.
tilð OE 'cultivated land'.
timber OE 'timber'.
tjǫrn ON 'tarn, small lake'.
*todd OE 'bushy mass'.
toft ODan 'building site'.
toll-both ME 'toll-booth'.
torr OE 'rocky outcrop'.

*tōt-ærn OE 'guard house'.
trani ON 'crane'.
træppe OE 'snare'.
trēow OE 'tree'.
trog OE 'valley'.
truht OE 'trout'.
*tullo- Brit 'hole, pit'.
tūn OE 'enclosure, village'.
twisting ModE 'twisting'.
tyri ON 'resinous wood'.
þorn OE 'thorn-tree'.
þorp ON 'outlying farmstead'.
þrēap OE 'dispute'.
þrēo OE 'three'.
þriðjungr ON 'third part'.
þrop ON 'hamlet'.
þrostle OE 'thrush'.
þveit ON 'clearing, meadow'.
þyrne OE 'thorn-bush'.
þyrre OE 'dry, withered'.
ūle OE 'owl'.
vangr ON 'garden, field'.
vatn ON 'water, lake'.
vað ON 'ford'.
veiðr ON 'hunting, fishing'.
vík ON 'creek, inlet'.
víðir ON 'willow'.
viðr ON 'wood'.
vrá ON 'nook, corner'.
wād OE 'woad'.
*walc OE 'fulling'.
wald OE 'wood'.

wall OE 'wall'.
wang OE 'meadow, open field'.
*wæsse OE 'wet place'.
weg OE 'road'.
welle OE 'spring, stream, well'.
welm OE 'spring'.
wēod OE 'weed, herb'.
ge-weorc OE 'work, building structure'.
wer OE 'wier'.
west OE 'west'.
westan OE 'west of'.
wīc OE '(dairy) farm'.
wīd OE 'wide, spacious'.
wicga OE 'beetle'.
wild-bor ME 'wild boar'.
wilde OE 'wild'.
*wilig OE 'willow'.
wind[1] OE 'wind'.
windig OE 'windy'.
wīðig OE 'willow'.
*wīðign OE 'growing with willows'.
Wōden OE 'the god Woden'.
wōh OE 'crooked'.
worð OE 'enclosure'.
worðign OE 'enclosure'.
wudu OE 'wood'.
wulf OE 'wolf'.
wyrhta OE 'wright'.
*yfre OE 'brow of a hill'.

General Index

This index lists relevant forms that are not given as headwords in the main body of the text. As an aid to tracing words by their modern equivalents, it includes all the OED forms from the text (cited here as ModE, even when this is not strictly the case). It also includes all the headwords omitted or altered from the forms used by Smith (EPNE), the county surveys which have been completed since 1956 (Db, YW, Gl, We, Ch, Brk, Ru) and published *corrigenda*. Where there is simply a change in spelling, readers are directed to the new head-form by the symbol >. Where the form is discussed as a variant or alternative in another entry, the instruction is to 'see'. Where evidence is lacking, poor or late (i.e. later than c.1750), this is noted. Where a word may appear in one or two p.ns, but the evidence is considered weak, the p.ns have been recorded here.

abadie OFr 'abbey', see **abbaie**.
abbacy ModE, see **abbaie**.
abbas Lat 'abbot', see **abbod**.
abbatess ModE, see **abbesse**.
abbatie ModE, see **abbaie**.
abbat OFr 'abbot', see **abbod**.
abbaye > **abbaie**.
abbess ModE, see **abbesse**.
abbey ModE, see **abbaie**.
abbodesse OE 'abbess', see **abbesse**.
abbodie ME 'abbey', see **abbaie**.
*aßon > **abonā**.
abbot ModE, see **abbod**.
abbotess ModE, see **abbesse**.
abūfan OE 'above' > **bufan**.
*ācen OE 'oaken', see **æcen**.
-āco- > **-āko-**.
acorn ModE, see **æcern**.
acre ModE, see **æcer**.
acre-land ModE, see **æcer**.
acreman ModE, see **æcer-mann**.
ācweorna OE 'squirrel', see **æcern**.
addle ModE, see **adela**.
affadille ModE 'daffodil', late.
āfor OE 'bitter', possible in Awre Gl.
airge > **ǽrgi**.
aise OFr 'ease', see **mesaise**.
akr ON 'acre', see **æcer**.
ál > **áll**.
alder ModE, see **alor**.

aldermun ModE, see **aldormann**.
aldern ModE, see **ælren**.
alfr ON 'elf', late.
alh OE, see **ealh**.
alius Lat 'other', no evidence.
allan ModE 'water-meadow', see **ēa**.
alley ModE, see **alee**.
*alma ?pre-Celtic r.n., see ***alaventa**.
almarie > **almerie**.
*almenn ON 'everybody', possible in Almondbury YW.
almoner ModE, see **aumoner**.
almonry ModE, see **almerie**.
almosnerie OFr 'almonry', see **almerie**.
almoyn ME 'alms', possible in Almond Royd YW:7·152.
alms ModE, see **ælmesse**.
alms-land ModE, see **ælmesse**.
alms-house ModE, see **ælmesse**.
*alo- Brit 'swift', no evidence.
*alren OE 'of alder', see **ælren**.
alter Lat 'other', no evidence.
alterior Lat 'higher', no evidence.
altus Lat 'high', no evidence.
*alūn > ***alaunā**.
ambry ModE, see **almerie**.
amore > **amer**.
anachorist ModE, see **anchorite**.
anchor ModE, see **ancor**.

ancra > ancor.
anddyri ON 'porch', no evidence.
angel > angle.
angr ON 'inlet', see *anger.
*ān-hūs OE 'lonely house', see ān.
anlepi ModE, see ānlēpig.
ant ModE, see æmette.
ant-hill ModE, see æmett-hyll.
apaldr ON 'apple-tree', no evidence.
apaldr(s)-garðr > appel-garth.
apple ModE, see æppel.
apple-tree ModE, see æppel-trēow.
ar > *are-.
*ara ?pre-Celtic r.n., see *arva.
archdeaconModE, see arce-dīacon.
*ardu- > *ardwo-.
ark > arc.
*armīsa ?pre-Celtic r.n., see *arva.
*arna ?pre-Celtic r.n., see *arva.
arnut ModE 'earth-nut', see eorðe.
arrow-smith ModE, see arwe-smith.
ash ModE, see æsc.
ashen ModE, see æscen.
asker > askre.
asp ModE, see æspe.
aspen ModE, see æspe, æspen.
ass ModE, see assa.
assart OFr 'clearing' > essart.
assize ModE, see assise.
at ModE, see æt.
*āten OE 'oaten', see āte.
atheling ModE, see æðeling.
au(l)ter ME 'altar', poor evidence.
auncien OFr 'ancient', late.
aunt ME 'aunt', late.
austarr ON 'more easterly', see austr.
avenue ModE, late.
average ModE, see *averys.
awl ModE, see āwel.
ǣdre OE 'water course' > ēdre.
æfesn OE 'pasturage', possible in

Hognaston Db.
ǣl OE 'eel' > ēl¹.
ǣling OE 'burning', possible in Ellenwray We.
*ǣling OE 'eel fishery' > *ēling.
*ǣlret OE 'alder copse', see *alret.
*æpplen OE 'growing with apple-trees', possible in Eppleton Du.
ærne-weg OE 'race course', see *ærne-ford.
ǣte OE 'oats', see āte.
ætstall OE 'camp', no evidence.
æðele OE 'noble', possible in Eddlestow Db.
ǣw(i)ell, see ǣwylm.
ǣwylle OE 'spring', see ǣwylm.
bache ModE, see bæce.
back ModE, see bæc.
back-house ModE, see bæc-hūs.
ba(c)ksyde > bak-side.
bad ModE, see badde.
badger ModE, see baggere.
badger > *bagger.
bäee OFr 'opening', see bay.
bag ModE, see *bagga.
bai OFr 'bay coloured', see bay.
baie OFr 'berry', see *beg.
bail ModE, see *bēgel.
bailey ModE, see baille.
bailie ModE, see baillif.
bailiff ModE, see baillif.
bailiffwick ModE, see bailli-wik.
baillie > bailliff.
bain ModE, see beinn.
bairn ModE, see barn.
bait ModE, see beit.
baiting ModE, see beiting.
bake see beak, *burn-bake.
bakehouse ModE, see bæc-hūs.
baker ModE, see bæcere.
bakestone ModE, see bæc-stān.
bakki ON, see banke.
bald ModE, see balled.
bale ModE, see bál.

blete ModE, see **blēat**.
blew > **bleu**.
blithe ModE, see **blīðe**.
blo ModE, see **blár**.
blob ModE 'blob', late.
block ModE, see **blok**.
blōd-lǣs OE 'blood-letting', see **blōd-lēas**.
blok(e ModE, see **blæc**.
blóm ON 'bloom, blossom', see **blōma**.
blood ModE, see **blōd**.
bloodless ModE, see **blōd-lēas**.
bloody ModE, see **blōdig**.
bloom ModE, see **blōma**.
bloomery ModE, see ***blōmere**.
blossom ModE, see **blōstm**.
blōt ME 'bare, desolate', late.
blou ME 'gust', see ***blāw**.
blow ModE, see ***blāw**.
blower ModE, see **blāwere**.
blubber ModE, see **bluber**.
blue ModE, see **bleu**.
blue-button ModE plant-name, late.
bluecap ModE plant-name, late.
bly ModE, see **blēo**.
boar ModE, see **bār**.
board ModE, see **bord**.
bob ModE, see **bobbe**.
bōcere OE 'scribe', no evidence (Hough 1994:24).
bod W 'dwelling', late.
boda OE 'messenger', possible in Bodeford Gl.
boeth W 'burnt', in a Welsh name.
boggin ModE 'goblin, ghost', late.
bogi ON 'bow', see **boga**.
bōl OE 'eel', possible in Bollin Ch:1·15, Bowmont Nb.
***bola** > **bol**.
bolace > **bolas-tre**.
bold OE 'building, house', see **boðl**.
bole ModE, see **bol**.

***bolig** ME 'full of logs', possible in Bonnywoods Ch:1·188.
boli ON 'bull', see **bula**.
boll ModE, see **bolla**.
bollere ME 'tippler', cf. ***bolled**.
bǫllr ON 'ball', see ***ball**.
bolr ON 'tree-trunk', see **bol**.
bolster OE 'bolster, pillow', no evidence.
ból ON 'homestead' > **bøli**.
bombast ModE 'cotton-down', late.
bond ModE, see **bóndi**.
bone ModE, see **bān**.
bone-dust ModE 'bone-meal', late.
bonny ModE, late.
book ModE, see **bōc²**.
bookland ModE, see **bōc-land**.
boon ModE, see **bón**, **bēn**.
boose ModE 'cowshed', see **báss**, ***bōs**.
boosing ModE 'cowshed', see **bōsig**.
boosy ModE 'cowshed', see **bōsig**.
boot ModE, see **bōt**.
booth ModE, see **bōð**.
boothall ModE, see **both-hall**.
bord OFr 'cottage', see **bord**, **bordel**.
borded ModE 'boarded up, made of boards', late.
bordure ME 'border', late.
bǫrkr ON 'bark', see **bark**.
borrow ModE, see **borg**.
borstall ModE, see **borg-stall**.
bote ME 'boat', late.
boteille OFr 'bottle', see **botiler**.
boterie OFr 'buttery', see **botilerie**.
***bōthere** ME 'booth-keeper, -dweller', late.
botm-lēas OE 'bottomless', late.
bottle ModE, see **boðl**, **boðen**.
bottler ModE, see **botiler**.
bottom > **botm**.
bott > **bot**.

bōtye ModE 'booty, common spoils', see **booty**.

bouge OFr 'heath', possible in Boulge Sf.

boul ModE, see **boga**.

boulder ME 'boulder' see **bulder**.

bound(ary) ModE, late.

bouverie > **boverie**.

bow ModE, see **boga**.

bowker > **bouker**.

bowl ModE, see **bolla**.

bowsen ModE, 'cowshed', late.

boy ModE, see ***boia**.

bright ModE, see **berht**.

buck ModE, see **bouker**.

buddle ModE, see **boðen**.

bullace ModE, see **bolas-tre**.

bullester ModE, see **bolas-tre**.

bully ModE, see **bolas-tre**.

bur ModE, see ***bors**.

burn-beat ModE, see ***bete**.

burning ModE, see **bærning**.

burre ME 'bur', see ***bors**.

butcher ModE, see **bocher**.

butchery ModE, see **bocherie**.

butler ModE, see **botiler**.

buttery ModE, see **botilerie**.

búð OWN 'booth', see **bekkr**, **bōð**.

by ModE, see **bī**.

ēacen OE 'increased, huge', see **ǣcen**.

eald OE 'old', see **ald**.

earc OE 'chest', see **arc**.

earn ModE, see **ærn**.

***elre* OE 'alder clump', see **alor**.

***elren* OE 'of alder', see **ælren**.

***elret* OE 'alder copse', see ***alret**.

emmet ModE, see **ǣmette**.

ende ModE 'duck', see **æned**.

ened OE 'duck', see **æned**.

eystri ON 'more easterly', see **austr**.

gist ModE, see **agistement**.

gistment ModE, see **agistement**.

justment ModE, see **agistement**.

oak ModE, see **āc**.

oaken ModE, see **ǣcen**.

oast ModE, see **āst̩**.

oat ModE, see **āte**.

old ModE, see **ald**.

one ModE, see **ān**.

ǫngull ON 'hook', see **angle**.

onlepy ModE, see **ānlēpig**.

onset ModE, see **ānsetl**.

ǫsp ON 'aspen-tree', see **æspe**.

woodbine ModE, see **binde**.

yellow-hammer ModE, see **amer**.